GUN CONTROL

RESTRICTING RIGHTS
OR PROTECTING PEOPLE?

GUN CONTROL
RESTRICTING RIGHTS OR PROTECTING PEOPLE?

Jeffrey Ferro

INFORMATION PLUS® REFERENCE SERIES
Formerly published by Information Plus, Wylie, Texas

Detroit
New York
San Francisco
London
Boston
Woodbridge, CT

GUN CONTROL: RESTRICTING RIGHTS OR PROTECTING PEOPLE?

Jeffrey Ferro, *Author*

The Gale Group Staff:

Editorial: John F. McCoy, *Project Manager and Series Editor*; Andrew Claps, *Series Associate Editor*; Jason M. Everett, *Series Associate Editor*; Michael T. Reade, *Series Associate Editor*; Rita Runchock, *Managing Editor*; Luann Brennan, *Editor*

Image and Multimedia Content: Barbara J. Yarrow, *Manager, Imaging and Multimedia Content*; Robyn Young, *Project Manager, Imaging and Multimedia Content*

Indexing: Lynne Maday, *Indexing Specialist*; Amy Suchowski, *Indexing Specialist*

Permissions: Margaret A. Chamberlain, *Permissions Specialist*; Maria Franklin, *Permissions Manager*

Product Design: Michelle DiMercurio, *Senior Art Director*; Kenn Zorn, *Product Design Manager*

Production: Evi Seoud, *Assistant Manager, Composition Purchasing and Electronic Prepress*; NeKita McKee, *Buyer*; Dorothy Maki, *Manufacturing Manager*

ISBN 0-7876-5103-6 (set)
ISBN 0-7876-5394-2 (this volume)
ISSN 1534-1909 (this volume)
Printed in the United States of America
10 9 8 7 6 5 4 3 2 1

TABLE OF CONTENTS

CHAPTER 1

Few issues in American society provoke stronger emotions than the debate over gun control. Dating back to colonial times, Americans felt that individual ownership of guns was essential to the formation of a militia. In modern times, the gun control debate includes such issues as gun registration, waiting periods on gun purchases, and the ban on certain types of firearms.

CHAPTER 2

Studies estimate that there are 260 million guns privately owned or available for sale in the United States. Although some weapons are manufactured in the United States, many come from foreign countries. The majority of gun owners are men, and they own different types of guns for varying reasons. Some gun owners belong to organizations that promote the right to own guns.

CHAPTER 3

The debate over the federal government's role in the regulation of firearms still rages after more than half a century. Over the years, Congress has passed many laws regulating the sale and use of firearms, with major legislation including the Gun Control Acts of 1968 and 1986 and the Brady Handgun Violence Prevention Act. State and local governments have also passed laws that regulate the sale and use of guns.

CHAPTER 4

Federal and state courts have upheld the rights of the federal government, states, and local communities to require the registration of firearms, to determine how these weapons may be carried, and even to forbid the use of some weapons under certain circumstances. This chapter presents selections of court cases which include landmark decisions and recent rulings on gun regulations at the federal, state, and local levels.

CHAPTER 5

Guns and crime are often linked. Guns are frequently used to commit robbery and murder, crimes in which human life is either threatened or taken. The misuse of guns places most Americans at some risk.

This chapter deals with the frequency and ways in which guns are used to commit crimes.

CHAPTER 6

Each year thousands of Americans are injured or killed due to gun-related incidents. These incidents have become major public health issues, which have led some public health agencies, scholars, and gun rights groups to attempt to track information on weapons-related injuries and deaths. A growing number of organizations are trying to reduce both deliberate and unintentional firearm injuries and deaths.

CHAPTER 7

An increasing number of youth are growing up in neighborhoods with high levels of violence. Although in recent years, firearm homicides among youth have declined, increasing numbers of young people carry and possess weapons. Recent shootings at schools have stepped up the debate over gun control.

CHAPTER 8

Some Americans are convinced that the regulation of firearms is necessary to reduce firearm related injuries and deaths. However, others support the right to private ownership of guns and argue that it is guaranteed by the Second Amendment. Opinion polls directed toward all segments of the population illustrate different concerns and attitudes toward gun control.

CHAPTER 9

This chapter presents a sample of the arguments used by the proponents of strong federal gun control to support their position over the last several decades.

CHAPTER 10

This chapter presents a sample of the arguments used by the opponents of strong federal gun control to support their position over the last several decades.

PREFACE

Gun Control: Restricting Rights or Protecting People? is the latest volume in the ever-growing *Information Plus Reference Series*. Previously published by the Information Plus company of Wylie, Texas, the *Information Plus Reference Series* (and its companion set, the *Information Plus Compact Series*) became a Gale Group product when Gale and Information Plus merged in early 2000. Those of you familiar with the series as published by Information Plus will notice a few changes from the 1999 edition. Gale has adopted a new layout and style that we hope you will find easy to use. Other improvements include greatly expanded indexes in each book, and more descriptive tables of contents.

While some changes have been made to the design, the purpose of the *Information Plus Reference Series* remains the same. Each volume of the series presents the latest facts on a topic of pressing concern in modern American life. These topics include today's most controversial and most studied social issues: abortion, capital punishment, care for the elderly, crime, health care, the environment, immigration, minorities, social welfare, women, youth, and many more. Although written especially for the high school and undergraduate student, this series is an excellent resource for anyone in need of factual information on current affairs.

By presenting the facts, it is Gale's intention to provide its readers with everything they need to reach an informed opinion on current issues. To that end, there is a particular emphasis in this series on the presentation of scientific studies, surveys, and statistics. This data is generally presented in the form of tables, charts, and other graphics placed within the text of each book. Every graphic is directly referred to and carefully explained in the text. The source of each graphic is presented within the graphic itself. The data used in these graphics is drawn from the most reputable and reliable sources, in particular from the various branches of the U.S. government and from major independent polling organizations. Every effort was made to secure the most recent information available. The reader should bear in mind that many major studies take years to conduct, and that additional years often pass before the data from these studies is made available to the public. Therefore, in many cases the most recent information available in 2001 dated from 1998 or 1999. Older statistics are sometimes presented as well, if they are of particular interest and no more-recent information exists.

Although statistics are a major focus of the *Information Plus Reference Series* they are by no means its only content. Each book also presents the widely held positions and important ideas that shape how the book's subject is discussed in the United States. These positions are explained in detail and, where possible, in the words of those who support them. Some of the other material to be found in these books includes: historical background; descriptions of major events related to the subject; relevant laws and court cases; and examples of how these issues play out in American life. Some books also feature primary documents, or have pro and con debate sections giving the words and opinions of prominent Americans on both sides of a controversial topic. All material is presented in an even-handed and unbiased manner; the reader will never be encouraged to accept one view of an issue over another.

HOW TO USE THIS BOOK

The right to bear arms, and in particular firearms, is one of the most controversial issues in modern America. Many Americans feel that guns are a threat to public safety, and that their sale and use should be tightly controlled. Many other Americans feel that gun ownership is an essential form of protection, that guns help ensure safety rather than threatening it. For this reason they believe that competent, law-abiding, citizens should be free to purchase guns without government regulation, registration, or scrutiny. Both sides have compelling arguments and statistical studies that support their views. These studies and opinions are explored in detail in this book, as are the history of gun control in the United States and recent trends in gun violence, so that the reader can see the evidence and decide for themselves what, if any, gun control measures are necessary and legal.

Gun Control: Restricting Rights or Protecting People? consists of ten chapters and four appendices. Each chapter is devoted to a particular aspect of the issue of gun control in the United States. For a summary of the information covered in each chapter, please see the synopses provided in the Table of Contents at the front of the book. Chapters generally begin with an overview of the basic facts and background information on the chapter's topic, then proceed to examine sub-topics of particular interest. For example, Chapter 4: Court Rulings on Firearms begins with an overview of some generally accepted legal doctrines regarding gun control. It then examines major federal court rulings on the Second Amendment. From there it progresses through rulings on other, more specific, federal laws, such as those that prohibit the ownership of machine guns, the bringing of guns into "school zones," and laws requiring certain amounts of jail time for those who use firearms during drug-related crime. Following the section on federal laws is a similar section on state laws, and then one on local laws. The chapter concludes with legal opinions on who can be held liable for firearm-related injuries, deaths, and medical costs. Readers can find their way through a chapter by looking for the section and sub-section headings, which are clearly set off from the text. Or, they can refer to the book's extensive index, if they already know what they are looking for.

Statistical Information

The tables and figures featured throughout *Gun Control: Restricting Rights or Protecting People?* will be of particular use to the reader in learning about this issue. These tables and figures represent an extensive collection of the most recent and important statistics on gun control and related issues; for example: the number of guns Americans own, how many guns are used to commit crimes and in self-defense each year. Excerpts of gun control regulations and related documents are also featured. Gale believes that making this information available to the read-

er is the most important way in which we fulfill the goal of this book: To help readers understand the issues and controversies surrounding guns and gun control in the United States and reach their own conclusions about them.

Each table or figure has a unique identifier appearing above it, for ease of identification and reference. Titles for the tables and figures explain their purpose. At the end of each table or figure, the original source of the data is provided.

In order to help readers understand these often complicated statistics, all tables and figures are explained in the text. References in the text direct the reader to the relevant statistics. Furthermore, the contents of all tables and figures are fully indexed. Please see the opening section of the index at the back of this volume for a description of how to find tables and figures within it.

In addition to the main body text and images, *Gun Control: Restricting Rights or Protecting People?* has four appendices. The first is a listing of the "right to bear arms" provisions found in the U.S. Constitution and in the constitutions of those states which have such provisions. The next appendix is the Important Names and Addresses directory. Here the reader will find contact information for a number of organizations that advocate influential opinions and policies on guns and gun control. The third appendix is the Resources section, which is provided to assist the reader in conducting his or her own research. In this section, the author and editors of *Gun Control: Restricting Rights or Protecting People?* describe some of the sources that were most useful during the compilation of this book. The final appendix is this book's index. It has been greatly expanded from previous editions, and should make it even easier to find specific topics in this book.

COMMENTS AND SUGGESTIONS

The editor of the *Information Plus Reference Series* welcomes your feedback on *Gun Control: Restricting Rights or Protecting People?* Please direct all correspondence to:

Editor
Information Plus Reference Series
27500 Drake Rd.
Farmington Hills, MI, 48331-3535

ACKNOWLEDGEMENTS

The editors wish to thank the copyright holders of the excerpted material included in this volume and the permissions managers of many book and magazine publishing companies for assisting us in securing reproduction rights. We are also grateful to the staffs of the Detroit Public Library, the Library of Congress, the University of Detroit Mercy Library, Wayne State University Purdy/Kresge Library Complex, and the University of Michigan Libraries for making their resources available to us. Following is a list of the copyright holders who have granted us permission to reproduce material in this volume of Gun Control: Restricting Rights or Protecting People?. Every effort has been made to trace copyright, but if omissions have been made, please let us know.

COPYRIGHTED MATERIAL IN GUN CONTROL: RESTRICTING RIGHTS OR PROTECTING PEOPLE? **WAS REPRODUCED FROM THE FOLLOWING PERIODICALS:**

1997–1998 National Gun Policy Survey of the National Opinion Research Center: Research Findings, by Tom W. Smith. National Opinion Research Center, University of Chicago. Reproduced by permission.

1999 National Gun Policy Survey of the National Opinion Research Center: Research Findings by Tom W. Smith. National Opinion Research Center, University of Chicago, 1999. Reproduced by permission.

Gun Acquisition and Possession in Selected Juvenile Samples, Office of Juvenile Justice and Delinquency Prevention. Reproduced by permission.

Missing in Action: Health Agencies Lack Critical Data Needed for Firearm Injury Prevention. Reproduced by permission of Handgun Epidemic Lowering Plan (HELP) Network.

National Institute of Justice Research Brief, by Philip J. Cook and Jens Ludwig. From National Institute of Justice. Reproduced by permission.

New England Journal of Medicine, vol. 35, no. 19, November 7, 1996. Copyright © 1996 by Massachusetts Medical Society. All rights reserved. Reproduced by permission.

Paper Tiger? Will the Brady Law Work After Instant Check? Violence Policy Center. Reproduced by permission.

The Harris Poll #38, by Humphrey Taylor. Louis Harris and Associates, Inc. Reproduced by permission.

COPYRIGHTED MATERIAL IN GUN CONTROL: RESTRICTING RIGHTS OR PROTECTING PEOPLE? **WAS REPRODUCED FROM THE FOLLOWING BOOKS:**

Diaz, Tom. Making a Killing: The Business of Guns in America. The New Press, 1999. Copyright © 1999 by The New Press. Reproduced by permission.

CHAPTER 1

THE HISTORY OF THE RIGHT TO BEAR ARMS

Few issues incite Americans more than gun control. The debate over gun ownership has provoked strong emotions for years and shows no sign of abating. Are gun ownership rights guaranteed by the U.S. Constitution, or should guns be banned or restricted because they are used to commit many crimes? Some people argue that the individual right to bear arms is not as vital to freedom today as it was in 1791, nor that it applies to individuals; others argue that it is an individual right guaranteed by the Constitution.

The right of the individual to keep and bear arms has a long tradition in Western civilization. The Greek philosopher Aristotle (384–322 B.C.E.) thought that bearing arms was necessary for true citizenship and participation in the political system (Aristotle, *Politics*). On the other hand, Plato (427?–347 B.C.E.) believed in a hierarchical monarchy with few liberties and saw the disarming of the populace as essential to the maintenance of his orderly and autocratic system (Plato, *Republic*). Cicero (106–43 B.C.E.), one of the leading advocates of Roman republicanism, supported bearing arms for self-defense of the individual and for public defense against tyranny (Cicero, *De Offices*). Machiavelli (1469–1527), the Italian political philosopher, advocated an armed populace of citizen soldiers to keep headstrong rulers in line (Machiavelli, *Discourse*).

AN EARLY PRECEDENT—MILITIA AND THE OWNERSHIP OF WEAPONS

Perhaps the first document linking the bearing of arms with the militia (an army composed of citizens called to action in time of emergency) was the *Assize of Arms* of 1181, which directed every free man to provide himself with weaponry. This ordinance, issued by Henry II of England, was intended to permit the rapid creation of a militia. Apparently, it also permitted carrying arms in self-defense and forbade the use of arms only when the

intention was to "terrify the King's subjects." In 1328, under the reign of King Edward III, Parliament enacted the Statute of Northampton, which prohibited the carrying of arms in public places. This law, however, apparently did not overrule the right to carry arms in self-defense.

EARLY GUN CONTROL LAWS

The 17th century was a period of considerable turmoil in England. Civil war was followed by a republic that degenerated into a dictatorship (1649–1660) led by Oliver Cromwell and supported by the weapons of a disciplined standing army. With the passage of the Game Act of 1671, lands that had formerly been held for public use and hunting were restricted for use only by those who earned £40–100 per year. Persons not permitted to hunt, or those with land valued at less than £100, were not allowed to keep weapons of any kind. This is the first recorded example of a gun control law. It was enacted to keep the ownership of hunting lands and weaponry in the hands of the wealthy and to restrict hunting and gun ownership among the peasants. Persons without an income of at least £40–100, a large amount at the time, could no longer legally keep weapons, even for self-defense.

THE ENGLISH BILL OF RIGHTS

When William and Mary of Holland were invited to occupy the throne of England in 1689, they were presented with an English Bill of Rights, which limited the monarch's rights and guaranteed the rights of Englishmen. This Bill of Rights included a specific right of "Protestants [to] have arms for their defense suitable to their conditions and as allowed by law." The English Bill of Rights also attacked abuses committed by standing armies and declared "that the raising and keeping of a standing army within the kingdom in time of peace, unless it be with consent of Parliament, is against the law."

THE AMERICAN MILITIA AND THE RIGHT TO BEAR ARMS

Much of American law is rooted in English common law. Most American colonists came from England, bringing with them English values, traditions, and legal concepts. Many of the English were familiar with the famous jurist Sir William Blackstone (1723–1780), who listed in his *Commentaries* the "right of having and using arms for self-preservation and defense." This right, brought to America by the English, is older than the American Constitution. In fact, if the colonists had not exercised this right during the Revolutionary War, the United States Constitution might never have been written.

A primary cause of the Revolutionary War was the king's attempt to disarm the colonists. The British army's encounter with the Massachusetts militia—"the shot heard round the world"—the eventual seizure of arms and munitions held by the militia at Lexington, and the Boston Massacre, in which British soldiers shot and killed unarmed citizens in the streets of Boston, made the colonists conscious of the danger of a standing army. At the same time, they were even more concerned about the "security of a free state." The formation of a militia was considered necessary to achieve this security.

At that time, individual colonies did not have enough money to purchase weapons, and, therefore, each citizen had to maintain a firearm to enable himself to report immediately for duty and form a militia. In *The Federalist, No. 24,* Alexander Hamilton spoke of the right to bear arms in the sense of an "unorganized militia," which consisted of the "people-at-large." He suggested that this militia could mobilize against the standing army if the army usurped the government's authority or if it supported a tyrannical government. Such a standing army, declared Hamilton, could "never be formidable to the liberties of the people while there is a large body of citizens, little, if any, inferior to them in discipline and the use of arms, who stand ready to defend their rights and those of their fellow-citizens" (*The Federalist, No. 29*).

Many colonists felt that the right to bear arms was inseparable from the right to form a militia. Thomas Jefferson stated, "No freeman shall be debarred the use of arms within his own land," and Richard Henry Lee observed that "to preserve liberty, it is essential that the whole body of the people always possess arms." Many colonists felt that individual ownership of weapons was essential to the formation of a militia; without this privilege, the right to organize a militia would have little meaning.

James Madison, who would later write the first 10 amendments (the Bill of Rights) to the U.S. Constitution, attributed the colonial victory to armed citizens. In *The Federalist, No. 46,* he wrote, "Americans [have] the right and advantage of being armed—unlike citizens of other countries whose governments are afraid to trust the people with arms."

THE U.S. CONSTITUTION, THE RIGHT TO BEAR ARMS, AND THE MILITIA

In 1787, following the Revolutionary War, 39 men gathered in Philadelphia to sign the Constitution. Three of them refused to sign because it did not include a Bill of Rights. One of the reluctant signers protested that, without a Bill of Rights, Congress "at their pleasure may arm or disarm all or any part of the freemen of the United States."

When James Madison wrote the constitutional amendments that eventually became known as the Bill of Rights, he was influenced by state bills of rights and numerous amendment suggestions from the state conventions that ratified the Constitution. Overall, four basic beliefs were assimilated into the Second Amendment: the right of the individual to possess arms, the fear of a professional army, the dependence on militias regulated by the individual states, and the control of the military by civilians.

The ratifying state conventions offered similar suggestions about the militia and the right to bear arms. While New Hampshire did not mention the militia, it did state,

> . . . no standing Army shall be Kept up in time of peace unless with the consent of three-fourths of the Members of each branch of Congress, nor shall Soldiers in Time of Peace be quartered upon private Houses without the consent of the Owners.

Another New Hampshire amendment read, "Congress shall never disarm any Citizen unless such as are or have been in Actual Rebellion." Maryland proposed five separate amendments, which Virginia consolidated by stating,

> . . . the people have a right to keep and bear arms; that a well regulated Militia composed of the body of the people trained to arms is the proper, natural and safe defence of a free State. That standing armies in time of peace are dangerous to liberty, and therefore ought to be avoided, as far as the circumstances and protection of the community will admit; and that in all cases the military should be under strict subordination to and governed by the Civil power.

The New York convention offered more than 50 amendments, including the following: "That the People have a right to keep and bear Arms; that a well regulated Militia, including the body of people capable of bearing Arms, is the proper, natural and safe defence of a free state."

The constitutions of several states guaranteed the rights of individuals to bear arms, while forbidding the maintenance of a standing army. Pennsylvania's constitution ensured "that the people have a right to bear arms for the defense of themselves and the state; and as standing armies in the time of peace are dangerous to liberty, they ought not to be kept up; and that the military should be kept under the strict subordination to, and governed by, the civil power." (See Appendix for state constitution articles concerning weapons.)

Because of their fear of tyranny and repression by a standing army, the colonists preferred state militias to provide protection and order; these militias could also act as a counterbalance against any national standing army. Some people believe the individual right to bear arms was implied when such laws stated that the militia would be composed of the body of the people trained to arms.

The Bill of Rights was adopted in 1791. The Second Amendment states,

A well regulated Militia, being necessary to the security of a free State, the right of the people to keep and bear Arms, shall not be infringed.

THE MODERN GUN CONTROL DEBATE

The modern debate includes many issues, such as gun registration, waiting periods on gun purchases, and a ban on certain types of firearms. In the early 1930s, Franklin Roosevelt tried unsuccessfully to pass legislation requiring the registration of handguns. Sixty years later, in 1992, gun control advocates succeeded in enacting the Brady Handgun Violence Prevention Act, which imposed a five-day waiting period on handgun purchases and a criminal background check on buyers.

The required background check was never rigidly enforced, however, because Congress did not fund the mandate. In 1997 the Supreme Court ruled that the federal government cannot require state, county, and municipal officials to conduct background checks on prospective handgun purchasers. (See Chapter 4 for more details on *Printz v. United States.*) A national database for such background checks was established on November 30, 1998, as part of Phase II of the Brady Act. Known as the National Instant Criminal Background Check System (NICS), this computerized system is managed by the Federal Bureau of Investigation and is used to make presale background checks for purchases of both handguns and long guns from federal firearms licensees. As of one year after the implementation of NICS, about 72 percent of background checks were approved within 30 seconds after the purchaser's identifying information was input into the system. If a background check cannot be completed in three business days, the sale is automatically allowed to proceed by default.

"Collective Rights" versus "Individual Rights"

In *The Politics of Gun Control* (Chatham House, Chatham, NJ, 1995) Robert Spitzer wrote that the debate has been split between gun control proponents, who favor a "collective rights" interpretation of the Second Amendment, and gun control opponents, who take an "individual rights" interpretation.

Proponents of the collective rights argument hold that the Second Amendment guarantees the rights of states—not individuals—to maintain well-regulated militias. Gun control proponents, therefore, say that this right is represented by the National Guard: because the National Guard is responsible for the security of a free state, it is not vital for individuals to keep and bear arms in order to protect states' security.

In contrast, proponents of individual rights hold that individuals have a right to keep and bear arms. Gun control opponents add that the phrase "right of the people" is used in other amendments in the Bill of Rights, and in each case it refers to a right of individuals. (See Chapter 4 for more information on Second Amendment interpretations.)

Gary Wills, in "To Keep and Bear Arms" (*The New York Review of Books,* September 21, 1995), agreed with the collective rights advocates on the issue of militias but pointed out that, although Congress passed a militia law in 1792 requiring all able-bodied men to own a musket so that they could serve in the militia, it served little purpose since there was no provision for organized training.

Is Handgun Control Unconstitutional?

Often referred to as the "weapon of choice" for criminals, as well as for those who say they use them for self-defense, handguns are a particular point of contention. While gun rights advocates argue that a ban on, or restriction of, handgun use is unconstitutional, others argue that no gun control legislation—including legislation affecting handguns—has ever been struck down by the Supreme Court as unconstitutional under the Second Amendment.

The Slippery Slope

Spitzer (see above) claims that handguns are used in self-defense in 80,000 cases per year. In 2000 the Justice Department put the number at 108,000, while gun control critics suggest a figure as high as 2.5 million. Regardless of the number, Spitzer argues that the defensive use of handguns does not justify the use of handguns by criminals for offensive purposes, which he claims accounts for 35,000 deaths and up to 245,000 injuries annually.

Spitzer illustrates his argument against handgun use on a smaller scale: A convenience store employee working the late shift is shot and killed by a thug using a handgun. The employee has been denied the use of a handgun and, hence, the ability to defend himself and perhaps save his life. At the same time, however, a depressed woman who was also denied a handgun cannot commit suicide, and a child whose parents were denied a handgun cannot accidentally find a handgun and perhaps kill himself or a friend. So, overall, society is safer.

Gun rights advocates—many of whom interpret any gun control measure as the slippery slope to disarmament—argue that the convenience store employee has the same right to life as the depressed woman. She can choose to kill herself with poison or by driving off a cliff. Furthermore, the child can accidentally find and drink toxic insect repellant or fall into a swimming pool, yet no background check or waiting period is required for the purchase of cars, toxic insect repellants, or swimming pools. The right to keep and bear these items is not constitutionally protected, and society might very well be safer without these as well.

Spitzer offers another view of the dangers of interpreting the Second Amendment as an individual right. He believes that gun proliferation and carrying among law-abiding citizens will start an arms race with criminals, who will upgrade their weapons and be more willing to kill with them. This, Spitzer believes, will inevitably result in an increase in gun-related crimes and accidents. Many law enforcement officers across the nation claim that they are already outgunned by criminals who often have much more powerful weapons than they do.

The Bellevue, Washington–based Second Amendment Foundation, a gun rights organization, counters that only law-abiding citizens observe laws. To use a misinterpretation of the Second Amendment to control or restrict gun use by law-abiding citizens would leave them perilously exposed to those who do not obey laws. (See Chapters 9 and 10 concerning arguments for and against gun control.) Furthermore, just because the quality of handguns, like most consumer products, has improved is no reason to override the Second Amendment.

CHAPTER 2
HOW MANY GUNS ARE THERE, AND WHO OWNS THEM?

OWNERSHIP BY PRIVATE CITIZENS

Only Estimates

The actual number of privately owned guns in the United States is impossible to accurately determine. Many guns are unregistered, and there is no reliable method for counting them. Each state has its own method of gun registration, and overlapping categories make it difficult to arrive at an accurate count of the total number of guns American citizens hold.

Weapons, Crime and Violence in America (Washington, D.C., 1981), a two-year research study conducted by the Social and Demographic Research Institute of the University of Massachusetts at Amherst for the National Institute of Justice (NIJ), concluded there were roughly 80 million (plus or minus 20 million) guns in private hands in 1968. A decade later, in 1978, the study put the estimate at about 120 million (plus or minus 20 million). In both years, handguns accounted for an estimated 25 to 30 percent of the total number of weapons, while shoulder weapons (rifles and shotguns) accounted for the rest. In 1994, according to an NIJ survey, Americans owned 192 million guns. By the end of 1996, the Bureau of Alcohol, Tobacco and Firearms (ATF) estimated that approximately 242 million firearms were available for sale or were owned by private citizens. Since then, 4.5 million new firearms, including two million handguns, and two million secondhand firearms have been added to those numbers each year through 1999, bringing the total number of guns privately owned or available for sale in the United States to over 260 million.

ATF Estimates

The ATF's mission includes regulatory and law enforcement duties relating to firearms. The ATF arrives at the total number of firearms by adding domestic firearms production and imports since 1899, then subtracting firearms exports during the same period. They do not take into account guns that are destroyed or no longer function. Higher depreciation rates would result in a lower estimated current stock. The ATF statistics also do not account for guns smuggled into or out of the United States or guns manufactured illegally. Therefore, no one really knows how many firearms are in the United States.

According to the ATF and the Bureau of Justice Statistics (*Commerce in Firearms in the United States,* February 2000), during the 99-year period from 1899 to 1998, 243 million guns became available for sale in the United States. These included over 86 million rifles, 84 million handguns, and 71 million shotguns. The ATF estimated that there were 54 million guns for sale in the United States in 1950, 104 million in 1970, 165 million in 1980, 206 million in 1990, and 260 million at the end of 1998. It concluded that the increase in the total number of firearms in the United States was due primarily to a sharp rise in imports rather than from increases in domestic production. From 1990 to 1999, ATF data suggests that the net import of rifles, shotguns, and handguns combined averaged up to one million per year, with handguns accounting for roughly half that figure.

U.S. FIREARM MANUFACTURING

The upward trend in annual firearms sales in the United States surged in the early 1990s to a peak in 1993 of some eight million small arms, half of which were handguns. Since then, sales have fallen back to about half that level, which accounts for the steady trend seen in recent manufacturing statistics. In 1997 manufacturers produced 1,036,077 pistols and 370,428 revolvers. Other firearms produced included rifles (1,251,341), shotguns (915,978), machine guns (67,844), and miscellaneous firearms (19,669). A comparison with the same figures for 1998 (see Table 2.1) showed relatively minor fluctuations. For example, the number of pistols was down slightly for 1998 (960,365), as was the number of revolvers (324,390), while the numbers of rifles and shotguns man-

TABLE 2.1

Annual firearms manufacturing report, 1998

Pistols		Revolvers	
TO .22	184,836	TO .22	68,108
TO .25	50,936	TO .32	2,602
TO .32	62,338	TO .39 SPEC	77,289
TO .380	98,266	TO .357 MAG	73,905
TO 9MM	284,374	TO .44 MAG	64,236
TO .50	279,615	TO .50	38,250
Total	**960,365**	**Total**	**324,390**

Rifles	1,345,899
Shotguns	1,036,520
Machine guns	32,866
Any other weapon	645
Misc. firearms	24,506

* For purposes of this report only, "production" is defined as: firearms, including separate frames or receivers, actions or barreled actions, manufactured and disposed of in commerce during the calendar year.

SOURCE: *Annual Firearms Manufacturing and Export Report 1998*, U.S. Bureau of Alcohol, Tobacco and Firearms, Washington, D.C., 1999

ufactured in 1998 were slightly higher than the same figures for the year before. Table 2.2 describes the various kinds of firearms.

Despite the stabilizing trend in the sale and manufacture of firearms since 1993, the ATF points out that sales per adult are higher today than in the 1950s and the early 1960s, even with increases in population factored in. In the past few years, the bureau has detected a growing demand for U.S. firearms. Basing its conclusions on industry newsletters, trade publications, and media reports, the agency attributes the recent increase to:

- Concern that various legislative proposals would prohibit or restrict the availability of firearms

- Acquisition of firearms for home/self-defense because of concern over increasing violent crime

- Increasing exportation of U.S. firearms

- Generally increased interest in firearms

The bureau concluded that the production of large-caliber semiautomatic pistols has more than tripled, due in part to more law enforcement agencies adopting these types of weapons.

IMPORTS

From 1899 to 1999, the United States imported 60.2 million firearms and exported 2.3 million. In 1999 about 892,000 firearms were imported—nearly 308,000 handguns, 198,000 rifles, and 386,000 shotguns. These numbers are down significantly from their peak in 1993, when over three million firearms were imported, including four times as many handguns and almost eight times as many rifles. Table 2.3 illustrates the rise in gun imports in the U.S. civilian market from 1978 to 1994, the year after the peak.

TABLE 2.2

What are the different types of firearms?

Types	
Handgun	A weapon designed to fire a small projectile from one or more barrels when held in one hand with a short stock designed to be gripped by one hand.
Revolver	A handgun that contains its ammunition in a revolving cylinder that typically holds five to nine cartridges, each within a separate chamber. Before a revolver fires, the cylinder rotates, and the next chamber is aligned with the barrel.
Pistol	Any handgun that does not contain its ammunition in a revolving cylinder. Pistols can be manually operated or semiautomatic. A semiautomatic pistol generally contains cartridges in a magazine located in the grip of the gun. When the semiautomatic pistol is fired, the spent cartridge that contained the bullet and propellant is ejected, the firing mechanism is cocked, and a new cartridge is chambered.
Derringer	A small single- or multiple-shot handgun other than a revolver or semiautomatic pistol.
Rifle	A weapon intended to be fired from the shoulder that uses the energy of the explosive in a fixed metallic cartridge to fire only a single projectile through a rifled bore for each single pull of the trigger.
Shotgun	A weapon intended to be fired from the shoulder that uses the energy of the explosive in a fixed shotgun shell to fire through a smooth bore either a number of ball shot or a single projectile for each single pull of the trigger
Firing action	
Fully automatic	Capability to fire a succession of cartridges so long as the trigger is depressed or until the ammunition supply is exhausted. Automatic weapons are considered machineguns subject to the provisions of the National Firearms Act.
Semiautomatic	An autoloading action that will fire only a single shot for each single function of a trigger.
Machine gun	Any weapon that shoots, is designed to shoot, or can be readily restored to shoot automatically more than one shot without manual reloading by a single function of the trigger.
Submachine gun	A simple fully automatic weapon that fires a pistol cartridge that is also referred to as a machine pistol.
Ammunition	
Caliber	The size of the ammunition that a weapon is designed to shoot, as measured by the bullet's approximate diameter in inches in the United States and in millimeters in other countries. In some instances, ammunition is described with additional terms, such as the year of its introduction (.30/06) or the name of the designer (.30 Newton). In some countries, ammunition is also described in terms of the length of the cartridge case (7.62 x 63 mm).
Gauge	For shotguns, the number of spherical balls of pure lead, each exactly fitting the bore, that equals one pound.

SOURCE: *Guns Used in Crime*, U.S. Bureau of Justice Statistics, Washington, D.C., 1995

The increase in the number of firearms imported in the mid-1990s is partially attributable to increased levels of trade with China and the former Communist countries. Imports of inexpensive Chinese rifles increased dramatically between 1992 and 1994. In 1992 China sold 164,271 rifles to the United States; in 1993 it sold 490,399. Chinese rifles accounted for nearly two-thirds (64 percent) of all imported rifles in 1993. (See Table 2.4.) In 1994 President Bill Clinton imposed a ban on the import of Chinese guns as a condition of renewing China's "most favored nation" trading status. Since then, gun imports from

TABLE 2.3

Guns imported into the U.S. civilian market

	1978	1994	Percent Change
Handguns	180,275	1,395,320	674%
Rifles	204,401	698,907	242%
Shotguns	362,462	145,233	- 60%
Total	**747,138**	**2,239,460**	**200%**

SOURCE: Copyright 1999 *Making a Killing,* by Tom Diaz. Reproduced by permission of The New Press, 450 W. 41st St., New York, NY 10036

TABLE 2.4

Rifle imports from China to the United States, 1987–94

	Total rifles imported	Chinese rifles imported	Percent Chinese
1987	452,059	100,897	22%
1988	484,976	182,935	38%
1989	350,012	141,382	40%
1990	273,102	31,370	11%
1991	339,966	115,902	34%
1992	420,085	164,271	39%
1993	764,498	490,399	64%
1994	698,907	344,648	49%
Total	**3,783,605**	**1,571,804**	**42%**

SOURCE: Copyright 1999 *Making a Killing,* by Tom Diaz. Reproduced by permission of The New Press, 450 W. 41st St., New York, NY 10036

TABLE 2.5

Leading handgun exporters to the United States, 1991–96

1991		1992		1993	
Brazil	218,382	Brazil	316,160	Brazil	319,281
Austria	115,430	Italy	178,318	Austria	184,283
Germany	90,842	Austria	164,034	Germany	155,374
Italy	71,616	Germany	114,032	Italy	120,055
Spain	68,706	Hungary	72,253	Spain	112,473
1994		1995		1996	
Brazil	372,003	Brazil	213,859	Austria	213,387
Russia	215,585	Austria	202,259	Brazil	182,775
Austria	209,820	Germany	181,711	Germany	113,632
Germany	165,302	Italy	74,650	Italy	57,149
Spain	95,014	Spain	53,849	Spain	22,476

SOURCE: Copyright 1999 *Making a Killing,* by Tom Diaz. Reproduced by permission of The New Press, 450 W. 41st St., New York, NY 10036

TABLE 2.6

Annual firearms export report, 1998

Pistols	29,537
Revolvers	15,788
Rifles	65,807
Shotguns	89,699
Machine guns	12,529
Any other weapon	23
Misc. firearms	2,513

Amended 3-08-2000 by NES
Rifle & shotgun totals change

SOURCE: *Annual Firearms Manufacturing and Export Report 1998,* U.S. Bureau of Alcohol, Tobacco and Firearms, Washington, D.C., 1999

China, as well as from other countries, has dropped from an average of 2.9 million for the years 1992–94 to an average of 940,000 for the years 1997–99.

Nonetheless, many Chinese-made firearms are imported illegally. In May 1996 the ATF and U.S. Customs Service found that thousands of guns had been manufactured and shipped by two state-controlled companies in China to the United States—a clear violation of a trade pact between the two countries. The two companies had covered up the origin of the guns by shipping them out of rarely policed ports in the Philippines, Thailand, and Cambodia.

After the collapse of the former Soviet Union, the United States removed import restrictions on the former Iron Curtain countries (Russia, Poland, Hungary, Czechoslovakia, and East Germany). Consequently, the number of guns these countries shipped to the United States increased immediately and significantly. According to ATF figures, the number of rifles imported from Russia grew from fewer than 3,000 in 1993 to more than a quarter of a million in 1994.

For nearly two decades, five countries—Brazil, Germany, Italy, Spain, and Austria—were the top exporters of handguns to the United States. Brazil remained at the top until 1996, when Austria sold the most handguns to the United States. Two former Iron Curtain countries, Hungary and Russia, were among the top five in 1992 and 1994, respectively. (See Table 2.5.)

EXPORTS

In 1998 the United States exported 215,896 guns. About one-fourth were handguns, nearly one-third were rifles, and almost half were shotguns. (See Table 2.6 for the actual numbers of each type.) The number of exported handguns (pistols and revolvers) dropped from an all-time high of 229,603 in 1995. The number of machine guns exported in 1998 decreased from 33,875 in 1996 and 40,940 in 1985. In 1993, however, only 7,012 machine guns were exported.

AUTOMATIC AND SEMIAUTOMATIC FIREARMS

The 1986 Firearms Owners' Protection Act (PL 99-308, revised in PL 99-360) banned the sale of machine guns made after May 19, 1986 (see Chapter 3). Not surprisingly, the ATF was flooded with 80,000 applications for licenses to sell or buy automatic firearms before the cutoff date. In 1989 the ATF issued an order permanently banning the importation of 43 of the 50 models of semiautomatic assault-type guns that President George Bush had conditionally banned several months earlier following a schoolyard shooting in Stockton, California, that killed five and wounded 29 (see Chapter 3). The ATF estimated that, at that time, Americans owned three million semiautomatic firearms, about one-fourth of which were imported. The ATF claimed that, without the ban, an estimated 700,000–1,000,000 semiautomatic assault guns would have been imported in 1989.

The Violent Crime Control Act of 1994 (PL 103-322) banned the sale and possession of 19 assault-type firearms and copycat models, including the Uzi, the TEC-9, and the Street Sweeper. The act also limited the capacity of newly manufactured magazines (a cartridge holder that feeds the gun chamber automatically) to 10 cartridges.

According to the ATF, assault guns account for less than 2 percent of all guns in the United States. Of those guns used in crimes each year, about 6–8 percent are assault guns. "As a type, they are a relatively new development, and their representation in the population of guns is small," said Jack Killorin, a bureau spokesperson. He further commented that their use in committing crimes is "vastly out of proportion to their number."

Gun control advocates believe that semiautomatic firearms should be banned because they are suitable for, or convertible to, military or criminal use. They claim that the guns are disproportionately being used as weapons for criminal purposes. The National Rifle Association defends the use of these firearms for hunting, informal target shooting, and many forms of competitive target shooting. It further claims that many other guns offer criminals the same capacity to kill and that the only way to stop their use is to control criminals.

Imported Assault Weapons

According to the Violence Policy Center, a national nonprofit educational foundation that conducts research on violence in America, efforts to keep foreign-made assault weapons out of the United States have not been successful. The center blames the ATF for failing to treat assault weapons as a distinct class of firearm. Because the agency relies on specific gun-by-gun analysis, manufacturers can make slight cosmetic modifications that change little, if any, of the gun's characteristics. To gain import approval, for example, foreign manufacturers often "sporterize" their weapons. This allows them to claim on the application for import approval that the particular firearm is suitable for "sporting purposes."

In 1997 the ATF approved import permits for 150,000 foreign-made assault rifles and was considering permits for another 600,000 assault rifles, including the Uzi. President Clinton reacted with an order to suspend all outstanding import permits and to review the ATF's interpretation and implementation of the "sporting purposes" test, a provision of the Gun Control Act of 1968 (see Chapter 3). In April 1998 Clinton ordered the ATF to prohibit the importation of modified semiautomatic assault rifles that possess the ability to accept large-capacity magazines holding more than 10 rounds, concluding that such weapons are unsuitable for "sporting purposes."

AMERICANS WHO OWN GUNS

Guns in the Home

In "Guns in America: National Survey on Private Ownership and Use of Firearms" (*National Institute of Justice Research in Brief*, May 1997) Philip J. Cook and Jens Ludwig reported on the findings of the 1994 *National Survey on Private Ownership and Use of Firearms* (NSPOF). The NSPOF indicated that about 35 percent of households owned guns, a number that contradicted the long-held belief that about half of American households had guns. In 1994, 44 million Americans owned nearly 200 million guns, enough to have provided every adult in the United States with one gun. However, only 25 percent of adults actually owned a gun; three-quarters of this number possessed two or more.

Persons who had several guns tended to have varied collections, including long guns (such as rifles and shotguns) and handguns (pistols and revolvers). One-third (65 million) of the guns owned were handguns. By comparison, the proportion of handguns used in crimes is more than twice that, at 77 percent, according to *Crime Gun Trace Reports* (1999), published by the ATF. (See Figure 2.1.)

In the *1999 National Gun Policy Survey of the National Opinion Research Center: Research Findings* (National Opinion Research Center, University of Chicago, July 2000) Tom Smith reported on the third annual gun policy survey by the National Opinion Research Center (NORC). According to this survey (NGPS), conducted about four years later than the NSPOF, about 40 percent of American households had at least one gun (see Table 2.7), including handguns and long guns. Nearly 17 percent owned long guns only, while almost 6 percent owned handguns only. About 18 percent of households owned both types of guns.

Gun Ownership Trends over the Past 25 Years

Table 2.8 includes NORC data from the 1973–96 *General Social Survey* and all three *National Gun Policy* surveys (1996, 1997–98, and 1999) to show the trends in private gun ownership over the past 25 years. Overall, the proportion of households with guns has been dropping slowly since 1977, despite the slight rise from an average of 34.7 percent in 1998 to 35.8 percent in 1999. In the early 1970s, about half of adults lived in households that kept a gun. This proportion fell to slightly less than 40

FIGURE 2.1

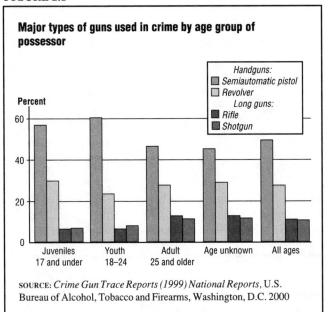

Major types of guns used in crime by age group of possessor

SOURCE: *Crime Gun Trace Reports (1999) National Reports,* U.S. Bureau of Alcohol, Tobacco and Firearms, Washington, D.C. 2000

TABLE 2.7

Levels of gun ownership and puchases

Have Gun in Household	39.9%
Respondent Owns Gun	27.2
Other Person Owns Gun	13.6
No Gun in Household	59.2
Have Handgun in Household	22.2
Respondent Owns Handgun	17.1
No Guns in Household	59.8
Handgun Only	5.6
Long gun Only	17.0
Both Types of Guns	17.6
Bought Handgun	21.1
Never Bought Handgun	77.8
Refused, etc.	1.1

SOURCE: Tom W. Smith, *1999 National Gun Policy Survey of the National Opinion Research Center: Research Findings,* National Opinion Research Center, University of Chicago, Chicago, IL, 2000

TABLE 2.8

Trends in gun ownership—overall

	Percent of adults in households with guns	Percent of households with guns	Percent of adults personally owning gun
1973	49.1	47.3	–
1974	47.9	46.2	–
1976	49.7	46.7	–
1977	54.0	50.7	–
1980	50.8	47.7	29.0
1982	48.9	45.5	29.1
1984	48.5	45.2	25.5
1985	48.1	44.3	30.7
1987	48.6	46.1	28.2
1988	43.4	40.1	25.2
1989	48.9	46.1	27.4
1990	45.8	42.7	28.7
1991	43.7	39.9	27.6
1993	45.5	42.1	29.4
1994	43.9	40.7	28.5
1996	43.4	40.2	27.2
1996	42.3	39.1	30.8
1997	38.6	37.4	28.7
1998	36.8	34.9	22.5
1998	37.8	34.5	25.4
1999	39.9	35.8	27.2

SOURCE: Tom W. Smith, *1999 National Gun Policy Survey of the National Opinion Research Center: Research Findings,* National Opinion Research Center, University of Chicago, Chicago, IL, 2000

TABLE 2.9

Trends in gun ownership–type of firearm

	Percent of adults in household with handguns	Percent of adults in household with long guns
1973	20.3	42.1
1974	20.3	40.4
1976	22.2	41.7
1977	21.3	45.8
1980	24.3	42.8
1982	22.4	41.5
1984	22.4	41.3
1985	24.2	39.5
1987	26.5	41.9
1988	24.4	35.9
1989	26.8	40.0
1990	24.9	37.3
1991	22.1	37.0
1993	26.1	36.7
1994	26.2	35.4
1996	23.7	34.8
1996	24.8	36.9
1997	24.0	31.1
1998	20.7	29.0
1998	23.1	31.9
1999	22.2	33.5

SOURCE: Tom W. Smith, *1999 National Gun Policy Survey of the National Opinion Research Center: Research Findings,* National Opinion Research Center, University of Chicago, Chicago, IL, 2000

percent in 1999, partly because of a decrease in household size. The proportion of households with guns has steadily dropped from a high of 50.7 percent in 1977.

In addition, there has been a shift in the types of guns that Americans own. Probably because of a decline in hunting as a recreational pursuit, the proportion of adults in households with long guns dropped from a high of nearly 46 percent in 1977 to 33.5 percent in 1999. On the other hand, the proportion of adults living in a household

with a handgun increased, from about 20 percent in 1973 to 22–26 percent in the 1990s. (See Table 2.9.)

Louis Harris and Associates conducted a poll on gun ownership and found that 39 percent of the respondents in 1999 reported owning a gun. (See Table 2.10.) This drop from 48 percent nearly two decades earlier, in 1980, may be due, at least in part, to an unwillingness to admit to having a gun in the home, following recent news stories about children getting and using such guns. Between 1996 and 1999, ownership of all types of guns declined, except shotguns, which rose from 27 percent in 1996 to 29 percent in 1999.

GUN OWNERSHIP AND HOMICIDE IN THE HOME

In "Gun Ownership as a Risk Factor for Homicide in the Home" (*New England Journal of Medicine,* October 1993) Kellermann et al. studied homicides in Shelby County, Tennessee, and King County, Washington, from 1987 to 1992 and in Cuyahoga County, Ohio, from 1990 to 1992. Firearms killed 50 percent of the victims. One-quarter (26 percent) were killed with knives or other sharp instruments, while the rest were bludgeoned (12 percent), strangled (6 percent), or killed by other means.

Reasons for Murder

Approximately 80 percent of the victims were killed by relatives or acquaintances. Quarrels or romantic triangles led to the deaths of 50 percent of the victims, while felonies accounted for 22 percent and drug dealing for another 8 percent. The rest were either murder–suicide cases or had unknown motives. In 44 percent of the cases, the victims attempted to defend themselves. In 5 percent of these cases, the victim unsuccessfully attempted to use a gun in self-defense.

Demographics of the Households

The study compared information about victims' households (called "case" households) with that of "control" households—those in which a homicide did not take place. In twice as many instances, case households had members with previous arrest records. Violent relationships were more common in case households than in the control homes. Approximately one-third (32 percent) of the case subjects admitted that someone in the household had been hit or hurt in a fight in the home, while only about 6 percent of control households admitted to domestic-violence episodes.

ALCOHOL AND DRUGS. The researchers found a correlation between drinking and drug use and homicides in the home. While only 56 percent of the control household members drank alcohol, nearly three-quarters (73 percent) of the case households did. One-quarter of the case subjects reported alcohol-related physical fights in the home, compared with only about 3 percent of the control subjects. Illicit drug use in the case households occurred more often than in the control households.

Guns in the Homes

The researchers found that 45 percent of the homes in which a homicide occurred had at least one firearm, compared with 36 percent of the control group homes. Case households were 50 percent more likely to have a handgun, while both control and case households had similar percentages of shotguns and rifles. Case households were about twice as likely to have loaded guns, and one-and-a-half times more likely to have guns kept unlocked, than the control households.

TABLE 2.10

Gun ownership, 1973–99

"Do you happen to have in your home or garage any guns or revolvers?"

If Yes
"Do you have a pistol or not?"
"Do you have a shotgun or not?"
"Do you have a rifle or not?"

	1973 %	1980 %	1988 %	1994 %	1996 %	1999 %
Have a gun or revolver in home	48	48	41	41	40	39
Have a pistol	20	23	23	25	25	25
Have a shotgun	28	30	24	24	27	29
Have a rifle	29	29	24	25	29	27
No, don't have guns	52	52	59	59	60	61

SOURCE: Humphrey Taylor, The Harris Poll #38, Wednesday, June 23, 1999, Harris Interactive, New York, NY, 1999

Security Measures

The researchers found that home-security measures and locks had little effect on the risk of home homicide. Family members and acquaintances committed most of the homicides, and they usually had easy access to the home. The researchers concluded that a gun kept in the home is much more likely to be involved in the death of a household member than it is to be used to kill in self-defense. They also considered illicit-drug use and a history of physical violence as important risk factors.

Disagreement with the Findings

Wayne La Pierre, Jr. (*USA Today,* October 11, 1993), then executive vice president of the National Rifle Association, thought the report was flawed. La Pierre claimed that the study emphasized instances in which firearms were used to kill someone and that it did not analyze the 99.8 percent of firearm use in which no one is killed. According to La Pierre, the study did not incorporate the 1.1 million cases annually in which he claimed people successfully used firearms for protection. (See below for the study upon which this claim is based.)

La Pierre also thought that the sample of people surveyed did not represent mainstream America. Half of the victim households had members with arrest records; one-third had members who used illegal drugs. La Pierre also considered the study biased because the Centers for Disease Control and Prevention (CDC), a government agency that he believed supports strict gun control measures, provided funding.

CHARACTERISTICS OF GUN OWNERS

In "Who Owns Guns? Criminals, Victims, and the Culture of Violence" (*American Economic Review,* Vol. 88, No. 2, May 1998) Edward L. Glaeser and Spencer Glendon reported their findings on the characteristics of

FIGURE 2.2

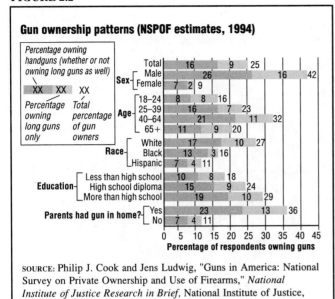

Gun ownership patterns (NSPOF estimates, 1994)

SOURCE: Philip J. Cook and Jens Ludwig, "Guns in America: National Survey on Private Ownership and Use of Firearms," *National Institute of Justice Research in Brief,* National Institute of Justice, Washington, D.C., 1997

gun owners. (The purpose of the article was to examine the existing studies and literature to understand in what situations private justice still dominates public protection of life and property.) They concluded that gun owners are most likely to be:

- White married men, over age 40, with teenage children (rather than infants or young children)

- High school graduates who make higher incomes and own their own homes

- Hunters

- Residents of the South who live away from large cities and in areas where police are less available

- Members of social groups in which gun ownership is the norm, perhaps because of a mistrust of public justice or because reliance on public justice is seen as a lack of individual competence

- Individuals with a tendency toward more violent types of retribution

In 1994, based on the *National Survey of Private Ownership of Firearms* (see above), far more men (42 percent) than women (9 percent) reported owning a gun. (See Figure 2.2.) Compared with 7 percent of women, 26 percent of men owned handguns; they may have owned long guns as well. Sixteen percent of men owned a long gun only, while only 2 percent of women reported owning just a long gun. Whites (27 percent) were substantially more likely than blacks (16 percent) or Hispanics (11 percent) to own guns. However, for handguns alone, the NSPOF found that ownership rates among whites and blacks were similar: 16.5 percent and 13.1 percent, respectively.

According to the survey, middle-aged, college-educated people of rural and small-town America were most likely to own guns. About one-third of the respondents between 40 and 64 years of age reported owning a gun. Those with more than a high school diploma were more likely to own a gun than those with less education. A significant predictor of gun ownership was the presence of a gun in the respondent's childhood home. Those whose parents had owned guns were three times as likely to own a gun themselves. Of the survey respondents, 36 percent of those who owned guns said their parents had a gun in the home. (See Figure 2.2.) In fact, 80 percent of all current gun owners said that their parents kept a gun in the home.

The *1999 National Gun Policy Survey* (see above) also showed that ownership is generally concentrated among certain sociodemographic groups. (See Table 2.11.) Men (44.4 percent) were far more likely to own guns than were women (11.6 percent). More respondents in the Midwest (46.9 percent) said they had a gun in the household, and handgun ownership was also highest there (29.7 percent), although only slightly higher than in the South (29.0 percent). In general, those who were married were more likely to have guns. According to the NGPS, personal gun ownership did not vary much by education level, though it was lowest for those with a college degree.

Table 2.11 indicates that gun ownership also varies with household income. Households with an income of $50,000–$59,000 reported the highest levels of gun ownership, with a drop-off in the $60,000–$79,000 bracket and a further drop-off at the highest level of household income.

Middle-aged Americans were more likely to own guns than those under 30 and over 65. The decline in gun ownership in the over-65 age category is partly due to the greater proportion of women among the elderly. (See Table 2.11.)

REASONS FOR OWNING A GUN

About half the respondents to the 1994 NSPOF survey reported using guns for recreation: either for hunting or for other sport shooting. (See Figure 2.3.) Self-protection was another important reason for gun ownership: 41 percent of men and 67 percent of women said they owned a gun primarily as protection against crime. A larger percentage, almost 75 percent of those who owned handguns, kept them primarily for self-defense.

Of those who did not own guns, about two-thirds were opposed to guns in their homes because they felt guns were dangerous, immoral, or otherwise objectionable. The other one-third reported they might obtain a gun if their financial condition or motivation became stronger. Close to 5 percent reported they planned to get a gun as protection against crime within a year.

TABLE 2.11

Gun ownership by socio-demographics

	Gun in household	Handgun in household	Personally owns gun
Men	45.2%	26.1%	44.4%
Women	35.1**	18.6**	11.6**
Northeast	26.9	15.1	21.0
Midwest	46.9	17.0	29.7
South	43.5	26.5	29.0
West	38.5**	26.7**	27.1**
Rural	66.7	34.7	43.7
Town, small city	43.2	21.3	26.8
Suburb	26.7	17.2	21.2
Large City	28.9**	18.6**	20.9**
Married	50.6	28.1	33.4
Divorced	27.4	18.4	22.5
Separated	28.4	26.7	28.9
Widowed	33.3	13.2	21.1
Never married	24.5**	13.2**	17.6**
Less than high school	43.9	20.4	32.2
High school	43.3	21.4	28.8
College	37.8	24.4	24.8
Greater than college	34.2	19.4	25.8
$0-9,999	26.6	15.0	21.0
$10,000-19,999	38.1	17.5	27.4
$20,000-29,999	43.0	16.1	29.1
$30,000-39,999	40.4	20.0	28.8
$40,000-49,999	40.3	20.3	20.1
$50,000-59,999	51.5	41.7	35.8
$60-000-79,999	44.6	24.3	33.0
$80,000+	37.9**	24.5**	31.5*
Less than 30 years old	30.6	12.9	21.1
30-39	37.9	21.8	23.2
40-49	45.8	21.5	29.5
50-65	47.5	30.2	33.1
65+	40.2**	26.0**	31.8*
No children in home	40.1	23.6	28.5
1 child	37.8	21.5	23.5
2 children	41.3	15.3	23.2
3 children	35.7	14.3	22.4
4+ children	49.8	38.7**	41.1
Republican	47.3	25.7	34.8
Independent	42.6	23.1	28.8
Democrat	31.7**	18.6*	20.4**
Liberal	29.6	15.5	19.7
Moderate	44.2	25.9	31.6
Conservative	41.3**	22.6*	27.0*

* Overall differences in distributions significant at .05-.002
** Overall differences in distributions significant at .001 or less

SOURCE: Tom W. Smith, *1999 National Gun Policy Survey of the National Opinion Research Center: Research Findings,* National Opinion Research Center, University of Chicago, Chicago, IL, 2000

Participants in the NGPS who did not personally own a gun were asked why not. (See Table 2.12.) The major reason, given by 39 percent, was a lack of interest in having a gun (never felt the need, don't participate in sports/hunting, and the like). One-third felt that guns were simply too dangerous (e.g., frequently involved in accidents and suicides). Other reasons included opposition to guns on ethical grounds, inexperience with guns, and cost.

Carrying Handguns

In the 1999 NGPS, participants were asked about carrying handguns away from home. Only 10 percent report-

FIGURE 2.3

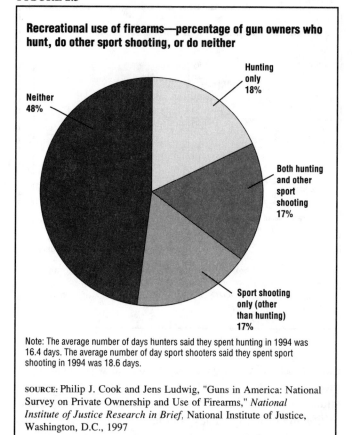

Recreational use of firearms—percentage of gun owners who hunt, do other sport shooting, or do neither

Neither 48%

Hunting only 18%

Both hunting and other sport shooting 17%

Sport shooting only (other than hunting) 17%

Note: The average number of days hunters said they spent hunting in 1994 was 16.4 days. The average number of day sport shooters said they spent sport shooting in 1994 was 18.6 days.

SOURCE: Philip J. Cook and Jens Ludwig, "Guns in America: National Survey on Private Ownership and Use of Firearms," *National Institute of Justice Research in Brief,* National Institute of Justice, Washington, D.C., 1997

ed that they had carried a gun away from home in 1999. Sixty-six percent of those said they carried the gun to a firing range or for target practice, followed by personal protection (63 percent), hunting (38 percent), and work-related (17 percent). (Most people gave more than one reason for carrying a handgun, with the average respondent giving two reasons.)

Of all handgun carriers, over half (55 percent) reported having their weapons loaded when carrying them, and those who did were more likely to be carrying the gun for protection. Fifty-five percent of handgun carriers possessed a permit for carrying a firearm in 1999, up from 42 percent in the 1997–98 NGPS. Those with permits were more likely to carry a handgun for work or for multiple reasons. Permits were not more common among carriers whose stated purpose was using the handgun for protection.

NATIONAL RIFLE ASSOCIATION MEMBERSHIP

The National Rifle Association (NRA) was founded in 1871 as an organization of hunters and shooters. Now a powerful political lobby, membership stands at approximately 3.5 million, up from 2.5 million in 1991 but down from 5 million in 1995. In 1995, after the bombing of a federal building in Oklahoma City, the NRA lost some of its lobbying power and public support when it lost its attempt to have Congress repeal the ban on assault

TABLE 2.12

Reasons for not owning a gun

Never felt the need for a gun	35.2%
Against guns/ethical reasons	11.6
Have children in the house	11.0
Felt guns more a threat than a help	8.4
Afraid of gun accident	6.2
Know someone killed/injured with gun	2.7
Afraid of suicide with gun	2.4
Don't participate in gun-type sports/hunting	2.3
Too expensive	2.0
Doesn't want/no interest	1.6
Can use spouse's, boyfriend's, other's	1.5
Don't know how to use	1.5
Bad temper/fear accident	1.1
Was stolen/destroyed	1.1
Gun may get in wrong hands	1.0
Has gun (e.g. at work)	1.0
Raised not to own gun	0.9
Lacks training/license	0.8
Spouse or girl/boyfriend against guns	0.3
Too young	0.3
Not allowed (e.g. in service)	0.3
Other	5.8
Unsure	1.1

SOURCE: Tom W. Smith, *1997–98 National Gun Policy Survey of the National Opinion Research Center: Research Findings,* National Opinion Research Center, University of Chicago, Chicago, IL, 1998

weapons. Former President George Bush, a lifetime NRA member, canceled his membership that same year after Wayne La Pierre, then president of the NRA, called federal agents "jack-booted thugs" who would stomp on citizens' Second Amendment rights.

In 1989 the NRA sponsored a survey to compare the characteristics of NRA members and gun owners who were not members. Of 605 respondents, 75 percent were men, 88 percent were white, and each owned at least one gun, with more than three-fourths (77 percent) owning more than one gun. Fewer than 2 in 10 of the respondents (17 percent) belonged to the NRA. The survey found no significant demographic differences between NRA members and those gun owners who were not members. However, handgun owners and those who owned more than one gun were more likely to belong to the NRA than those who owned long guns and only one firearm. Those who owned a gun for reasons other than protection were also more likely to be NRA members. In addition, the researchers found a positive correlation between NRA membership and formal training in the proper use of guns.

WOMEN AND GUNS

Gun groups such as the NRA believe that women are more likely to own guns today than they were at any point in the past century. Although the number of guns sold to women in the early part of the 20th century is unknown, studies show that women are buying guns in ever-increasing numbers. A 1988 poll sponsored by Smith & Wesson showed that the number of women who owned guns

increased 53 percent from 1983 to 1986. While not releasing sales figures, Ken Jorgensen, director of communications at Smith & Wesson, said that sales of the company's Lady Smith—first introduced in 1902 as a .22-caliber revolver and now a six-gun series that includes a 9mm pistol and five revolvers—doubled from 1991 to 1992. Several other companies, such as New England Firearms, Interarms, and Lorcin, also make guns for women.

In 1992, according to the NRA, at least 12 million women legally owned firearms. The NRA reported that 1.5 million were hunters and that women accounted for 15 percent of all competitive shooters. One observer noted that many women initially bought guns for self-defense and became recreational shooters later.

Organizations supporting private gun ownership actively recruit women for membership in an attempt to overcome the "males only" image of owning and handling a gun. Advertisements encourage women, particularly those who live alone, to learn how to select and properly use a handgun to protect themselves. In 1994 the Violence Policy Center published a report titled *Female Persuasion—Study of How the Firearms Industry Markets to Women and the Reality of Women and Guns.* The report showed how the National Shooting Sports Foundation, a firearms trade association, began a series of shooting competitions called the Ladies Charity Classic Events as a way of introducing women to guns.

According to the National Shooting Sports Foundation, all regional events operated by the Women's Shooting Sports Foundation include shooting clinics that are held before the tournament. The clinics are also associated with charitable causes. The clinics and charitable associations are said to have encouraged women to participate, even when they are not already shooters. These events have benefited shelters for abused women and children and facilities for breast cancer research and treatment. Handgun Control, Inc., and similar organizations that want to limit handgun ownership are trying to educate women on the dangers of possessing handguns.

Despite the efforts of organizations that support gun ownership to encourage women to purchase guns, and despite countless news reports about women buying guns in record numbers, a study by the University of Chicago's National Opinion Research Center showed that female gun ownership increased only slightly between 1980 and 1994. About 10.5 percent of women owned firearms in 1980, compared with 12.7 percent in 1994, an increase of 2.2 percent over 14 years. While 6.6 percent of women possessed handguns in 1980, only 8.3 percent did so in 1994. Meanwhile, the percentage of men who owned handguns increased from 27 percent in 1980 to 30.1 percent in 1994, while the percentage who possessed any type of firearm decreased from 52 percent in 1980 to 47 percent in 1994.

According to the Gallup Poll *Gun Laws and Women* (May 12, 2000), 22 percent of women respondents said that they personally owned a handgun, rifle, shotgun, or other kind of firearm. The figure for men in the same poll was more than double (46 percent).

The director of the National Opinion Research Center General Social Survey, Tom Smith, concluded that there is no proof that women are more likely to own guns or handguns in the past 14 years. He speculates that the idea of a record number of women rushing out to buy guns was created by gun groups to open a potential new market at a time when gun sales were decreasing and the male market had become saturated.

RETAIL SALES

By early 1996, Sears, JCPenney, Montgomery Ward, and Target had all stopped selling firearms because of the lack of profitability, concern over their liability should the guns be misused, and the difficulties involved in keeping track of the various local, state, and federal laws. Many of the stores removed firearms from their shelves because management thought guns did not fit the family image they were promoting. In fact, Kmart does not sell any handguns; and, Wal-Mart, while its customers can order them through the company's catalog, does not keep any handguns in stock.

On the other hand, Kmart and Wal-Mart do sell rifles and shotguns in their stores. Both companies are very concerned that they adequately train their sales staffs to comply with the various gun laws. In 1993 a Florida jury ordered the Kmart Corporation to pay $12.5 million for selling a firearm to a man so drunk the clerk had to fill out the forms for him. An appeals court later overturned the decision.

CHAPTER 3

FIREARM LAWS, REGULATIONS, AND ORDINANCES

The debate over the federal government's role in the regulation of firearms still rages after more than half a century. During the Roaring Twenties and into the 1930s, the nation was swept by a growing wave of crime committed by gangsters who had built criminal empires based on the illegal manufacture and sale of alcohol, which had been banned under the Nineteenth Amendment. In 1922 the American Bar Association (ABA) Committee on Law Enforcement called for a ban on the manufacture and sale of pistols except for government and official use.

In 1927, in an attempt to curb the mail-order business in handguns, Congress passed a law banning the mailing of handguns (18 USC 1715). Advocates of the new legislation claimed it would help the states to enforce their own state firearms regulations. During this period, many states did pass laws regulating the sale and use of handguns. However, supporters of the federal law could not get a law passed forbidding the shipment of handguns by a commercial carrier across state lines.

The National Firearms Act of 1934 (26 USC 5801 *et seq.*) was designed to make it more difficult to acquire especially dangerous "gangster-type" weapons such as machine guns, sawed-off shotguns, and silencers. The legislation placed heavy taxes on all aspects of the manufacture and distribution of these firearms and required registration of the firearm through the entire production, distribution, and sales process. This law is still in effect.

The Federal Firearms Act of 1938 (52 Stat. 1250) prohibited any manufacturer or dealer who was not federally licensed from sending or receiving of firearms across state lines. Firearms could not be sent to anyone who was a fugitive from justice or had been indicted or convicted of a felony. Furthermore, it was illegal to transport stolen guns from which the manufacturer's mark had been rubbed out or changed.

THE GUN CONTROL ACT OF 1968

In 1968 the Federal Firearms Act was repealed and the National Firearms Act substantially amended. In 1963 work had begun on what would become popularly known as the Gun Control Act of 1968 (PL 90-618). This legislation received a favorable response in the aftermath of the assassinations of President John F. Kennedy, Dr. Martin Luther King, Jr., and Senator Robert Kennedy.

The Gun Control Act of 1968 had two major titles. Title I (18 USC 921 *et seq*.) required anyone dealing in firearms or ammunition to be federally licensed. Title I also established tougher licensing standards than the previous law and prohibited the interstate mail-order sale of all firearms and ammunition, the interstate sale of handguns generally, and the interstate sale of long guns, except under certain conditions. It required dealers to keep records of all commercial gun sales. It forbade the sale of firearms or ammunition to minors or those with criminal records, generally outlawed the importation of nonsporting firearms, and established special penalties for the use or carrying of a firearm while committing a crime of violence or drug trafficking.

However, Title I did not forbid the importation of unassembled weapons parts, and some individuals and companies were suspected of importing separate firearms parts and then reassembling them into a complete weapon as a means of getting around the law. Title II extended the act's provisions to private ownership of so-called "destructive" devices such as submachine guns, bombs, and grenades.

Efforts to Amend the Gun Control Act of 1968

As a result of the passage of the Gun Control Act of 1968, Congress found itself under siege from both pro- and antigun groups. Firearms owners and dealers protested that some requirements of the act were burdensome and did not serve legitimate law enforcement purposes. Those urging tighter control on guns felt it did not go far enough in keeping firearms out of the hands of criminals. Others who advocated less control voiced concern that its restrictions penalized sportsmen. Every Congress from 1968 to 1986 introduced dozens of pieces of legislation to strengthen, repeal, or lessen the requirements of the 1968 act.

THE FIREARM OWNERS' PROTECTION ACT OF 1986

Nearly 20 years later, in 1986, the 99th Congress passed major legislation amending the 1968 firearms statute. The Firearm Owners' Protection Act of 1986 (PL 99-308, revised in PL 99-360) has become commonly referred to as the Gun Control Act of 1986 and is still in effect today. The following sections compare the Gun Control Act of 1968 with the Gun Control Act of 1986.

Prohibited Persons

The 1968 legislation prohibited a licensee (someone who had previously been permitted legal ownership) from transferring a firearm to any member of a specified high-risk category. Currently, it is unlawful for anyone, whether licensed or not, to sell or otherwise transfer a gun to any person included in the "high-risk" category—convicted felons, drug abusers, and persons with mental illnesses.

Interstate Sales

Under the 1968 act, it was unlawful to sell or deliver a firearm to anyone from another state, with the exception of long guns (rifles and shotguns), which could be sold to residents of contiguous (bordering) states with laws allowing such sales. Interstate over-the-counter sales of long guns by those licensed to sell them are now legal as long as the laws of both states permit them. A ban on the interstate sale of handguns is still in effect.

Purchasing Firearms and Ammunition

The Gun Control Act of 1968 stated that firearms and ammunition could be purchased only on the premises of a licensee, and licensees were required to record all firearms and ammunition transactions. The 1986 law made the purchase of ammunition and gun components by mail legal, as it had been prior to the Gun Control Act of 1968. Firearms dealers must keep records only of "armor-piercing" ammunition sales (see below). Establishments that sell only ammunition (no firearms) do not have to be licensed, so stores that previously may not have carried ammunition because of licensing requirements could now do so.

Jurisdictional Travel

The 1968 act was silent on the effects of state and local regulations concerning intrastate (within a state) transportation of weapons. The 1986 laws made it legal to transport any legally owned gun through a jurisdiction where it would otherwise be illegal, provided the possession and transporting of the weapon are legal at the point of origin and point of destination. The gun must be unloaded and placed in a locked container or in the trunk of a vehicle.

Federal Crimes

The 1968 legislation prohibited the carrying or use of a firearm during and in relation to a federal crime of violence. In addition, anyone convicted of this crime was subject to a minimum penalty over and above any sentence received for the primary offense. The 1986 act added serious drug offenses to the category of crimes and doubled the existing penalty if a machine gun or gun equipped with a silencer is used.

Forfeiture of Firearms and Ammunition

Prior to 1986, any firearm or ammunition involved in, used, or intended to be used in violation of the Gun Control Act or other federal criminal law could be taken away from the gun owner. The Gun Control Act of 1986 made forfeiture no longer automatic. For some offenses, a willful element must be demonstrated; for others, "knowledge" is enough. In the case of a firearm being "intended for use" in a violation, "clear and convincing evidence" of the intent must be shown. In addition, only specified crimes now justify forfeiture, including crimes of violence, drug-related offenses, and certain violations of the Gun Control Act. In all cases, forfeiture proceedings must begin within 120 days of seizure, and the court will award attorney's fees to the owner if the owner wins the case.

Criminal Penalties

The 1968 law stated that a demonstration of "willfulness" was not needed as an element of proof of violation of any provision of the act, while the Gun Control Act of 1986 requires proof of "willful" violation or a "knowing" violation in order to prosecute. It also reduced licensee record-keeping violations from felonies to misdemeanors.

Legal Disabilities

Under the 1968 law, any person convicted of a crime and sentenced to prison for more than one year was restricted from shipping, transporting, or receiving a firearm, and could not be granted a federal firearms license. State pardons could not erase the conviction for federal purposes. On the other hand, a convicted felon could make a special request to the secretary of the Treasury to be allowed to possess a firearm. The secretary of the Treasury must certify that the possession of a firearm by a convicted felon is not contrary to public interest and safety and that the applicant did not commit a crime involving a firearm or a violation of federal gun control laws.

Under the new law, state pardons can erase convictions for federal purposes, unless the person is specifically denied the right to possess or receive firearms. The 1986 law allows those who violated the laws to appeal, even those whose crime involved use of a firearm or a federal gun control conviction. This relief is not automatic; judicial review of the case must be requested.

Machine Gun Freeze

The National Firearms Act (1934) imposed production and transfer taxes, as well as registration requirements, on firearms typically associated with criminal activity. These restrictions specifically applied to machine guns, destructive devices such as bombs, missiles and grenades, and firearm silencers. A machine gun was defined as "any combination of parts designed and intended for use in converting a weapon to a machine gun."

The Firearms Owners' Protection Act of 1986 made it "unlawful for any person to transfer or possess a machine gun" unless it was manufactured and legally owned before May 19, 1986. In addition, the definition was revised to include any combination of parts "designed and intended solely and exclusively for use in conversion." The U.S. Supreme Court upheld the ban on machine gun ownership when it denied review in *Farmer v. Higgins* (907 F.2d 1041, 1990). (See Chapter 4.)

"COP-KILLER" BULLETS

The Law Enforcement Officers Protection Act of 1985 (PL 99-408) amended the 1968 Gun Control Act to ban the manufacture or importation of certain varieties of armor-piercing ammunition. The law defines the banned ammunition as handgun bullets made of specific hard metals: tungsten alloys, steel, brass, bronze, iron, beryllium copper, or depleted uranium. (Standard ammunition is made from lead.) It also decreed that the licenses of dealers who knowingly sold such ammunition should be revoked. The same legislation exempted bullets made for rifles and sporting purposes, as well as ammunition sometimes used in oil- and gas-well perforating devices.

The 1994 Violent Crime Control Act (see below) broadened the ban to include other metal-alloy ammunition. Both laws limit the sale of such bullets to the U.S. military or to the police.

This legislation banning armor-piercing ammunition was politically important because it created a situation in which two traditionally allied groups, the National Rifle Association and the nation's police officers, were on opposite sides. The police saw this as a very personal issue, since the alleged "cop-killer" bullets were intended to harm them. On the other hand, the NRA felt that police were in no more danger from armor-piercing bullets than from other bullets.

PLASTIC GUNS

The nation's concern for the hijacking of aircraft led to the eventual passage of the Undetectable Firearms Act of 1988 (PL 100-649), which bars the manufacture of guns that contain less than 3.7 ounces of metal and cannot be detected by the X-ray security systems used at airports. Although no such plastic firearms were yet being manufactured in the United States, Congress began hearings in 1986 to determine if such weapons represented a danger to airline passengers.

Several overseas firms manufacture plastic firearms, which, since they are light and noncorrosive, have advantages over current all-metal guns. Many American police departments were already buying these firearms, and it is likely that plastic will increasingly be substituted for metal parts. Unfortunately, while these weapons may be an improvement over current models, they have aroused the concern of many who fear terrorists might use them to pass through metal detectors and then hijack an airplane.

The National Rifle Association (NRA) opposed the proposed legislation as unnecessary and as the first step toward the banning of handguns. This time, however, the NRA lost the support of a valuable ally in the Reagan administration. The Law Enforcement Steering Committee, formed earlier in the year to support the "Brady Amendment" (see below), convinced then Attorney General Edwin Meese III that such weapons posed an unacceptable hazard to public safety, and that this was, therefore, a necessary piece of legislation.

The Undetectable Firearms Act of 1988 banned the manufacture, import, sale, transfer, or possession of a "plastic firearm." A "plastic firearm" was defined as "any firearm containing less than 3.7 ounces of electromagnetically detectable metal." However, the act also stated, "[I]f the major parts of the firearms do not permit an accurate X-ray picture of the gun's shape, the firearm is [also defined as] a plastic firearm, even if the firearm contains more than 3.7 ounces of electromagnetically detectable metal."

TOY GUNS

A law requiring that a "toy, look-alike, or imitation firearm shall have as an integral part, permanently affixed, a blaze orange plug inserted in the barrel of such toy, look-alike, or imitation firearm" was passed as Section 4 of the Federal Energy Management Improvement Act of 1988 (PL 100-615). The law provided for alternative markings if the orange plug could not be used.

Ending Sales of Look-alike Toy Guns

In November 1994 three major toy retailers announced that they would stop selling toy guns designed to look like real guns. After the look-alikes led to tragic consequences, Kay-Bee Toy Stores, Toys "R" Us, Inc., and Bradlees, Inc., made the decision, even though the sale of these guns had generated almost $250 million. In two separate incidents, a 13-year-old male was shot and killed and a 16-year-old male was seriously wounded when police mistook their look-alike toy guns for real weapons. The New York Police Department also found that realistic-looking toy guns had been used in 534 felonies by October 1994.

GUN-FREE SCHOOL ZONES

The Gun-Free School Zones Act [18 U.S.C. Sect. 921(a)(25, 26), 922(q)(1)], as part of the Crime Control Act of 1990 (PL 101-647), made it unlawful for anyone to knowingly possess firearms in school zones. It also made it illegal to carry unloaded firearms in an unlocked suitcase on public sidewalks in front of one's residence as long as that part of the sidewalk is within 1,000 feet of the grounds of any public or private school, whether or not school is in session.

In April 1995, however, the Supreme Court struck down the act (see Chapter 4) in *U.S. v. Lopez* (514 U.S. 549). In response to the court's ruling, Congress approved a slightly revised version of the Gun-Free School Zones Act in 1996 (PL 104-208), requiring prosecutors to prove an impact on interstate commerce as an element of the offense.

THE BRADY HANDGUN VIOLENCE PREVENTION ACT

A National Waiting Period Established

In November 1993, after years of debate, Congress passed the Brady Handgun Violence Prevention Act (PL 103-159) named for presidential press secretary James S. Brady, who was shot by John Hinckley during an attempted assassination of President Ronald Reagan in 1981. Hinckley was quickly apprehended and placed in custody. Brady was seriously wounded and suffers from injuries that generally confine him to a wheelchair. Despite his injuries, he nominally retained his position as press secretary for the Reagan administration. Today, Brady and his wife, Sara, lobby for greater control over guns and are leaders in Handgun Control, Inc., a gun control lobby.

The Brady Law, which went into effect February 28, 1994,

- Established a national five-day waiting period to allow local law enforcement to conduct background checks on handgun purchasers for instability or criminal backgrounds and to serve as a cooling-off period that might reduce gun-related crimes of passion

- Applies only to handgun sales by licensed dealers and not to sales by nondealers

- Requires dealers to send, within one day, a copy of the purchaser's sworn statement (see Figure 3.1) to the chief law enforcement officer where the purchaser resides. The dealer can complete the sale within five business days after sending the documents to the local officer unless the police notify the dealer that the sale would violate the law.

- Requires police to respond within 20 business days to any request for a written explanation if a request is denied

- Unless the sale was prohibited, requires the police to destroy the copy of the statement and any other record of the transaction within 20 business days

- Five years after enactment (1999), replaces the five-day waiting period with a national computerized instant criminal identification system to screen gun purchasers

The Brady Law prohibits firearms sales to a person who:

- Is under indictment for a crime punishable by imprisonment for more than one year or has been convicted of such a crime

- Is a fugitive from justice

- Is an unlawful user of a controlled substance

- Has been judged mentally ill or has been committed to a mental institution

- Has renounced United States citizenship

- Is subject to a court order restraining him or her from harassing, stalking, or threatening an intimate partner or a child

- Has been convicted of domestic violence

States with alternative waiting periods do not have to comply with the Brady Law. Table 3.1 and Figure 3.2 show which states must comply and which states have alternative plans. In the beginning, 32 states and Puerto Rico were required to follow the procedures set forth in the law. By the end of 1996, there were 23 Brady states and 27 Brady-alternative states. However, the law does not include criminal sanctions against law enforcement officials who deliberately do not enforce the law.

Support and Opposition

Members of the American Bar Association, the American Medical Association, the U.S. Conference of Mayors, and the American Federation of Labor-Congress of Industrial Organizations testified in support of the bill. Other supporters of the Brady Amendment, such as Handgun Control, Inc., the National Coalition to Ban Handguns, and a coalition of 11 police organizations known as the Law Enforcement Steering Committee, emphasized that the real issues are law enforcement and public safety.

On the other hand, the major opponents of the Brady Amendment, including the National Rifle Association, Gun Owners of America, the Second Amendment Foundation, and the Citizens' Committee for the Right to Keep and Bear Arms, focused their arguments on the Second Amendment to the Constitution, which, they said, forbids

FIGURE 3.1

Brady Handgun Purchase Form

Form Approved: OMB No. 1512-0520 (02/28/98)

DEPARTMENT OF THE TREASURY
BUREAU OF ALCOHOL, TOBACCO AND FIREARMS
STATEMENT OF INTENT TO OBTAIN A HANDGUN(S)
Prepare in duplicate. All entries must be in ink. Before completing, please see notices and instructions on the back of this form.

SECTION A - TO BE COMPLETED PERSONALLY BY THE TRANSFEREE (BUYER). THE BUYER MUST PRINT ITEMS 1, 2, 3, 4, AND 5 OF THIS SECTION.

1. TRANSFEREE'S (BUYER'S) NAME (Last, (*and maiden, if applicable*), first, middle)

2. DATE OF BIRTH (Month, day, year)

3. RESIDENCE ADDRESS (No., street, county, city, State, and ZIP code)

4. OPTIONAL INFORMATION - THE INFORMATION REQUESTED IN THIS ITEM (4) IS OPTIONAL BUT WILL HELP AVOID THE POSSIBILITY OF BEING MISIDENTIFIED AS A FELON OR OTHER PROHIBITED PERSON.

SOCIAL SECURITY NUMBER | HEIGHT | WEIGHT | SEX

PLACE OF BIRTH | ALIEN REGISTRATION NUMBER

A ____ ____   ____ ____ ____   ____ ____ ____

5. STATEMENT OF TRANSFEREE (BUYER), EACH QUESTION MUST BE ANSWERED WITH "YES" OR "NO" CHECKED IN THE APPROPRIATE BOX FOR EACH QUESTION

	YES	NO		YES	NO
a. Are you under indictment or information* in any court for a crime punishable by imprisonment for a term exceeding one year? *A formal accusation of a crime made by a prosecuting attorney, as distinguished from an indictment presented by a grand jury.			c. Are you a fugitive from justice?		
b. Have you been convicted in any court of a crime punishable by imprisonment for a term exceeding one year? (Note: A "YES" answer is necessary if the judge could have given a sentence of more than one year. A "YES" answer is not required if you have been pardoned for the crime or the conviction had been expunged or set aside, or you have had your civil rights restored, and under the law where the conviction occurred, you are not prohibited from receiving or possessing any firearm.)			d. Are you an unlawful user of, or addicted to, marijuana, or any depressant, stimulant, or narcotic drug, or any other controlled substance?		
			e. Have you ever been adjudicated mentally defective or have you ever been committed to a mental institution?		
			f. Have you been discharged from the Armed Forces under dishonorable conditions?		
			g. Are you illegally in the United States?		
			h. Are you a person who, having been a citizen of the United States, has renounced his/her citizenship?		

I hereby certify that the answers to the above are true and correct. I understand that a person who answers "Yes" to any of the above questions is prohibited from purchasing and/or possessing a firearm, except as otherwise provided by Federal law. I also understand that the making of any false oral or written statement or the exhibiting of any false or misrepresented identification with respect to this transaction is a crime punishable as a felony.

TRANSFEREE'S (BUYER'S) SIGNATURE | DATE

SECTION B - TO BE COMPLETED BY THE TRANSFEROR (SELLER) (SEE NOTICES AND INSTRUCTIONS ON REVERSE.)

6. TRADE/CORPORATE NAME, ADDRESS, AND TELEPHONE NUMBER OF TRANSFEROR (SELLER) | FEDERAL FIREARMS LICENSE NUMBER

7. THE TRANSFEREE (BUYER) HAS IDENTIFIED HIMSELF/HERSELF TO ME BY USING A DRIVER'S LICENSE OR OTHER IDENTIFICATION THAT CONTAINS THE TRANSFEREE'S (BUYER'S) NAME, DATE OF BIRTH, RESIDENCE ADDRESS AND PHOTOGRAPH.

TYPE OF IDENTIFICATION
☐ DRIVER'S LICENSE   ☐ OTHER (Specify) _____
NUMBER ON IDENTIFICATION

8. CONTENTS OF THE STATEMENT IN SECTION A OF THIS FORM WERE RECEIVED BY _____ OF _____ ON _____ BY
(Chief Law Enforcement Officer)   (Law Enforcement Agency)   (Date)
(Check the appropriate answer.)
☐ TELEPHONE   ☐ TELEFAX   ☐ IN PERSON   ☐ OTHER (Specify) _____

9. A COPY OF THE STATEMENT IN SECTION A OF THIS FORM WAS TRANSMITTED TO THE CHIEF LAW ENFORCEMENT OFFICER ON _____ BY
(Date)
(Check the appropriate answer.)
☐ MAIL   ☐ TELEFAX   ☐ IN PERSON   ☐ OTHER (Specify) _____

10. ON _____ , THE CHIEF LAW ENFORCEMENT OFFICER PROVIDED REASON TO BELIEVE THAT THIS TRANSFER
(Date)
☐ WOULD   ☐ WOULD NOT VIOLATE FEDERAL, STATE, OR LOCAL LAWS. AGENCY IDENTIFIER _____

11. TRANSFEROR'S (SELLER'S) SIGNATURE | TRANSFEROR'S TITLE | DATE

ATF F 5300.35 (2-95) (INTERIM)

SOURCE: *Gun Control—Implementation of the Brady Handgun Violence Prevention Act,* U.S. General Accounting Office, Washington, D.C., 1996

TABLE 3.1

States which must comply with the Federal 5-day waiting period and states which have alternative plans

ON NOVEMBER 30,1993, PUBLIC LAW 103-159 (107 STAT.1536) WAS ENACTED, AMENDING THE GUN CONTROL ACT OF 1968 (GCA), AS AMENDED (18 U.S.C. CHAPTER 44) TITLE I OF PUBLIC LAW 103-159, CITED AS THE "BRADY HANDGUN VIOLENCE PREVENTION ACT" (COMMONLY KNOWN AS THE BRADY LAW) PROVIDES IN PART FOR A NATIONAL WAITING PERIOD OF 5 DAYS BEFORE A LICENSED IMPORTER, MANUFACTURER, OR DEALER MAY LAWFULLY TRANSFER A HANDGUN TO A NONLICENSED INDIVIDUAL (INTERIM PROVISIONS) AND FOR THE ESTABLISHMENT OF A NATIONAL INSTANT CRIMINAL BACKGROUND CHECK SYSTEM TO BE QUERIED BY FIREARMS LICENSEES BEFORE TRANSFERRING ANY FIREARM TO NONLICENSED INDIVIDUALS (PER-MANENT PROVISIONS). THE PERMANENT SYSTEM WILL BE EFFECTIVE ON NOVEMBER 30,1998.

TITLES II AND III OF PUBLIC LAW 103-159 RELATE TO REPORTING REQUIREMENTS FOR MULTIPLE HANDGUN SALES, LABELING OF PACKAGES CONTAINING A FIREARM, THEFTS OF FIREARMS FROM LICENSED FIREARMS DEALERS, AND INCREASED LICENSE FEES FOR DEALERS IN FIREARMS.

BELOW IS A LIST OF STATES SUBJECT TO THE FEDERAL FIVE DAY WAITING PERIOD OR STATES HAVING ALTERNATIVE SYSTEMS AS DEFINED IN THE LAW.

STATES AND TERRITORIES WHICH MUST COMPLY WITH THE FEDERAL 5-DAY WAITING PERIOD:

Alabama	Mississippi*	Puerto Rico
Alaska*	Montana*	Rhode Island
Arizona*	Nevada	South Carolina
Arkansas*	New Mexico	South Dakota*
Kansas	North Dakota*	Texas*
Kentucky	Ohio	Vermont
Louisiana*	Oklahoma*	West Virginia
Maine	Pennsylvania*	Wyoming*

* In these states, the federal 5-day waiting period does not apply to transfers of handguns to persons holding valid permits/licenses to carry handguns issued within 5 years of the proposed purchase.

STATES WHICH MEET ONE OF THE ALTERNATIVES TO THE FEDERAL 5-DAY WAITING PERIOD:

California	Permit or other approval- type system
Colorado	"Instant check"
Connecticut	Permit or other approval-type system
Delaware	"Instant check"
Florida	"Instant check"
Georgia	"Instant check"
Guam	Permit or other approval-type system
Hawaii	Permit or other approval-type system
Idaho	Permit or other approval-type system
Illinois	Permit and "instant check"
Indiana	Permit or other approval-type system
Iowa	Permit or other approval-type system
Maryland	Permit or other approval-type system
Massachusetts	Permit or other approval-type system
Michigan	Permit or other approval-type system
Minnesota	Permit or other approval-type system
Missouri	Permit or other approval-type system
Nebraska	Permit or other approval-type system
New Hampshire	"Instant check"
New Jersey	Permit or other approval-type system
New York	Permit or other approval-type system
North Carolina	Permit or other approval-type system
Oregon	Permit or other approval-type system
Tennessee	Permit or other approval-type system
Utah	"Instant check"
Virginia	"Instant check"
Virgin Islands	Permit or other approval type system
Washington	Permit or other approval type system
Wisconsin	"Instant check" (except for pawn transactions)

SOURCE: *State Laws and Published Ordinances—Firearms,* 21st edition, U.S. Bureau of Alcohol, Tobacco and Firearms, Washington, D.C., 1998

such a law. They also believed that such a law would not stop criminals from getting guns.

By April 1994, five rural sheriffs in the South and West had filed suits in federal courts to overturn the Brady Law on grounds that it violated the Tenth Amendment of the Constitution, which reserves powers to the states and the people if not directly given to the federal government or prohibited to the states. Supporters of the lawsuits also believed the Brady Law violates the Second Amendment. Law enforcement officers opposing the law regard it as unenforceable. Sheriffs have reported that they do not have the time, personnel, or funds to verify all the information required by the Brady Law.

Court cases ended in verdicts that either upheld the constitutionality of the Brady Law or found it unconstitutional. Two of the sheriffs took their cases to the U. S. Supreme Court in December 1996, and the case was decided in 1997. In *Printz v. U.S.* (117 S. Ct. 2365) the Supreme Court declared unconstitutional the provision that required a chief law enforcement officer (CLEO) to conduct background checks on prospective handgun purchasers. (See "Is The Brady Law Constitutional?" in Chapter 4.)

Permit Denials

According to the U.S. Department of Justice (*Presale Handgun Checks, 1994–98,* Bureau of Justice Statistics,

FIGURE 3.2

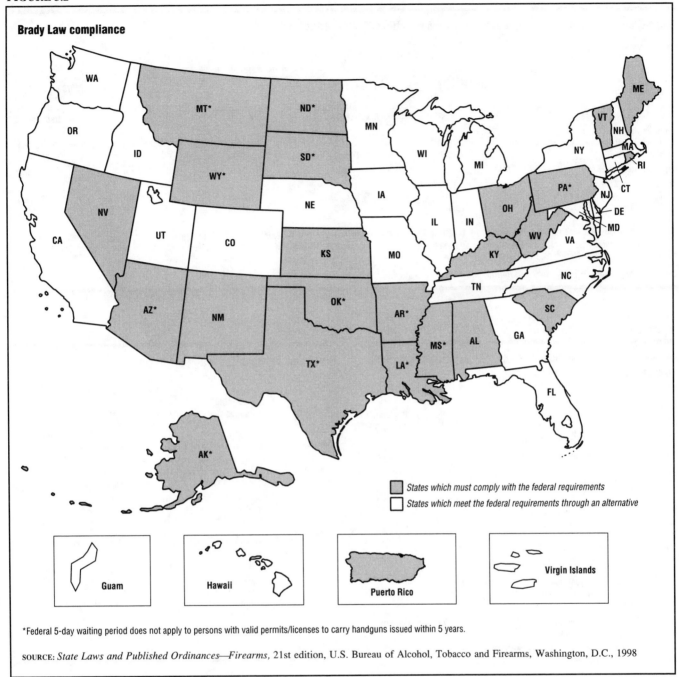

Brady Law compliance

[Map legend:]
■ States which must comply with the federal requirements
□ States which meet the federal requirements through an alternative

[Map inset boxes:] Guam, Hawaii, Puerto Rico, Virgin Islands

*Federal 5-day waiting period does not apply to persons with valid permits/licenses to carry handguns issued within 5 years.

SOURCE: *State Laws and Published Ordinances—Firearms,* 21st edition, U.S. Bureau of Alcohol, Tobacco and Firearms, Washington, D.C., 1998

Washington, D.C., June 1998), of the average 70,000 rejected applicants in 1997, about 44,000 were rejected because the intended purchasers had been indicted or convicted as felons. (See Table 3.2.) The data represent only attempted purchases from licensed firearm dealers and do not indicate whether rejected purchasers later obtained a gun through other means, or how many were rejected because of inaccurate information in the background check database.

When an application was submitted to purchase handguns, the chief law enforcement officer (CLEO) of the jurisdiction where the prospective buyer lived was to complete a background check. From March 1994, when the Brady Law took effect, through the end of November 1997 handgun sellers in the United States submitted approximately 12.7 million applications to purchase firearms. Of those, approximately 312,000 (about 2.5 percent) were blocked by CLEOs after background checks were made.

As shown in Table 3.3, during 1998, close to two-thirds (63.3 percent) of denials for a handgun purchase were based on a finding of a felony conviction or indictment. Domestic violence (13.3 percent) accounted for the next largest group of rejections, followed by persons prohibited by state laws (6.6 percent) and fugitives from justice (6.1 percent).

TABLE 3.2

Presale handgun checks: estimates of inquiries and rejections, 1998 and 1994–98

	Presale checks for handguns				
	1/1/98–11/29/98			3/1/94–11/29/98	
	All states	Original Brady states*	Brady states in 1998	All states	Original Brady states*
Inquiries and rejections					
Inquiries/applications	2,384,000	1,248,000	891,000	12,740,000	7,238,000
Rejected	70,000	47,000	29,000	312,000	203,000
Rejection rate	2.9%	3.8%	3.2%	2.4%	2.8%
Reasons for rejection					
Felony indictment/conviction	44,000	30,000	16,000	207,000	130,000
Other	26,000	17,000	13,000	105,000	73,000

Notes: All estimated counts are rounded. Percentages were calculated from unrounded data. Detail may not add to total because of rounding.

* Original Brady states were 32 states required to follow presale review procedures set out in the Brady Act when it became effective on February 28, 1994. At the end of the Brady interim period (11/29/98), 23 of the 32 were still Brady states.

SOURCE: *Bureau of Justice Statistics Bulletin, June 1999*, U.S. Bureau of Justice Statistics, Washington, D.C., 1999

TABLE 3.3

Reasons for rejection of handgun purchase applications: national estimates January–November 1998

Reason for rejection	All states	Original Brady states	Brady states during 1998
Total	100.0%	100.0%	100.0%
Felony (indictment/conviction)	63.3	68.7	54.8
Fugitive	6.1	7.5	13.4
Domestic violence			
Misdemeanor conviction	9.9	7.9	11.9
Restraining order	3.4	2.8	0.3
State law prohibition	6.6	2.5	6.2
Mental illness or disability	0.7	0.2	0.4
Drug addiction	0.9	1.1	2.4
Local law prohibition	0.3	0.1	0.1
Other*	8.8	9.2	10.5

* Includes illegal aliens, juveniles, persons discharged from the armed services dishonorably, persons who have renounced their U.S. citizenship, and other unspecified persons.

SOURCE: *Bureau of Justice Statistics Bulletin, June 1999*, U.S. Bureau of Justice Statistics, Washington, D.C., 1999

TABLE 3.4

Brady Law changes

	"Old" Brady (ended Nov. 30, 1998)	"New" Brady (started Nov. 30, 1998)
Firearms covered	Handguns	Handguns and long guns (rifles and shotguns)
Waiting period	Waiting period of up to five business days for completed background check	"Instant Check," with up to three business days to sort out ambiguous results of check
Background check	Local law enforcement checks "available criminal records." (Supreme Court removed requirement for local law enforcement to conduct checks, now check is optional for local government.)	Instant Check, by telephone or computer. In some states, firearm dealers query state "point of contact" or "POC." If state does not provide POC, dealer contacts FBI directly.
Exemptions	Individuals with valid state permits to "possess or acquire" firearms are exempt from background check.	Exemption from Instant Check is expanded to include concealed-carry license holders.

SOURCE: *Paper Tiger? Will the Brady Law Work After Instant Check?*, Violence Policy Center, Washington, D.C., 1998

THE "PERMANENT" BRADY LAW

On November 30, 1998, as required by the Brady Handgun Violence Prevention Act of 1993, the five-day waiting period for handgun purchasers was replaced by a national computerized criminal identification system to screen gun purchasers. The FBI operates the National Instant Criminal Background Check System (NICS). State criminal history records are provided through each state's central repository and the Interstate Identification Index. The index, also maintained by the FBI, instantly indicates any state criminal record, as well as any federal offenses. (See Figure 3.3.)

All firearms dealers and pawnshop owners are now required to run background checks on prospective buyers of both handguns and long guns (rifles and shotguns). In many states, some or all inquiries will be directed to a state's designated "point of contact" (POC), which will then conduct a background check directly through NICS. In states without a designated POC, gun dealers contact the FBI directly, and the FBI runs the check through NICS. When someone buys a gun, NICS provides information and advises the dealer to proceed with the sale, deny it, or delay it. If the sale is delayed, the FBI has three working days to decide to approve or deny the request. If denied, the buyer may appeal to find out the reason and to challenge the denial. NICS allows gun store owners to review applications in minutes rather than days. See Table 3.4 for a comparison of the "old" and the "new" Brady laws.

NICS checks do not override state laws. If a state has a waiting period or other requirements, these regulations must be followed. In most states, individuals with right-to-carry permits or permits to purchase that comply with the Brady Law will not have to undergo a NICS check at the time of transfer.

According to the United States General Accounting Office report *Gun Control: Implementation of the National Instant Criminal Background Check System,* February 2000, 26 states currently participate, either fully or partially, in NICS. In those states, the FBI performed a total of 4,402,291 NICS background checks from November 30, 1998, through November 30, 1999, with a 95.8 percent approval rate. Of the denials for the same period, 69.8 percent were due to felony indictments or convictions, followed by 14.5 percent for domestic violence misdemeanor convictions or restraining orders, and 3.8 percent for drug addiction. Twenty-two percent of all denials were ultimately reversed.

Cost of the New System

With an FBI estimate of 11.4 million annual background checks, the cost of NICS may be as much as $78 million each year. The Department of Justice proposed charging gun dealers a fee for each check, between $13 and $16. However, in the Omnibus Appropriations Act (PL 105-277), Congress specifically prohibited the FBI from charging a user fee for NICS checks. States that conduct checks through the designated "point of contact," however, could determine their own fees.

Controversies over the New Brady Provisions

Many observers worry that the rapid record-checking plan may help some Brady Law targets escape detection. Some critical state and local records may not be in the national database. NICS may miss individuals convicted of misdemeanor domestic violence cases, involuntary admissions to mental hospitals, and arrests too recent to be in the computer. Gun control advocates are against the elimination of the waiting period. They claim that waiting periods allow local police to search records that might not be in NICS and that waiting periods allow "cooling-off" periods, thereby preventing many crimes of passion. They support legislation to establish a minimum three-day waiting period.

Under a pending proposal, the Bureau of Alcohol, Tobacco, and Firearms (ATF) would exempt a gun buyer from a background check if he or she holds a state permit to carry concealed weapons. The Violence Policy Center, a research foundation that grew out of the National Coalition to Ban Handguns, strongly opposes this exemption. Research conducted by the center showed massive errors in background checks for these permits, including applicants with criminal records who were still granted permits. The center also found permit holders who committed crimes but kept their permits for months or even years. States where concealed-weapons permits would exempt a gun buyer from the background check include Florida, Georgia, Pennsylvania, Texas, and Virginia.

After the establishment of NICS, the National Rifle Association (NRA) immediately filed a lawsuit in an effort to stop the FBI from keeping records of gun transactions on people who had not committed a crime. The Department of Justice says the records will be kept for no more than six months or the time needed to conduct audits to make sure gun dealers are following the law and to check for fraud and abuse of the system. The NRA contends the Brady Law specifically bans the federal government from retaining records and keeping a central registry of gun buyers. The NRA also intends to lobby Congress to revise the law to remove rifles and shotguns from the list of weapons that lead to background checks.

The background check requirement applies only to federally licensed gun dealers, manufacturers and importers, and pawnshop brokers. Sales at gun shows or flea markets, through classified ads, and through personal sales are unregulated under current law. President Bill Clinton called for stricter regulation of gun shows, and legislation has been introduced to license gun shows and apply the Brady Law and other gun laws to them.

On November 7, 2000, voters in Colorado and Oregon overwhelming approved statewide ballot initiatives closing the so-called gun show loophole, largely in response to the failure of both state legislatures to do so in response to school shootings at Columbine High School (Colorado) and Thurston High School (Oregon). Both states now require background checks on all sales of firearms at gun shows in addition to the checks that are currently in place.

VIOLENT CRIME CONTROL ACT

Banning Assault Weapons

In 1994 Congress passed the Violent Crime Control Act (PL 103-322). Although the law has several different provisions pertaining to guns, the debate focused on the banning of semiautomatic assault weapons. In 1989 Patrick Pard, armed with a semiautomatic rifle, killed 5 children and wounded 29 others and a teacher at an elementary school in California. In response, several states banned the sale and possession of semiautomatic rifles (see below). At the federal level, President George Bush banned the importation of 43 firearms, although he permitted companies within the United States to continue to make them. Nonetheless, American Colt Industries, maker of the AR-15, said it would no longer sell them to the public, although the law did not pertain to the AR-15.

The Violent Crime Control Act bans the manufacture, transfer, or possession of semiautomatic rifles. This provi-

FIGURE 3.3

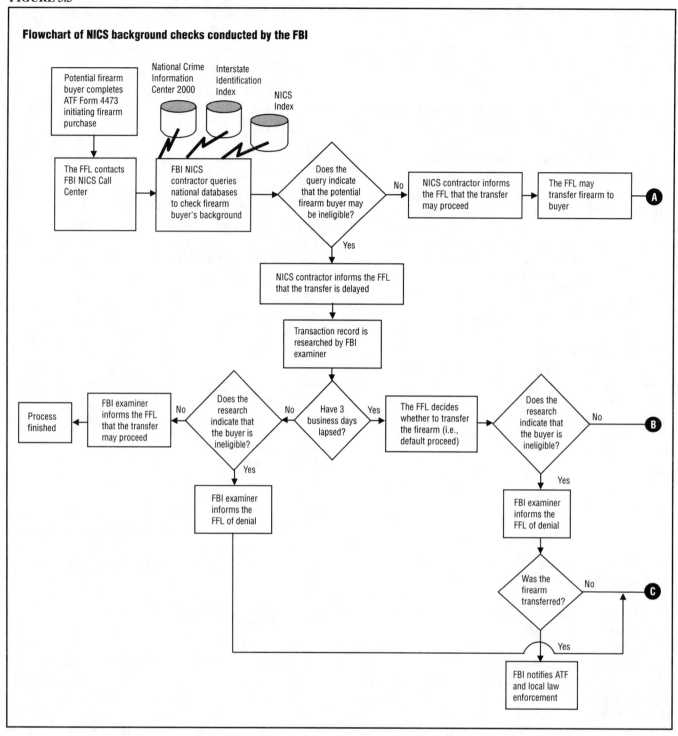

Flowchart of NICS background checks conducted by the FBI

sion does not outlaw firearms lawfully possessed before the enactment of this law. The legislation defines semiautomatic rifles and lists 19 types, such as the Uzi, the TEC-9, the Street Sweeper, and their copycats. The crime law also exempts at least 650 different sporting rifles and limits the capacity of newly manufactured magazines to 10 cartridges.

The law defines an assault rifle as a firearm that can accept a detachable magazine and that has at least two of the following features: a folding or telescoping stock, a pistol grip, a bayonet mount, a flash suppressor or threaded barrel, or a grenade launcher. An assault pistol can accept a detachable magazine and has at least two of the following: a magazine that attaches to the pistol outside of the pistol grip, a threaded barrel capable of accepting a barrel extender, a flash suppressor, a forward handgrip, or a silencer; a barrel shroud that allows the shooter to hold the gun with the nontrigger hand without being burned; a manufactured weight of 50 ounces or more when unloaded; or a semiautomatic version of a machine gun. A

FIGURE 3.3

Flowchart of NICS background checks conducted by the FBI [CONTINUED]

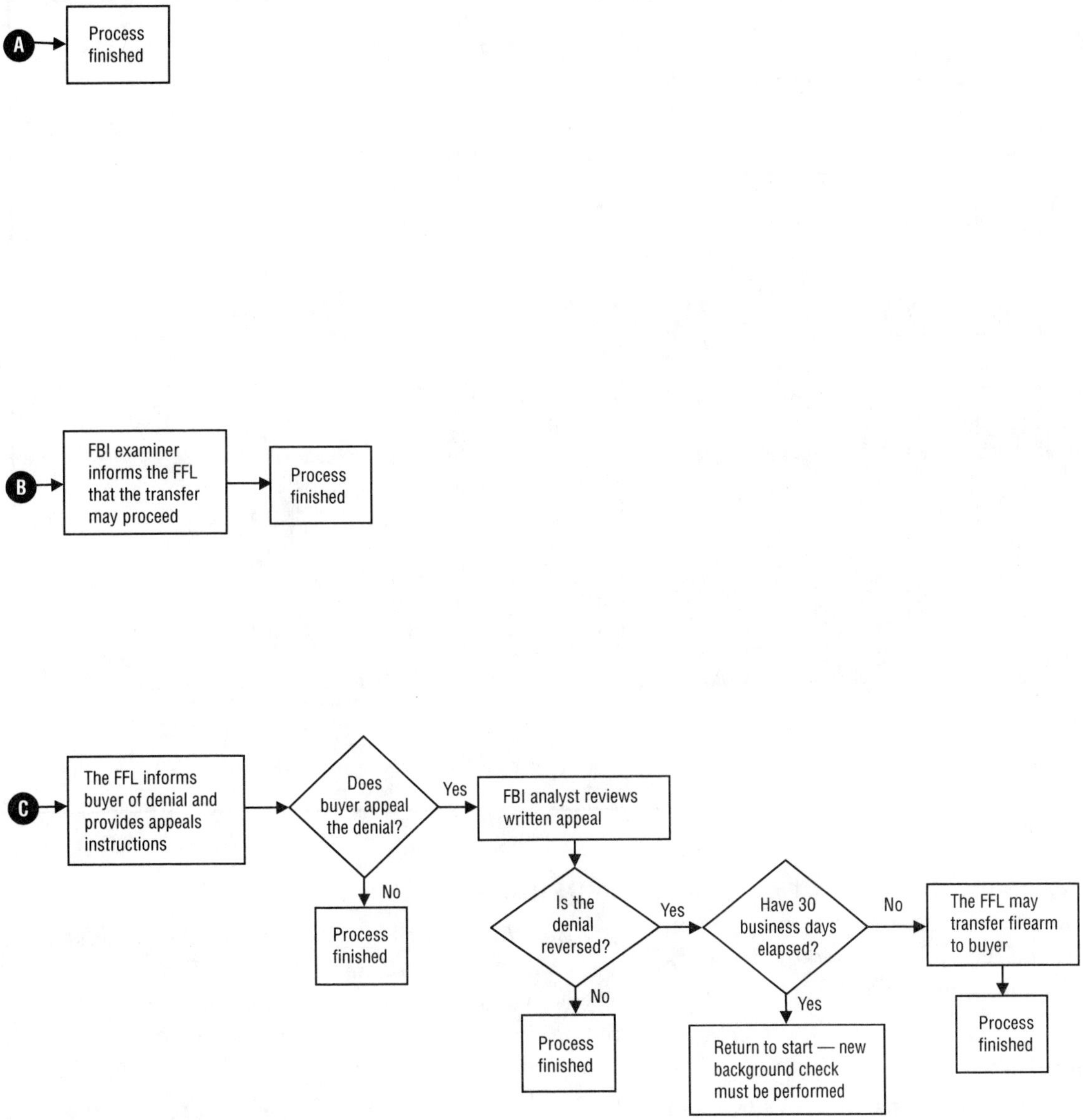

* NICS contract personnel are not authorized to review actual criminal history records. The database query results seen by these personnel are simply an indicator that there either is no match (therefore, a proceed) or a potential match on one or more of the databases (therefore, a delay).

SOURCE: *Gun Control—Implementation of the National Instant Criminal Background Check System*, U.S. General Accounting Office, Washington, D.C., 2000

semiautomatic shotgun must have at least two of the following: a folding stock, a pistol grip that shows conspicuously beneath the action of the firearm, a fixed magazine capacity of more than five rounds, and the ability to accept a detachable magazine.

In 1997 and 1998 the importation of assault weapons again became an issue, after the ATF approved the impor-

tation of about 60 makes and models of semiautomatic rifles. In November 1997 a group of senators asked President Clinton to prohibit this importation, since they felt that these guns fell under the assault weapons ban in the Violent Crime Control Act. After a six-month review, the president and the secretary of the Treasury imposed a ban on the importation of these 60 assault rifles. The Omnibus Appropriations Act of 1999 (PL 105-277) authorized

FIGURE 3.4

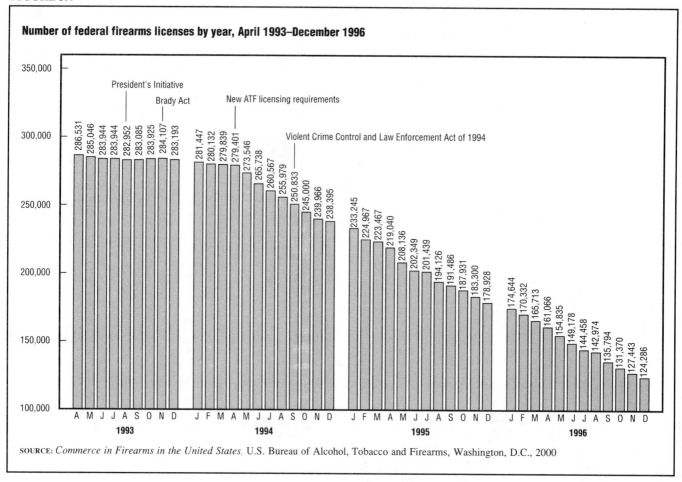

Number of federal firearms licenses by year, April 1993–December 1996

SOURCE: *Commerce in Firearms in the United States,* U.S. Bureau of Alcohol, Tobacco and Firearms, Washington, D.C., 2000

reimbursement to firearms importers who had been granted authority to import the semiautomatic assault rifles on November 14, 1997, and who had released the firearms under bond to the Customs Service by February 10, 1998.

Youth Handgun Safety

Subtitle B of the 1994 Violent Crime Control Act prohibits the possession of a handgun or ammunition or the sale or private transfer of a handgun or ammunition to a juvenile under 18 years of age. Exemptions include those cases in which the juvenile temporarily uses the handgun for employment, such as in ranching or farming where predatory animals often kill livestock, with the permission of the owner. Other exemptions include using a handgun for target practice, hunting, or a course of instruction on the safe and lawful use of a handgun. Minors who are members of the Armed Forces of the United States or the National Guard are also exempt from this regulation.

OTHER PROVISIONS. The Violent Crime Control Act imposes stiffer penalties for using a gun during a violent crime or drug felony. It also prohibits the possession of firearms by persons who have committed domestic abuse and tightens rules for firearms dealers (see below).

FEDERAL LICENSING

Beginning in 1993—even before the changes in the 1994 Violent Crime Control Act—the Bureau of Alcohol, Tobacco and Firearms was tightening the procedures for obtaining a federal firearms license, which allows a person to buy or sell firearms. Until late 1992 the ATF received each month between 2,500 and 3,000 new applications for federal firearms licenses (FFLs) and between 4,500 and 5,000 applications for renewals. Between late 1992 and early 1993, several well-publicized news stories revealed how easy it was to get an FFL. A three-year license cost only $30, and the only check was a cursory computer criminal history query. As a result, the number of FFL applications rose dramatically, peaking in March 1993 with new applications totaling 7,001 and renewals reaching 8,753.

Because of the rising number of applications, the ATF began contacting every applicant to help eliminate the number of criminals obtaining licenses. The Brady Law (see above) raised the fee to $200 for a three-year license and $90 for a three-year renewal. In March 1994 the ATF sent out new application forms requiring the applicant to submit fingerprint cards and a photograph. These new regulations, as well as the requirement to check that the

FIGURE 3.5

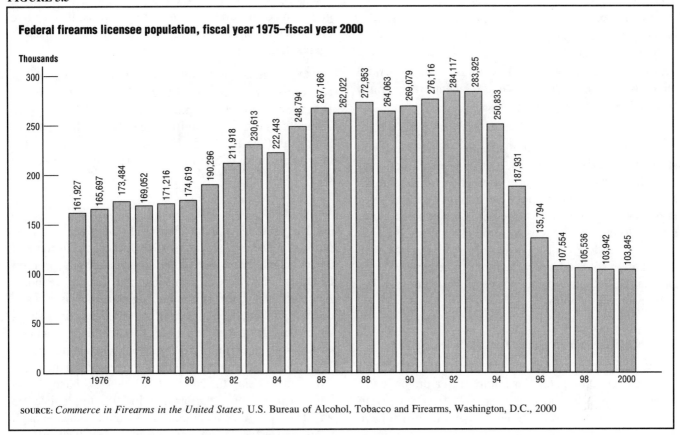

Federal firearms licensee population, fiscal year 1975–fiscal year 2000

SOURCE: *Commerce in Firearms in the United States,* U.S. Bureau of Alcohol, Tobacco and Firearms, Washington, D.C., 2000

person applying complies with state and local laws, had been approved as part of the Violent Crime Control Act.

The crime law also required each licensee to report the theft or loss of a firearm within 48 hours. The Clinton administration worked with the trade associations to get support for these reforms. The Collector and Arms Dealers Association and the National Alliance of Stocking Gun Dealers supported the measure to ensure that only individuals who were really firearms merchants and who intended to actively sell firearms were licensed.

In *Federal Firearms Licensees* (General Accounting Office, Washington, D.C., March 1996) the GAO reported that, because of the revisions, the number of licensed firearms dealers and the number of license applications submitted dropped sharply. That decline is reflected in the declining numbers of federal firearms licenses issued from April 1993 to December 1996. (See Figure 3.4.) However, as illustrated in Figure 3.5, that decline appears to have abated beginning in 1996, as the overall numbers of federal firearms licensees stabilized from fiscal years 1996 to 2000.

RECENT AMENDMENTS TO THE GUN CONTROL ACT OF 1968

Under the Gun Control Act of 1968, persons convicted of felony crimes are prohibited from buying or possessing firearms. The Lautenberg amendment to the Omnibus Consolidated Appropriations Act for 1997 (PL 104-208) prohibits the purchase or possession of firearms by anyone convicted of a misdemeanor crime of domestic violence or child abuse. This law became effective on September 30, 1996; however, the ban applies to persons convicted of this misdemeanor crime at any time, even if the offense occurred before the effective date. Legislation has been introduced that would apply the ban only to those convicted after September 30, 1996, and that would exempt government employees, such as military and police.

Section 121 of the Omnibus Appropriations Act for 1999 (PL 105-277) amended the Gun Control Act of 1968 to prohibit aliens admitted to the United States under a nonimmigrant visa from obtaining firearms. This includes persons traveling temporarily in the United States, persons studying in the United States but who maintain a residence abroad, and some foreign workers. Exceptions include persons entering the United States for lawful hunting or sporting purposes, an official representative of a foreign government, and foreign law enforcement officers from friendly foreign governments who enter the United States on official business. In addition, the U.S. attorney general has the authority to waive the prohibition by approving a petition that an alien submits.

OTHER ISSUES

In 1997 President Clinton directed firearms dealers to post signs alerting the public about risks posed by guns. In addition, dealers must notify buyers in writing of the dangers guns pose to juveniles. In 1998 he directed that all handguns held by federal law enforcement officers must be equipped with child safety locks.

The Omnibus Appropriations Act for 1999 (PL105-277) includes a requirement that dealers agree to sell gun storage and safety devices. Other issues frequently brought up by Congress are whether to limit handgun sales to an individual to only one a month, to license or register handgun owners, to require dealers to fit handguns with locking devices or some other form of childproofing, and to raise taxes on the firearms and ammunition sold and apply the funds to health-care costs associated with gun violence. None of these proposals has ever become federal law.

STATE FIREARM CONTROL LAWS

Most firearms regulations have been enacted by state and local governments. Laws may differ dramatically from state to state and just as sharply from county to county and town to town. In fact, state laws might have little bearing on the gun regulations where a person lives. For example, the laws of New York State, by themselves, are of little use in understanding the firearms restrictions placed on someone living in New York City, which has significant additional restrictions on the use and possession of guns. Most states have laws prohibiting the possession of explosive weapons, machine guns, and short-barrel firearms. Some states, such as Texas and Vermont, have outlawed the use of silencers.

With the passage of the 1993 Brady Law, all states had a waiting period. They either complied with the federal waiting period of five business days or had alternative requirements. As of 2000 all states except Hawaii have some form of instant background checks. Sixteen states, plus the District of Columbia, require permits or licenses to purchase handguns, while five states and the District of Columbia require permits for long guns. (Firearms licenses are issued to individuals and allow them to purchase, receive, or possess firearms. Registration is a record of the transfer or ownership of a specific firearm.) Some of the permits are for certain cities only and are not required statewide; some of the long gun permits apply only to semiautomatic weapons. (See Table 3.5.)

A semiautomatic firearm is not an automatic gun or a machine gun. A machine gun shoots out a stream of bullets every time the trigger is pulled. A semiautomatic gun allows the user to shoot one bullet each time the trigger is pulled without having to pull back the hammer or use a bolt to put the bullet into the chamber. The user can fire as fast as he or she can pull the trigger. Some semiautomatic guns can be converted to automatic firearms. It is legal to buy conversion accessories, but the conversion itself is against federal law.

Only three states and the District of Columbia actually require registration for handguns; two states and the District of Columbia require registration for long guns. Some cities or towns require registration of handguns or long guns. (See Table 3.5.) Forty-four states have "right to bear arms" provisions in their state constitutions (see Appendix).

Banning Firearms

Eleven states and the District of Columbia have laws prohibiting certain weapons. (See Table 3.5.) In some of these states, only certain local jurisdictions prohibit firearms. In 1989 California banned assault weapons. Although the California state legislature was already debating the question of assault guns because drug gangs were using them, the murders of schoolchildren by a killer armed with an assault rifle in Stockton, California, in 1989 added to the public concern and pressured the legislature into passing the ban. In 1990 the New Jersey legislature also passed a similar law. In 1992 the legislature voted to repeal the law but, in 1993, could not get enough votes to override the governor's veto. In 1992 Connecticut passed a ban on assault weapons. In 1993 Virginia outlawed the Street Sweeper shotgun.

Since 1977 residents of the District of Columbia cannot acquire any additional handguns; existing handguns registered prior to the ban may be reregistered. The District of Columbia also banned semiautomatic firearms with magazines capable of holding more than 12 rounds. In 1988 the Maryland General Assembly passed a law banning the manufacture and sale of cheap, low-caliber handguns and, in 1994, outlawed "assault pistols." In 1992 Hawaii banned assault pistols and pistol ammunition magazines holding more than 10 rounds.

Many hunting rifles are semiautomatic. They generally have longer barrels than assault weapons so that the hunter can aim a great distance and the bullet can go farther more accurately. In addition, the magazine usually holds five or fewer bullets. Many opponents of controls on assault weapons do not believe that the differences between automatic rifles and hunting rifles are significant. As a result, they fear that controls could lead to bans on hunting rifles.

Concealed Weapons

As of 1996, all 50 states had concealed-carry laws. Thirty-one states have a "shall-issue" permit system, which makes it easy for almost anyone to carry a hidden gun. Vermont requires no concealed-weapon permit at all. Twelve states have a discretionary "may-issue" system,

TABLE 3.5

Statutory and constitutional provisions relating to the purchase, ownership, and use of firearms

By state, Aug. 1, 2000

State	NICS instant background check[a]	Exemptions to NICS	State waiting period (in days) Hand-gun	State waiting period (in days) Long gun	License or permit to purchase Hand-gun	License or permit to purchase Long gun	Registration Hand-gun	Registration Long gun	Record of sale sent to police	License or identification card	Certain firearms prohibited	State firearms preemption law[b]	Constitutional provision	Concealed carry law	Carrying openly prohibited	Hunter protection law[c]	Range protection law[d]	Firearm industry lawsuit preemption[e]
Alabama	Y[f]								Y[g]			Y[h]	Y	Y[i]	Y[j]	Y		Y
Alaska	Y[f]	(k)										Y	Y	Y		Y	Y	Y
Arizona	Y[f]	(k)										Y	Y	Y		Y	Y	Y
Arkansas	Y[f]	(m)										Y	Y	Y[n]	Y[n]	Y	Y	
California	Y[f]		10	10					Y[g]		Y[o]	Y	Y[p]	Y[q]	Y	Y	Y	Y
Colorado	Y[f]												Y	Y[p]		Y		
Connecticut	Y[f]	(m)	14[f,s]	14[f,s]	Y[t]				Y[g]		Y[o]		Y	Y[p]	Y	Y	Y	
Delaware	Y[f]	(m)										Y	Y	Y		Y	Y	Y
Florida	Y[f]		3[f,s]									Y	Y	Y	Y	Y	Y	
Georgia	(w)	(k)			Y[t]		Y[x]	Y[x]	Y[g]		Y[o]	Y[v]	Y	Y[p]	Y	Y	Y	Y
Hawaii	Y[f]	(w)			Y[t]	Y[t]	Y	(y)		Y			Y	Y[r]	Y	Y	Y	
Idaho	Y[f]											Y	Y	Y[r]	Y	Y	Y	
Illinois	Y[w]	(k)	3	1	Y[t]	Y[t]	(y)	(y)	Y[g]	Y	Y[o]	Y[aa]	Y[p]	Y	Y	Y	Y	
Indiana	Y[w]	(k,w)			Y[t]		(ab)		Y[g]			Y	Y	Y[r]	(ab)	Y	Y	Y
Iowa	Y[f]		(ab)		(ab)							Y	Y	Y		Y	Y	Y
Kansas	Y[f]	(m)							Y[g]			Y	Y[p]	Y	Y	Y	Y	
Kentucky	Y[f]	(m)							Y[g]			Y	Y	Y	Y	Y	Y	Y
Louisiana	Y[f]								Y[g]			Y	Y	Y		Y	Y	Y
Maine	Y[f]		7[ac]		(t)							Y	Y	Y		Y		
Maryland	Y[w]	(m)	7	7	Y[t]	Y[t]			Y[g]		Y[o]	Y	Y[p]	Y[p]	Y	Y	Y	Y
Massachusetts	Y[f]	(m)	7		Y[t]				Y[g]			Y[u]	Y	Y[p]	Y	Y	Y	
Michigan	Y[w]	(w)			Y[t]		Y			Y		Y	Y	Y[p]	Y[i]	Y	Y	Y
Minnesota	Y[f]	(m)	7[r]	(r)	Y[t]	Y[t]			Y[g]		Y[o]	Y	Y	Y	Y	Y	Y	
Mississippi	Y[f]	(k)			Y[t]							Y	Y	Y[z]		Y	Y	Y
Missouri	Y[f]	(m)	7		Y							Y	Y	Y[z]		Y	Y	Y
Montana	Y[f]	(k)										Y	Y	Y		Y		
Nebraska	Y[w]	(w)	(ab)		Y		(ab)		Y[g]			Y	Y	Y[z]		Y	Y	Y
Nevada	Y[w]	(k)										Y	Y	Y[z]	Y	Y	Y	Y
New Hampshire	Y[f]				Y[t]				Y[g]		Y[o]	Y[u]	Y	Y[z]		Y		
New Jersey	Y[f]				Y[t]	Y[t]	Y		Y[g]	Y	Y[o]	Y[u]	Y[p]	Y[z]	Y	Y		
New Mexico	Y[f]	(w)			Y[t]				Y[g]	Y	(o)	Y[v]	Y	Y[z]		Y	Y	
New York	Y[w]	(k,w)			Y[t]		Y	(ad)	Y[g]			Y[v]	Y[p,t]	Y	Y	Y	Y	Y
North Carolina	Y[f]	(m)							Y[g]		(o)	Y	Y	Y[z]	Y[p]	Y	Y	Y
North Dakota	Y[f]		(ab)		(t)		(ab)		(ab)	(u)	(o)	Y	Y	Y[z]	(ab)	Y	Y	Y
Ohio	Y[f]	(m)							Y[g]			Y	Y	Y[z]	Y[p]	Y	Y	
Oklahoma	Y[f]	(m)							Y[g]			Y	Y	Y[z]	Y	Y	Y	Y
Oregon	Y[w]	(m)							Y[g]			Y	Y	Y[z,ae]		Y	Y	
Pennsylvania	Y[f]								Y[g]			Y	Y	Y[p]	Y[i]	Y	Y	Y
Rhode Island	Y[f]		7	7					Y[g]			Y	Y	Y[z]	Y	Y	Y	Y
South Carolina	Y[f]	(k)	(s)		(t)				Y[g]		Y[o]	Y	Y	Y[z]	Y	Y	Y	Y
South Dakota	Y[f]	(m)	2						Y[g]			Y	Y	Y[z]	Y	Y	Y	Y
Tennessee	Y[f]	(k)										Y	Y	Y	Y[n]	Y	Y	Y
Texas	Y[f]	(k)										Y	Y	Y	Y[p]	Y	Y	Y
Utah	Y[f]											Y	Y	Y[z,af]	Y[n]	Y	Y	Y
Vermont	Y[f]		(s,ab)		(t)				(ab)			Y	Y	Y	(ab)	Y	Y	
Virginia	Y[w]	(m)	5[ag]						Y[g]		Y	Y	Y	Y		Y	Y	Y
Washington	Y[f]											Y	Y	Y		Y	Y	
West Virginia																	Y	

TABLE 3.5

Statutory and constitutional provisions relating to the purchase, ownership, and use of firearms [CONTINUED]

By state, Aug. 1, 2000

State	NICS instant background check [a]	Exemptions to NICS	State waiting period (in days) Hand-gun	State waiting period (in days) Long gun	License or permit to purchase Hand-gun	License or permit to purchase Long gun	Registration Hand-gun	Registration Long gun	Record of sale sent to police	License or identifica-tion card	Certain firearms pro-hibited	State firearms pre-emption law [b]	Consti-tutional provision	Con-cealed carry law	Carrying openly prohibited	Hunter protection law [c]	Range protection law [d]	Firearm industry lawsuit preemption [e]
Wisconsin	Y[w]		2									Y	Y	Y[z]			Y	Y
Wyoming	Y[f]	(k)										Y	Y	Y[z]		Y	Y	Y
District of Columbia	Y[f]	(m)			Y[t]	Y[t]	Y[t]	Y	Y[h]	Y	Y[o]		(ah)	Y[o]	Y			

Note: These data were compiled by the National Rifle Association of America, Institute for Legislative Action. In addition to state laws, the purchase, sale, and in certain circumstances, the possession and interstate transportation of firearms are regulated by the Federal Gun Control Act of 1968 as amended by the Firearms Owners' Protection Act and other federal laws. Also, cities and localities may have their own firearms ordinances in addition to federal and state laws. A "Y" in the table indicates the existence of a state law or constitutional provision. However, many qualifications may apply. The source notes that state firearms laws are subject to frequent change. State and local statutes and ordinances, as well as local law enforcement authorities, should be consulted for full text and meaning of statutory provisions.

a A long gun is a rifle or shotgun. The source defines "constitutional provision" by citing Article 1, Section 15 of the Connecticut State Constitution as an example of the basic feature contained in the constitutions of many states. It reads: "Every citizen has a right to bear arms in defense of himself and the state."

a The National Instant Check System (NICS), conducting records checks on retail firearm purchasers, took effect November 1994, replacing the Brady Act requirement that retail handgun sales be delayed until law enforcement authorities completed a check, or 5 business days passed, whichever came first.

b A state firearms preemption law prohibits local statutes more restrictive than the state's law regulating firearms.

c Hunter protection laws prohibit interference with lawful hunting activities.

d Range protection laws protect firearm ranges from nuisance and noise control actions intended to prevent a range's operation.

e Prohibits local jurisdictions from suing entities of the firearm industry.

f Checks are conducted by the FBI for retail firearm sales.

g On some or all firearm sales.

h Applies to handgun ordinances only.

i "Shall issue" permit system, liberally administered discretion by local authorities over permit issuance, or no permit required.

j Carrying a handgun in a motor vehicle requires a license, with exceptions.

k Firearm-carrying permit holders are exempt. In Indiana, holders of personal protection or hunting and target shooting permits are exempt. Those not exempt: in Mississippi, permits issued to security guards; in Texas, peace officer licenses issued after NICS start date.

l Checks are conducted by the state for retail firearm sales.

m Holders of firearm-carrying permits issued before Nov. 30, 1998, are exempt.

o Arkansas prohibits carrying a firearm with a purpose to employ it against a person. Tennessee prohibits carrying "with the intent or purpose of injuring another." Vermont prohibits carrying with "the intent to go armed." Ohio restricts "assault weapons." Hawaii restricts "assault pistols." Illinois prohibits federal firearms licensees from manufacturing or selling a handgun certain parts of which are made of certain metals and melt or deform below 800 degrees Fahrenheit; some cities prohibit other kinds of firearms. Maryland

o California, Connecticut, New Jersey, New York, New York City, other local jurisdictions in New York, and some local jurisdictions in Ohio restrict "assault weapons." Hawaii restricts "assault pistols." Illinois prohibits federal firearms licensees from manufacturing or selling a handgun any part of which is made of certain metals and melt or deform below 800 degrees Fahrenheit; Chicago, Evanston, Oak Park, Morton Grove, Winnetka, Wilmette, and Highland Park prohibit handguns; some cities prohibit other kinds of firearms. Maryland prohibits several small, low-caliber, inexpensive handguns and "assault pistols." Minnesota prohibits licensed firearm dealers from selling a handgun any part of which melts below 1,000 degrees Fahrenheit or has an ultimate tensile strength less than 55,000 p.s.i. Ohio: Some cities prohibit handguns of certain magazine capacities. South Carolina prohibits new acquisition of handguns and any semi-automatic firearm capable of using a detachable ammunition magazine of more than 12 rounds capacity. (With respect to some of these laws and ordinances, individuals may retain prohibited firearms owned previously, with certain restrictions.)

p Restrictively administered discretion by local authorities over permit issuance, or permits are unavailable and carrying is prohibited in most circumstances.

q Loaded.

r The state waiting period does not apply to a person holding a valid permit or license to carry a firearm. In Connecticut, a hunting license also exempts the holder for long gun purchases. In Indiana, only persons with unlimited carry permits are exempt.

s Purchases from licensed dealers only.

t A permit to purchase or a carry permit is required.

u Preemption through judicial ruling. Local regulation may be instituted in Massachusetts if ratified by the legislature.

v Previously by judicial ruling, adopted by law.

w Indiana, New Hampshire, Oregon, Washington, Wisconsin: state check for handguns, FBI check for long guns. Iowa, Michigan, Nebraska, North Carolina: permit suffices for handguns, FBI check for long guns. Maryland: state check for handguns and assault weapons, FBI check for other long guns. Hawaii: permit suffices for all firearms transactions.

x Every person arriving in Hawaii is required to register any firearm(s) brought into the state within 3 days of arrival of the person or firearm(s), whichever occurs later. Handguns purchased from licensed dealers must be registered within 5 days.

y In Chicago and the District of Columbia, no handgun not previously registered may be lawfully possessed.

z No permit system exists and concealed carry is prohibited.

aa Except for ordinances in Gary, East Chicago, and those enacted before January 1994.

ab Local ordinance in certain cities or counties.

ac Maryland subjects purchases of "assault weapons" to a 7-day waiting period.

ad New York City only.

ae Prior to 1995, the law did not apply to Philadelphia.

af No permit is required to carry for lawful purposes.

ag Extended to 60 days if purchaser does not have a Washington driver's license.

ah The District of Columbia is subject to the U.S. Constitution's Second Amendment.

SOURCE: *Sourcebook of Criminal Justice Statistics, 1999*, Bureau of Justice Statistics, Washington, D.C., 1999

which allows law enforcement officials or the licensing authority to approve or deny an application for a concealed-carry permit, based on the applicant's record. In some of these states, the owners must show they need a concealed weapon; an example would be a security guard who must carry large amounts of money. In seven states, no permit system exists; concealed carrying is prohibited. (See Tables 3.5 and 3.6.)

In 1995 Texas, Virginia, Arkansas, Oklahoma, and Utah passed laws making it easier for law-abiding citizens to obtain permits to carry concealed handguns. Some of these states ban the carrying of firearms into schools, bars, government buildings, or sporting events and allow businesses to post "No Guns" signs if desired. In Texas, between January 1, 1996, and January 1, 1997, about 116,000 citizens took training courses—one of the prerequisites for acquiring a permit-to-carry license—and obtained permits to carry concealed handguns.

Carrying Firearms Openly

Twenty-eight states and the District of Columbia prohibit the open carrying of firearms. Arkansas bans carrying a firearm "with a purpose to employ it as a weapon against a person." Tennessee forbids carrying "with the intent to go armed," and Vermont outlawed the carrying of a firearm "with the intent or purpose of injuring another." California prohibits carrying loaded firearms. (See Table 3.5.)

Minors

Because of the increase in the number of homicides committed by young people with guns, many states are passing tougher laws prohibiting juveniles from possessing firearms and/or punishing those who provide them with guns. As of 1994, 20 states and the District of Columbia had such laws. These are in addition to the federal law that prohibits federal firearms licensees from selling or delivering "any firearm or ammunition to any individual who the licensee knows or has reasonable cause to believe is less than eighteen years of age, and if the firearm is other than a shotgun or rifle or ammunition for a shotgun or rifle, to any individual who the licensee knows or has reasonable cause to believe is less than twenty-one years of age" [18 U.S.C. Sect. 922(b)(1)].

In July 1996 President Clinton established a federal computer system to track the illegal sale of guns to minors in an effort to help police limit the supply of those firearms and stop the rise in gun violence among young people. In Boston, one of the cities that already had a gun-tracking system in place, police found that all the handguns gang members in one neighborhood were buying came from Mississippi. A student at Mississippi State University, who was bringing the guns home to sell on weekends, was convicted. According to Boston's police commissioner, the city's comprehensive violence preven-

TABLE 3.6

Permanent Brady Permit Chart

State	Qualifying permits
Alabama	None
Alaska	Concealed weapons permit
American Samoa	None
Arizona	Concealed weapons permit
Arkansas	Concealed weapons permits issued prior to November 30, 1998, and concealed weapons permits issued on or after April 1, 1999. Permits issued November 30, 1998 through March 31, 1999 DO NOT QUALIFY.
California	No permits that qualify under state law as an alternative to a background check
CNMI	Weapons ID cards issued on or after 11/30/98
Colorado	None
Connecticut	**Grandfathered only** - concealed weapons permits
Delaware	**Grandfathered only** - concealed weapons permits
D.C.	**Grandfathered only** - firearms purchase certificates
Florida	**Grandfathered only** - concealed weapons permit
Georgia	Concealed weapons permit
Guam	**Grandfathered only** - firearms identification card
Hawaii	Permits to acquire and licenses to carry
Idaho	Concealed weapons permit
Illinois	Firearm owners ID card (**NOTE:** under state law, licensees still need to do a background check through FTIP)
Indiana	Personal protection and hunting and target permits
Iowa	Permit to purchase a handgun and concealed weapons permit
Kansas	None
Kentucky	**Grandfathered only** - concealed weapons permits issued after July 15, 1998
Louisiana	**Grandfathered only** - concealed weapons permits
Maine	None
Maryland	**Grandfathered only** - concealed weapons permits
Massachusetts	**Grandfathered only** - license to carry
Michigan	Permit to purchase a handgun (**NOTE:** concealed weapons permit does **not** qualify)
Minnesota	**Grandfathered only** - Permit to acquire and permit to carry
Mississippi	Concealed weapons permit issued to individuals (**NOTE:** the permit issued to security guards does **not** qualify)
Missouri	**Grandfathered only** - permit to acquire a concealable firearm
Montana	Concealed weapons permit
Nebraska	Handgun purchase certificate
Nevada	Concealed weapons permit
New Hampshire	None
New Jersey	None
New Mexico	None
New York	Licenses to carry and possess handguns
North Carolina	Permit to purchase a handgun; concealed handgun permit
North Dakota	Concealed weapons permits issued prior to November 29, 1998, and concealed weapons permits issued on or after December 1, 1999. **Permits issued beginning November 30, 1998 through November 30, 1999 do not qualify.**
Ohio	None
Oklahoma	**Grandfathered only** - concealed weapons permits issued after 5/16/96
Oregon	**Grandfathered only** - concealed weapons permits
Pennsylvania	**Grandfathered only** - licenses to carry (**NOTE:** state background check is still required with grandfathered permits)
Puerto Rico	None
Rhode Island	None
South Carolina	Concealed weapons permits
South Dakota	**Grandfathered only** - concealed weapons permits
Tennessee	None
Texas	Concealed weapons permit (**NOTE:** Texas Peace Officer license, TCLEOSE card, is **grandfathered only**)
U.S. Virgin Islands	All permits
Utah	Concealed weapons permit
Vermont	None
Virginia	None
Washington	**Grandfathered only** - concealed weapons permits issued after July 1, 1996
West Virginia	None
Wisconsin	None
Wyoming	Concealed weapons permits

SOURCE: U.S. Bureau of Alcohol, Tobacco and Firearms, Washington, D.C., 2000

tion plan has been so successful that no juveniles were killed by guns in 1996.

Colorado has banned the possession of handguns by minors. Violators can be sentenced to a minimum of five days in jail; second-time offenders face felony charges. Utah outlawed the sale of firearms to minors unless they are accompanied by an adult. After the second felony offense involving the use of a handgun by minors 16 years of age and older, the juvenile can be tried as an adult in Utah.

Florida's laws allow police to seize guns from minors and charge them with first-degree misdemeanors. Violators can have their driving privileges suspended and be sentenced to community service. The law also provides tougher penalties for adults who illegally provide juveniles with firearms, especially dealers who sell the weapons to minors.

Kentucky's law barring weapons on school grounds took effect on July 15, 1994. Schools must post warning signs or be subject to a fine. In September 1994, police made their first arrest under the new law, apprehending a 16-year-old boy for bringing a .25-caliber semiautomatic Raven pistol to school. A teenager found guilty of such charges can be sentenced to up to five years in prison and fined $10,000.

North Dakota forbids the selling of handguns to minors but does not prohibit a person from lending or giving a handgun to a minor "if the minor will be using the handgun under the direct supervision of an adult and for the purpose of firearm safety training, target shooting, or hunting." Louisiana prohibits "the unlawful sales to minors . . . by anyone over the age of seventeen of any firearm or other instrumentality customarily used as a dangerous weapon, to any person under the age of eighteen. Lack of knowledge of the minor's age shall not be a defense."

Other states prohibiting the possession of handguns by juveniles include Arizona, Arkansas, California, Illinois, Massachusetts, Minnesota, Nebraska, New Jersey, New York, North Carolina, North Dakota, Oregon, Rhode Island, South Carolina, Utah, Virginia, West Virginia, and Wisconsin. Many other states are debating the issue.

In Florida "it is unlawful and punishable by imprisonment and fine for any adult to store or leave a firearm in any place within the reach or easy access of a minor [anyone under 16 years]." Stores selling firearms must post signs informing buyers of this law. California has a similar statute, requiring licensed gun dealers to post signs in block letters not less than one inch in height stating, "If you leave a loaded firearm where a child obtains and improperly uses it, you may be fined or sent to prison."

Other Issues

At the same time that Congress has been debating the gun control issue, so have many state legislatures. In 1997

Maryland passed legislation banning assault pistols. In 1993 the Virginia legislature passed a law allowing residents to buy only one handgun each month. (In 1992 registered gun dealers in Virginia had reported 3,525 sales of two or more handguns to the same person within five days. The state gained a national reputation as a "source state" for guns used in crimes in northeastern cities.) Maryland passed a "one-gun-a-month" law in 1996. In 1999 Los Angeles became the first big city to limit residents to one handgun purchase per month.

As of October 1, 1994, all handgun transfers in Connecticut, whether by sale or gift, were to be reported to the state police. The measure made it illegal for anyone to sell a handgun to any person without a permit to carry a handgun or a license to own one. To get a license, applicants must submit to background checks for criminal records and complete a gun safety course. In the fall of 1993, Nebraska adopted a measure requiring the state's gun shop owners to distribute safety information to all gun purchasers and hang posters demonstrating ways to prevent children from getting hold of loaded guns.

Connecticut and Maryland require traces on all guns seized by police in connection with a crime in order to identify traffickers (people who buy guns in one state with the purpose of selling those guns in another state). Illinois requires the tracing of all guns found in the possession of individuals under 21.

LOCAL ORDINANCES

Many laws regulating guns are local ordinances passed by town and city governments. Most of these statutes regulate the sale of weapons. For example, Salt Lake County, Utah, restricts the possession of "any device or attachment of a kind designed, used or intended for use in silencing the report of any firearm." Richmond, Virginia, requires buyers to obtain a permit to purchase "before a firearm may be sold or delivered to the purchaser or recipient." Many jurisdictions, such as Joliet, Illinois; Cumberland, Maryland; and Omaha, Nebraska, have similar requirements. Cheyenne, Wyoming, and Akron, Ohio, restrict the transfer of possession of "any firearm from which the manufacturer's identification mark or serial number has been removed."

Many jurisdictions restrict who can buy firearms. Examples include municipalities in Kansas (Junction City, Kansas City, Lawrence), Maine (Portland, Falmouth, Cape Elizabeth), and New Mexico (Albuquerque, Alamogordo, Grants) that "prohibit the sale, possession, or receipt of any type of firearm to or by any of a particular class of persons (e.g., convicted felons, fugitives from justice, illegal aliens, mental incompetents, unlawful drug users and addicts)." Evanston, Illinois, allows no firearms to be sold.

Municipalities requiring gun sellers to have a state or local license include Highland Park, Illinois; St. Louis, Missouri; Las Vegas, Nevada; Fargo, North Dakota; Pendleton and Springfield, Oregon; and Alexandria, Virginia. Some cities require longer waiting periods than those required by the Brady Law. Buyers in Atlanta, Georgia, must wait 15 days, while Cape Elizabeth and Westbrook, Maine, require a seven-day waiting period until the gun can be delivered. Brunswick County, Virginia, has a 30-day waiting period, while Fairfax County, Virginia, has a 30-day waiting period for nonstate residents.

Baltimore County, Maryland, holds the parents or guardians "of underage persons liable for acts wrongfully committed with firearms." Boston, Massachusetts, restricts the sale of replica firearms. New York City outlaws the sale to a minor of any toy pistol that can be loaded with powder, and bans the sale and possession of any toy or imitation pistol that duplicates a real pistol unless the replica is in a color other than black, blue, silver, or aluminum.

Banning Handguns

In 1981 the Chicago suburb of Morton Grove, Illinois, made national headlines when it passed Ordinances 81-10 and 81-11, which banned machine guns, sawed-off shotguns, and handguns. The ordinances excluded police officers, jail and prison authorities, members of the armed forces, licensed gun collectors, and gun clubs that maintain the guns on their premises. East St. Louis, Illinois, also outlawed the possession of handguns.

San Francisco, California, enacted a local ordinance prohibiting handguns to all but those who could display a compelling need. Individuals who could not show such a need were supposed to surrender their handguns, but few citizens complied with the request, and the courts eventually threw out the regulation. Since then, Cleveland

Heights, Ohio, and University Park and Skokie, Illinois, voted down similar proposed bans.

Requiring Handguns

Some towns have required residents to own guns. In 1982, when Morton Grove, Illinois, enacted the ban on gun ownership, city officials of Kennesaw, Georgia, located 24 miles northwest of Atlanta, passed a law requiring the head of every household in the 8,500-person town to "maintain a firearm, together with ammunition therefore." Exemptions were granted to residents with a physical or mental infirmity that would prohibit their using a firearm, to heads of households who were paupers, to those whose religious doctrine or belief forbids the possession of a firearm, and to convicted felons. Officials conceded that the ordinance was basically unenforceable.

Local Banning of Semiautomatic Assault Weapons

Many of the legislative battles over the issue of gun control can be traced to a gruesome murder. On January 17, 1989, a gunman using a semiautomatic assault rifle entered a Stockton, California, school yard and murdered 5 children and wounded 29 others and a teacher. As a result of the slayings, the Stockton city council enacted a ban on the sale and possession of semiautomatic firearms, including semiautomatic pistols or rifles with magazines that hold 20 or more rounds of ammunition, such as AK-47s, AR-15s, or Uzis. Los Angeles and Palo Alto passed similar laws. Other cities followed.

On February 18, 1989, the city council of Cleveland, Ohio, passed a similar ban on the sale or possession of assault weapons. Cincinnati, Columbus, and Dayton, Ohio, and East Chicago and Gary, Indiana, also have similar laws. In 1991 New York City passed a law banning the possession of assault guns, and, in 1992, Chicago outlawed assault weapons and ammunition magazines holding more than 12 rounds. In 1993 Philadelphia and Pittsburgh, Pennsylvania, banned the possession of assault weapons.

CHAPTER 4
COURT RULINGS ON FIREARMS

Although the U.S. Constitution and most state constitutions guarantee the right to bear arms (see Appendix), that right may be strictly controlled. In some cases, certain kinds of guns may be outlawed altogether.

Federal and state courts have upheld the rights of the federal government, states, and local communities to require the registration of firearms, to determine how these weapons may be carried, and even to forbid the use of some weapons under certain circumstances. Courts have also been asked to decide if manufacturers, dealers, or, sometimes, even relatives should be held responsible when guns are used to commit crimes.

Despite the general acceptance that gun ownership may be denied to convicted felons, mentally incompetent persons, and the insane, challenges to these restrictions are often made. The following selections of court cases include landmark decisions and recent rulings on gun regulations at the federal, state, and local levels.

SECOND AMENDMENT INTERPRETATIONS

The Second Amendment has undoubtedly been the least ruled-upon amendment. Most legal scholars believe few cases have been tried under this amendment because it remains tied to the U.S. Supreme Court decision *Baron v. Mayor of Baltimore* (32 U.S. 243, 1833), in which the High Court ruled that the Bill of Rights did not apply to or restrict the states. This means the guarantees of the Bill of Rights applied only to the federal government. For example, unless the state constitution guaranteed the right of free speech, the state did not have to permit free speech. Federal law enforcement officials could not arrest a person exercising the right of free speech, but state or local authorities could. This interpretation applied to all of the amendments and dominated American legal history during its formative years. However, during the years of Chief Justice Earl Warren's court (1953–69), most of the

provisions of the Bill of Rights were held to be applicable to the states through the Fourteenth Amendment.

This change, however, did not affect interpretations of the Second Amendment. This Amendment is still interpreted through the findings of *Baron v. Baltimore,* which ruled that the Constitution was a limitation only on the federal government and did not restrict state legislation. Therefore, most cases dealing with guns have been ruled upon according to state constitutions rather than the Second Amendment of the U.S. Constitution.

FEDERAL COURT CASES

United States v. Cruikshank

The first major federal case dealing with the Second Amendment was *United States v. Cruikshank* (92 U.S. 542, 1876). The defendants were convicted under the Enforcement Act of 1870 of conspiracy to deprive two black men of their right of assembly and free speech and their right to keep and bear arms as guaranteed by the First and Second Amendments of the U.S. Constitution. At that time, the Supreme Court, consistent with its opinion in the *Slaughterhouse Cases* (83 U.S. 36, 1873), denied that the federal Bill of Rights applied to the states via the Fourteenth Amendment. The Court ruled that

> Bearing arms for a lawful purpose is not a right granted by the Constitution. Neither is it in any manner dependent upon that instrument for its existence. The Second Amendment declares that it shall not be infringed; but this . . . means no more than it shall not be infringed by Congress. This is one of the amendments that has no other effect than to restrict the powers of the national government.

This finding has been interpreted in two ways. One is that the states, if they so desire, may limit, if not ban, the possession of arms. Others interpret the statement, "This is not a right granted by the Constitution," as meaning that the right to bear arms preceded the Constitution and therefore exists independently of the Constitution.

United States v. Miller

The Supreme Court has closely examined the Second Amendment only once in the 20th century. Following the passage of the National Firearms Act of 1934, Jack Miller and Frank Layton were convicted of going from Oklahoma to Arkansas while carrying a double-barreled, sawed-off, 12-gauge shotgun, a favorite weapon of the nation's gangsters at that time. They appealed, citing the Second Amendment, and the judges dismissed the charges. The two defendants were released, never to be seen again. In *United States v. Miller* (307 U.S. 174, 1939) the Supreme Court reversed the lower court's ruling and upheld the federal law. The High Court cited the militia argument, noting that

> In the absence of any evidence tending to show that possession or use of a "shotgun having a barrel of less than eighteen inches in length" at this time has some reasonable relationship to the preservation or efficiency of a well-regulated militia, we cannot say that the Second Amendment guarantees the right to keep and bear such an instrument. Certainly it is not within judicial notice that this weapon is any part of the ordinary military equipment or that its use could contribute to the common defense.

Referring back to the debates of the Constitutional Convention and discussion of the militia, the Court observed that the debates showed

> . . . plainly enough that the Militia comprised all males physically capable of acting in concert for the common defense, "A body of citizens enrolled for military discipline." . . . Ordinarily when citizens enrolled for service these men were expected to appear bearing arms supplied by themselves and of the kind in common use at the time.

Because Miller fled and did not appear to plead his case, the Supreme Court heard only the government's side of the issue and did not hear a strong argument for permitting a citizen to maintain the weapon. Nonetheless, *Miller* remains the major High Court ruling and precedent concerning gun control.

INTENT OF THE WEAPON. *United States v. Miller* denied Miller the right to carry a sawed-off shotgun because it could not be shown "at this time" that the weapon had

> . . . some reasonable relationship to the preservation or efficiency of a well-regulated militia. . . . Certainly it is not within judicial notice that this weapon is any part of the ordinary military equipment or that its use could contribute to the common defense.

That ruling raises some interesting questions. The sawed-off shotgun was used in Vietnam as an effective military weapon. Does this mean that, today, it could be shown to contribute to the common defense? And what of the machine gun, which is now forbidden under federal law? Could that weapon, too, be considered as potentially helpful to the common defense? If so, should American citizens be allowed to bear those types of weapons?

UPHOLDING MILLER. In *United States v. Tot* (131 F.2d 261, 1942) a .32-caliber gun was seized in a search of the home of a previously convicted felon while he was being arrested for a crime. The Third Circuit Court of Appeals did not accept Tot's argument that the Second Amendment prohibited the state of New Jersey from denying him the right to own a gun because he was a convicted felon. Using *Miller* as a precedent, the court reasoned,

> One would hardly argue seriously that a limitation upon the privilege of possessing weapons was unconstitutional when applied to a mental patient of the maniac type. The same would be true if the possessor were a child of immature years. . . . Congress has prohibited the receipt of weapons from interstate transaction by persons who have previously, by due process of law, been shown to be aggressors against society. Such a classification is entirely reasonable and does not infringe upon the presentation of the well regulated militia protected by the Second Amendment.

The Third Circuit Court of Appeals noted that the Second Amendment,

> . . . unlike those providing for protection of free speech and freedom of religion, was not adopted with individual rights in mind, but as a protection for the States in the maintenance of their militia organizations against possible encroachment by the Federal power.

Citing *U.S. v. Miller,* the First Circuit Court of Appeals, in *Cases v. United States* (131 F.2d 916, 1942), also upheld the Federal Firearms Act. Cases had been convicted of a violent crime and, under the federal law, could not own a gun. The circuit court observed,

> The Federal Firearms Act undoubtedly curtails to some extent the right of individuals to keep and bear arms, but it does not follow from this as a necessary consequence that is bad. . . . The right to keep and bear arms is not a right conferred upon the people by the federal constitution.

Gun Possession by a Convicted Felon

In a similar case involving the possession of a firearm by a convicted felon, the Eighth Circuit Court of Appeals concluded, in *U.S. v. Synnes* (438 F.2d 764, 1971), concerning the Second Amendment, that

> We see no conflict between it [a law prohibiting the possession of guns by convicted criminals] and the Second Amendment since there is no showing that prohibiting possession of firearms by felons obstructs the maintenance of a "well regulated militia."

Virtually all supporters of handgun possession have accepted the right of federal and state governments to deny weapons to former felons, drug abusers, and mentally incompetent persons.

Possession of a Machine Gun

In *United States v. Warin* (530 F.2d 103, 1976) the defendant tried to convince the Sixth Circuit Court of Appeals that a federal law prohibiting the possession of an unregistered machine gun violated his Second Amendment rights. The court upheld the defendant's conviction, stating,

> It would unduly extend this opinion to attempt to deal with every argument made by defendant and *amicus curiae* [a "friend of the court" that is not a party to the litigation but gives its opinions to the Court], Second Amendment Foundation, all of which are based on the erroneous supposition that the Second Amendment is concerned with the rights of individuals rather than those of the States.

Enhanced Penalties for "Use" of Firearms in a Drug Crime

In *Smith v. U.S.* (508 U.S. 223, 1993) the Supreme Court ruled that the federal law authorizing stiffer penalties if the defendant "during and in relation to . . . [a] drug trafficking crime uses . . . a firearm" includes not only the use of firearms as weapons but also firearms used as commerce, such as in a trade. John Angus Smith and his companion went from Tennessee to Florida to buy cocaine, which they planned to resell for profit. During a drug transaction, an undercover agent posing as a pawnshop dealer examined Smith's MAC-10, a small, compact, lightweight firearm that can be equipped with a silencer—"a favorite among criminals." Smith told the agent he could have the gun in exchange for two ounces of cocaine. The officer said he would try to get the drugs and return in an hour. In the meantime, Smith fled, and after a high-speed chase, officers apprehended him.

A grand jury indicted Smith for, among other offenses, drug-trafficking crimes and knowingly using the MAC-10 in connection with a drug-trafficking crime. Under 18 U.S.C. Sec. 924(c)(1)k, a defendant who so uses a firearm must be sentenced to 5 years' imprisonment, and if the "firearm is a machine gun or is equipped with a firearm silencer," as it was in this case, the sentence is 30 years. The jury convicted Smith on all counts.

On appeal, the defendant argued that the law applied only if the firearm was used as a weapon. The Eleventh Circuit Court disagreed, ruling that the federal legislation did not require that the firearm be used as a weapon—"any use of 'the weapon to facilitate in any manner the commission of the offense' suffices."

In a similar case, the Court of Appeals for the District of Columbia Circuit had arrived at the same conclusion

(*United States v. Harris,* 959 F.2d 246, 1993). On the other hand, the Court of Appeals for the Ninth Circuit (*United States v. Phelps,* 877 F.2d 28, 1989) had held that trading a gun in a drug-related transaction was not "using" it within the meaning of the statute. To resolve the conflict among the different circuit courts, the Supreme Court heard Smith's appeal.

In a 6–3 decision, in *Smith v. U.S.*, the Court ruled that the "exchange of a gun for narcotics constitutes 'use' of a firearm 'during and in relation to . . . [a] drug trafficking crime' within the meaning" of the federal statute. Delivering the opinion of the majority, Justice Sandra Day O'Connor wrote that "when a word is not defined by statute, we normally construe it in accord with its ordinary or natural meaning." Definitions for the word "use" from various dictionaries and *Black's Law Dictionary* showed the word to mean "convert to one's service; to employ; to carry out a purpose or action by means of." In trying to exchange his MAC-10 for drugs, the defendant "used" or employed the gun as an item of trade to obtain drugs. The words "as a weapon" do not appear in the statute. O'Connor reasoned that if Congress had so wanted the narrow interpretation of "use" as a weapon, it would have worded the statute so.

Writing in dissent, Justice Scalia viewed the normal usage of a gun as discharging, brandishing, or using as a weapon. He observed,

> Court does not appear to grasp the distinction between how a word can be used and how it ordinarily is used. It would, indeed, be "both reasonable and normal to say that petitioner 'used' his MAC-10 in his drug trafficking offense by trading it for cocaine." . . . It would also be reasonable and normal to say that he "used" it to scratch his head. When one wishes to describe the action of employing the instrument of a firearm for such unusual purposes, "use" is assuredly a verb one could select. But that says nothing about whether the ordinary meaning of the phrase "uses a firearm" embraces such extraordinary employments. It is unquestionably not reasonable and normal, I think, to say simply "do not use firearms" when one means to prohibit selling or scratching with them.

New Interpretation of "Use"

In April 1995 the High Court agreed to hear further arguments on the interpretation of the federal statute that enhances the penalty for the commission of a drug offense while using a firearm. In *U.S. v. Bailey* and *U.S. v. Robinson* (116 S.Ct. 501) the Court of Appeals for the D.C. Circuit (36 F.3d 106) consolidated the two very similar cases and established a new "use" test that would require a jury to find that a gun was accessible to an individual engaging in drug activity. The appellate court explained, "Whenever one puts or keeps the gun in a particular place from which one can gain access to it if and when needed to facilitate a drug crime," an individual has used the gun and should be held to the principles of Sec. 924 (c)(1). The cases prompting the new test involved guns and drugs, but no evidence that the guns were actually used as weapons in drug crimes.

U.S. v. Bailey involved a 1988 incident in which Washington, D.C., police officers stopped Roland J. Bailey in his car because he was missing a front license plate and an inspection sticker. When Bailey could not produce a driver's license, the officer searched Bailey's car and found ammunition and 30 grams of cocaine. Another officer found a loaded pistol and more than $3,200 in small bills in the trunk. At his trial, Bailey was convicted of possession of cocaine with intent to deliver and using or carrying a firearm in connection with a drug offense. On appeal, Bailey argued that there was no evidence that he had used the gun in connection with a drug offense.

U.S. v. Robinson involved an incident in which Larry Hale, a police officer buying drugs undercover, saw Candisha Robinson handing crack cocaine to another person. In the same room, the person who took the cocaine from Robinson sold the drug to the officer, who paid for it with $20 in marked money. Later, while executing a search warrant on Robinson's apartment, officers found a .22-caliber derringer, two rocks of crack cocaine, and the marked money. Robinson was found guilty of cocaine distribution, and, among other things, the use or carrying of a firearm during and in relation to a drug-trafficking offense. On appeal, Robinson argued that during the drug sale to the officer, the gun was unloaded and in a locked trunk and was not used in the commission or in relation to a drug-trafficking offense.

Using the new use test described in *Smith,* the appellate court explained,

> Using a gun to protect one's drugs, drug paraphernalia, or the proceeds of one's drugs sales is . . . clearly a prohibited use of the gun. . . . Whenever there is sufficient evidence for a jury to find the defendant at some time during the commission of the . . . drug offense put or kept a firearm in a place where it would be proximate to and accessible from a place that is clearly connected to . . . drug trafficking, the jury may also infer that the gun was being used to protect the drug-trafficking operation. . . .

In December 1995, however, the Supreme Court overrode the term "use" as defined after *Smith.* The Court unanimously held that to establish "use," the government must show that the defendant actively employed a firearm so as to make it an "operative factor in relation to the predicate offense." This definition includes hiding a gun in a shirt or pants, threatening to use a gun, or actually using the gun during the commission of a drug crime. The Court also found that Bailey's and Robinson's "use" convictions could not be supported because the evidence did

not indicate that either defendant actively employed firearms during drug crimes.

In 1998, in *U.S. v. Muscarello* (118 S.Ct. 1911), the Supreme Court put a much broader interpretation on the federal law, which subjects a person who "uses or carries" a gun "during and in relation to" a "drug trafficking crime" to a five-year mandatory prison term. The three defendants in this case carried guns in the trunks of their cars. The Court ruled that having a gun in a car from which a person is dealing drugs fits the meaning of "carries" for purposes of the sentencing statutes.

Possession of a Firearm Near a School

The Gun-Free School Zones Act of 1990 [18 U.S.C. Sec. 921(a)(25, 26), (22(q)(1)] makes it unlawful for any individual knowingly to possess a firearm in a school zone, defined as within 1,000 feet of the school grounds, whether or not school is in session. Two federal appellate courts came to different conclusions about the constitutionality of this bill.

THE LAW IS UNCONSTITUTIONAL. The U.S. Court of Appeals for the Fifth Circuit, in *U.S. v. Lopez* (2 F.3rd 1342, 1993), ruled that Congress had exceeded its power under the commerce clause of the U.S. Constitution. The commerce clause gives Congress the power to regulate conduct that crosses state borders. According to the court, with few specific exceptions, "Federal laws proscribing firearm possession require the government to prove a connection to commerce." In the debates before the law was enacted, and in the law itself, Congress made no attempt to link the Gun-Free School Zones Act to commerce. The appeals court asserted,

> Both the management of education and the general control of simple firearms possession by ordinary citizens have traditionally been a state responsibility. . . . We are unwilling to . . . simply assume that the concededly intrastate conduct of mere possession by any person of any firearm substantially affects interstate commerce, or the regulation thereof, whenever it occurs, or even most of the time that it occurs, within 1000 feet of the grounds of any school whether or not then in session. If Congress can thus bar firearms possession because of such a nexus to the grounds of any public or private school, and can do so without supportive findings or legislative history, on the theory that education affects commerce, then it could also similarly ban lead pencils, "sneakers," Game Boys, or slide rules.

Following this reasoning, the appeals court found the Gun-Free School Zones Act unconstitutional.

THE LAW IS CONSTITUTIONAL. On the other hand, in *U.S. v. Edwards* (13 F.3d 291, 1993), the U.S. Court of Appeals, Ninth Circuit, ruled that the commerce clause of the Constitution did, indeed, give Congress the power to pass such a law as the Gun-Free School Zones Act. In

1991 Sacramento police officers and school officials approached Ray Harold Edwards II and four other males at Grant Union High School. The officers discovered a .22 rifle and a sawed-off bolt-action rifle in the trunk of Edwards's car. One of the charges against Edwards was violation of the Gun-Free School Zones Act.

Edwards appealed, claiming the law violated the Tenth Amendment because Congress did not have the authority under the commerce clause or any other delegated power to enact the Gun-Free School Zones Act. The Tenth Amendment says that "the powers not delegated to the United States by the Constitution, or prohibited by it to the States, are reserved to the States respectively, or to the people."

Disagreeing with *U.S. v. Lopez,* the court of appeals ruled that the Gun-Free School Zones Act

> . . . does not expressly require the Government to establish a nexus [connection] between the possession of a firearm in a school zone and interstate commerce. . . . It is unnecessary for Congress to make express findings that a particular activity or class of activities affects interstate commerce in order to exercise its legislative authority pursuant to the commerce clause.

The judges used as a precedent a case upholding legislation making it illegal to possess an unregistered machine gun. In that case, the appeals court ruled that "violence created through the possession of firearms adversely affects the national economy, and consequently, it was reasonable for Congress to regulate the possession of firearms pursuant to the commerce clause."

In 1995 the Supreme Court, in *United States v. Lopez* (514 U.S. 549, 1995), struck down the act, saying that Congress had overstepped its bounds because it had based the law on the commerce clause of the U.S. Constitution. The commerce clause empowers Congress to regulate interstate commerce, but Congress had failed to connect gun-free school zones with commerce. Chief Justice William Rehnquist wrote that Congress had used the commerce clause as a general police power in a way that is generally retained by states. He also warned that the Gun-Free School Zones Act

> . . . is a criminal statute that by its terms has nothing to do with "commerce" or any sort of economic enterprise, however broadly one might define those terms. . . . If we were to accept the Government's arguments, we are hardpressed to [find] any activity by an individual that Congress is without power to regulate.

In 1996 Congress approved a slightly revised version of the Gun-Free School Zones Act in PL 104-208. These amendments require prosecutors to prove an impact on interstate commerce as an element of the offense. This version of the act has yet to be tested.

Is the Brady Law Unconstitutional?

In December 1996 the U.S. Supreme Court began hearing arguments concerning the constitutionality of the Brady Handgun Violence Prevention Act of 1993 (PL 103-159). (See Chapter 3 for more information on the Brady Law.) Under the Brady Law, Congress ordered local chief law enforcement officials (CLEOs) nationwide to conduct background checks on prospective handgun purchasers buying their guns through federally licensed dealers. Two sheriffs, Jay Printz of Ravalli County, Montana, and Richard Mack of Graham County, Arizona, appealed verdicts from lower courts, which gave the two similar cases different rulings, to a U.S. Court of Appeals.

The two cases, *Printz v. U.S.* (117 S.Ct. 2365) and *Mack v. U.S.* (66 F.3rd 1025), were consolidated for the purposes of the appeal. The sheriffs charged that Congress exceeded its powers under the Tenth Amendment of the U.S. Constitution, which defines the separate powers and relationship between the federal government and the sovereign powers of the individual states. They argued that the federal government had placed federal burdens on local police agencies with no federal compensation. Representing the federal government, Acting Solicitor General Walter Dellinger argued that the government had the right to require local agencies to carry out federal orders as long as those agencies were not forced to make policy.

In June 1997 the Supreme Court, in *Printz v. U.S.,* struck down the Brady Law provisions that require a CLEO to conduct background checks on prospective handgun purchasers and to accept the form on which that background check is based. They declared that these provisions violated the Tenth Amendment to the United States Constitution. Justice Scalia wrote,

> The Federal Government may neither issue directives requiring the States to address particular problems, nor command the States' officers, or those of their political subdivisions, to administer or enforce a federal regulatory program.

Because no mention was made of the Second Amendment, this decision will have no effect on other gun control laws.

The Court unanimously upheld the Brady Law's five-day waiting period for handgun purchases, however, since the waiting period is directed at gun store owners and is not a federal mandate to state officials. Most CLEOs continued to voluntarily conduct background checks until the National Instant Check System (NICS), instituted by the Brady Law, became effective in November 1998.

Selling Guns without a License

The Firearm Owners' Protection Act (PL 99-308, 1986) prohibits any person other than a licensed dealer from dealing in firearms. Anyone who "willfully violates" this law is subject to a fine and up to five years in prison. Sillasse Bryan bought several pistols in Ohio, using "straw purchasers" (legally qualified buyers who purchase for someone not legally qualified). After filing the serial numbers off the guns, he resold the guns in New York City, in areas known for drug dealing. After his arrest the defense argued that Bryan could be convicted only if he knew of the specific federal licensing requirement of the law. Nonetheless, Bryan was convicted. In 1998 the Supreme Court, in *U.S. v. Bryan* (118 S.Ct. 1939), interpreted "willfully violates" to mean that the defendant only needs to know that he was selling guns illegally and upheld Bryan's conviction.

STATE LAWS

Most state constitutions guarantee the right to bear arms (see Appendix). Some states clearly tie this right to the militia, while other state constitutions and courts have ruled from the perspective of personal defense or self-protection; no single position on this issue is common among all the states. Two excellent examples of self-defense are *Schubert v. DeBard* (398 NE.2d 1339, 1980) and *State v. Kessler* (614 P.2d 94, 1980).

A Right to Self-Defense in Indiana

Joseph L. Schubert, Jr., felt he needed a weapon to protect himself from his brother, who, he believed, threatened his life. Indiana law required that "a person desiring a license to carry a handgun shall apply to the chief of police or corresponding police officer," in this case Robert L. DeBard, superintendent of the Indiana State Police. Upon investigation, Superintendent DeBard's office found Schubert had done nothing to clear up the problem and that the claimed need for a weapon was probably unjustified. For example, he had not tried to talk about the problem with his brother. DeBard further claimed that Schubert was a "chronic liar" suffering from a "gigantic police complex."

The defense accepted the conclusion of the police investigation that Schubert had some psychological problems but felt that they were totally irrelevant to the matter at hand. Article 1, Section 32, of the Indiana Constitution guarantees that "the people shall have a right to bear arms, for the defense of themselves and the State." Therefore, when self-defense was properly indicated as the reason for desiring a firearms license, and the applicant was otherwise qualified, the license could not be withheld because an administrative official had subjectively determined that the applicant's need to defend himself was not justified. (At this point, no one had claimed Schubert was mentally incompetent, which is an accepted reason to deny permission for a gun.)

The Third District Court of Appeals of the State of Indiana, in *Schubert v. DeBard* (398 NE.2d 1339, 1980), agreed

with Schubert. After studying the debates at the time of the creation of the Indiana Constitution in 1850, the majority concluded that "it is clear that our constitution provides our citizenry the right to bear arms for their self-defense." If it were left to a police official to determine a "proper reason" for a person to claim self-defense, "it would supplant a right with a mere administrative privilege."

The state constitution grants an individual the right to obtain a weapon for self-defense. If an administrator could determine when "self-defense" was really necessary, then it would no longer be a right but a privilege to be ruled upon by a government official. Therefore, the court reversed a lower ruling upholding DeBard's right to determine what was "self-defense" and sent it back to the lower court, asking the court it to determine if Schubert was mentally incompetent, an accepted basis for denying him the right to purchase a weapon.

Oregon Upholds the Right to Possess Weapons for Self-Defense

The Constitution of the state of Oregon is identical to that of Indiana concerning possession of weapons. Randy Kessler had an argument with his apartment manager, which escalated into name-calling, swearing, and throwing things at each other. The police were called, and Kessler was arrested. He asked the police to get his coat from his apartment. While getting Kessler's coat, the police found two "billy clubs" in the apartment. They charged Kessler with disorderly conduct and possession of a "slugging weapon."

After studying the history of the Indiana Constitution and the *Schubert v. DeBard* decision, the Supreme Court of Oregon, in *State v. Kessler* (614 P. 2d 94, 1980), found the state regulation forbidding ownership of the billy clubs to be unconstitutional. After noting that the term "arms" applied only to hand-carried weapons such as muskets, knives, swords, and so forth and not to "cannon or other heavy ordnance," the court upheld Kessler's (state) constitutional (Article I, Section 27) right to possess the billy clubs or any other type of small weapon for his self-defense.

The reasoning of the courts is generally that a regulation is valid if the aim of public safety does not frustrate the guarantees of the state constitution. For example, many state courts have upheld statutes prohibiting concealed weapons and possession of firearms. The guarantees of the Oregon State Constitution were being unnecessarily violated by a state regulation, and the state constitution takes precedence.

Public Housing and the Right to Keep Firearms

A couple identified as John and Jane Doe, who had lived in public housing since 1981, were threatened with eviction after the Portland Housing Authority (PHA) in

Maine discovered guns in their apartment. John Doe was a veteran of the U.S. Marine Corps, a former firearms dealer, and a licensed hunter. Jane Doe, a target shooter, reported that she kept a handgun for self-protection when her husband worked late. The Does filed a petition to prevent the PHA from enforcing a provision in their lease that banned the possession of firearms.

The Does argued that a state law that regulates the possession of firearms preempted the lease. The preemption statute states,

> The State intends to occupy and preempt the entire field of legislation concerning the regulation of firearms. . . . No political subdivision of the State, including but not limited to municipalities, counties, townships, and village corporations, may adopt any [law] concerning . . . firearms, components, ammunition or supplies.

The PHA claimed that the state law could not preempt its resolutions because the PHA is not a political subdivision listed in the statute. In April 1995 the Maine Supreme Court, in *Doe v. Portland Housing Authority* (656 A.2d 1200), ruled that the PHA was indeed a political subdivision. The court also found that the state legislature intended to regulate uniformly the possession of firearms by all Maine residents whether they live in public housing or not. The case was appealed to the U.S. Supreme Court, but the High Court chose not to hear the case (cert. denied, 516 U.S. 861).

Mental Illness and the Right to Firearms

In 1991 the Circuit Court of Multnomah County, Oregon, ruled that a defendant who suffered from mental illness and had carefully planned a murder was a danger to himself and others. Because the defendant was unwilling, unable, or unlikely to seek voluntary treatment, he was committed to a psychiatric facility. The court then ordered that the defendant be prohibited from purchasing or possessing firearms for a period of five years, in accordance with Oregon statutes. The defendant, Patrick Owenby, appealed, challenging only the order that prohibited him from purchasing or possessing firearms.

The Oregon Court of Appeals, in *State v. The Defendant, Patrick Owenby* (826 P.2d 51, Or. App. 1992), ruled that the statute in question was a narrowly drawn and reasonable restriction on the right to bear arms, it was not in violation of the state constitution, clear and convincing evidence existed to support the order, and, finally, it did not violate the federal due process clause.

The court stated,

> The right to bear arms is not absolute. In the exercise of its police power, the legislature may enact reasonable regulations limiting the right and has done so.

> Given the nature of firearms . . . the danger that the statute seeks to avert is a serious one. The restriction on the right

of mentally ill persons to bear arms, on the other hand, is a relatively minor one. The statute is narrowly drawn and may be invoked only when it is shown that the prohibition is *necessary* "as a result of the mentally ill person's mental or psychological state," as demonstrated by past behavior than involves unlawful violence.

Connecticut—Banning Semiautomatic Firearms

In July 1995 the Supreme Court of Connecticut, in *Benjamin v. Bailey* (662 A.2d 1226), upheld a 1993 state law banning the sale, possession, or transfer of 67 automatic and semiautomatic or burst-fire firearms, ruling that the ban did not violate the state constitutional right to bear arms. One observer noted that the decision makes Connecticut one of the first states having the right of self-defense specified in its Constitution to have an assaults-weapons ban pass legal challenge.

Connecticut and Florida—Child Access Prevention

Florida was the first state to pass a "Child Access Prevention" (CAP) law. Often referred to as the "Safe Storage" law, the CAP law requires adults to either keep loaded guns in a place reasonably inaccessible to children or use a device to lock the gun. If a child, anyone under age 16, obtains an improperly stored, loaded gun, the adult owner is held criminally liable. Fourteen additional states—California, Connecticut, Delaware, Hawaii, Iowa, Maryland, Minnesota, Nevada, New Jersey, North Carolina, Rhode Island, Texas, Virginia, and Wisconsin—have passed similar laws.

In July 1993 three teenage boys found a loaded revolver in the bedroom of Joseph Wilchinski, a Connecticut college campus police officer. Soon after, a 15-year-old boy was shot in the face; he died two days later. Under the state's CAP law, Wilchinski was charged with criminal negligence and sentenced to three years probation. He appealed, claiming the law was unconstitutionally vague.

In July 1997 the Connecticut Supreme Court, in *Connecticut v. Wilchinski* (242 Conn. 211), upheld the law, declaring that the requirement to store firearms in a "securely locked box or other container . . . in a location which a reasonable person would believe to be secure" was sufficiently clear to inform Wilchinski of safe storage practices.

Kansas—Duty to Secure Handguns

In August 1998 the Kansas Supreme Court, in *Long v. Turk* (962 P.2d 1093), ruled that handgun owners have a duty to store guns safely in order to prevent juveniles and others from misusing them. Seventeen-year-old Matthew Turk took his father's .357 Magnum handgun that had been left in a cabinet. While out driving, he shot and killed Anthony Long, a passenger in another vehicle, during a traffic dispute. Long's mother filed a wrongful-death action against Matthew's father. The court held that since firearms are dangerous instruments, gun owners owe the public a duty to secure them. This case followed a similar case in Montana, *Strever v. Cline* (278 Mont. 165, 1996), which also resulted in a decision that firearms owners have a duty to secure their guns from theft.

New Jersey and California—Bans on Assault Weapons

In March 1999 the federal court in New Jersey rejected a challenge brought by a group of gun clubs and arms manufacturers seeking to overturn New Jersey's 1999 ban on assault weapons on the grounds of vagueness, free speech, and equal protection. The court held that the statute banning assault weapons was not vague because it "addresses an understandable core of banned guns and adequately puts gun owners on notice that their weapon could be prohibited" (*Coalition of New Jersey Sportsmen v. Whitman,* 1999, U.S. District Court). In their ruling, the court further held that the statute's ban on specifically named weapons "does not violate anyone's free speech," nor does the statute infringe upon equal protection rights "because the rationality of the link between public safety and proscribing assault weapons is obvious."

Across the country, the Supreme Court of California reversed the court of appeals and upheld the constitutionality of California's assault weapons law (*Kasler v. Lockyer,* June 29, 2000). The court held that the ban on such weapons "does not burden any fundamental right under the federal or state constitution" and that the California legislature "had a rational basis for enacting the statute." In addition, the court found that the ban did not violate the principles of equal protection, separation of powers, or due process.

Massachusetts—Gun Safety Regulations

In October 1997 Scott Harshbarger, the attorney general of Massachusetts, set forth regulations applying consumer product safety guidelines to all handguns made or sold within the state. On the day before implementation, the American Shooting Sports Council and a group of Massachusetts gun manufacturers sued to block the regulations from taking effect, arguing that the attorney general exceeded his authority. The case ultimately made its way to the Supreme Judicial Court of Massachusetts, which reversed the trial court's ruling in favor of the gun manufacturers and sent the matter back to the trial court to enter a final judgment in favor of the attorney general (*American Shooting Sports Council, Inc. v. Harshbarger,* 1999, Supreme Judicial Court of Massachusetts). On April 3, 2000, Attorney General Harshbarger announced that the implementation of the regulations would begin immediately.

LOCAL RULINGS

Salina, Kansas, Denies Individual Rights to Gun Ownership

In 1905 the Supreme Court of Kansas, in *City of Salina v. Blaksley* (83 P. 619, 1905), ruled that the right to possess or carry a handgun for self-defense was not absolute. Blaksley was convicted of carrying a pistol within the city while under the influence of alcohol. The Kansas High Court held that individual rights were not protected by the state constitutional provision and decided that "only to the people collectively as members of legitimate military organizations is the right guaranteed and then only to weapons of the type used in civilized warfare." The following cases indicate how various jurisdictions, like Salina, Kansas, have chosen to limit the right to own a weapon and how the courts have ruled on these laws.

Portland, Oregon, Regulates Possession of Guns

The city of Portland, Oregon, passed an ordinance prohibiting "any person on a public street or in a public place to carry a firearm upon his person, or in a vehicle under his control or in which he is an occupant, unless all ammunition has been removed from the chamber and from the cylinder, clip or magazine" (Portland Ordinance No. 138210, Sec. No. 14.32.010). In 1982 Michael Boyce was convicted of violating this statute, and he appealed, contending that the law violated Article I, Section 27, of the Oregon Constitution, which states,

> The people shall have their right to bear arms for the defense of themselves, and the State, but the Military shall be kept in strict subordination to the civil power.

Boyce based his case on *State v. Kessler* (see above) and *State v. Blocker* (630 P.2d 824, 1981), in which the State Supreme Court declared unconstitutional an Oregon law banning a number of weapons, including switchblades, billy clubs, and blackjacks. The court of appeals, however, in *State v. Boyce* (658 P.2d 577, 1983), did not see the similarities and upheld the lower court's conviction. The court observed that the statute in Kessler and Blocker forbids the "mere possession" of certain weapons and that was the characteristic that made it unconstitutional. The statute in this case regulates only the manner of possession, something both *Kessler and Blocker* recognized as permissible when the regulation was reasonable. The city of Portland could regulate use of weapons within its borders.

In fulfilling its obligation to protect the health, safety, and welfare of its citizens, a government body must sometimes pass legislation that touches upon a right guaranteed by the state or federal constitution. Such an encroachment is permissible when the unrestricted exercise of the right poses a clear threat to the "interests and welfare of the public in general" and the means chosen by the government body do not unreasonably interfere with the right.

The court agreed that individuals had a right to protect their property and themselves

> . . . when a threat to person or property arises in the victim's defense capacity. It is true, on the other hand, that, when the threat arises in a public place, the fact that a person must have any ammunition separated from his

firearm will hinder him to the extent that he is put to the trouble of loading the weapon.

However, given the magnitude of the city's felt need to protect the public from an epidemic of random shootings, we think that the hindrance is permissible.

Renton, Washington—Guns Not Permitted Where Alcohol Is Served

The city of Renton, Washington, enacted Municipal Ordinance 34-59, which states,

> It is unlawful for anyone on or in any premise in the City of Renton where alcoholic beverages are dispensed by the drink to . . . carry any rifle, shotgun or pistol, whether said person has a license or permit to carry said firearm or not, and whether said firearm is concealed or not.

Four residents, with the support of the Second Amendment Foundation, a nonprofit group that promotes the Second Amendment's right to bear arms, went to court seeking an injunction on the ordinance, claiming it violated state law and was unconstitutional. The Superior Court of King County upheld the city ordinance, and the Second Amendment Foundation appealed to the Court of Appeals of Washington.

Article 1, Paragraph 24, of the Washington Constitution states that

> The right of the individual citizen to bear arms in defense of himself, or the state, shall not be impaired, but nothing in this section shall be construed as authorizing individuals or corporations to organize, maintain or employ an armed body of men.

The Court of Appeals, in *Second Amendment Foundation v. City of Renton* (668 F.2d 596, 1983), indicated that "it has long been recognized that the constitutional right to keep and bear arms is subject to reasonable regulation by the State under its police power." Simply because something is guaranteed by either the state or federal Constitution does not mean that it cannot be regulated, declared the court:

> The scope of permissible regulation must depend upon a balancing of the public benefit to be derived from the regulation against the degree to which it frustrates the purposes of the constitutional provision. The right to own and bear arms is only minimally reduced by limiting their possession in bars. The benefit to public safety by reducing the possibility of armed conflict while under the influence of alcohol outweighs the general right to bear arms in defense of self and state.
>
> . . . On balance, the public's right to a limited and reasonable exercise of police power must prevail against the individual's right to bear arms in public places where liquor is served.

Furthermore, stated the court, the statutes "do not expressly state an unqualified right to be in possession of a firearm at any time or place." Had the city of Renton

instituted "an absolute and unqualified local prohibition against possession of a pistol by the holder of a state permit," it would have conflicted with state law and Washington's Constitution. This it did not do. Rather the city had instituted a law "which is a limited prohibition reasonably related to particular places and necessary to protect the public safety, health, morals and general welfare."

Finally, the court of appeals noted that "while 36 states have constitutional provisions concerning the right to bear arms, in none is the right deemed absolute." Furthermore, "those states with constitutional provisions similar to ours (Alabama, Michigan, Wyoming, Oregon, Indiana) have uniformly held the right subject to reasonable exercise of the police power." The city of Renton was within its rights when it passed the ordinance barring firearms from bars, and the court upheld the decision of the lower court.

Morton Grove, Illinois—Handguns Are Banned

Not surprisingly, as soon as Morton Grove, Illinois, a Chicago suburb, passed an ordinance banning handguns, handgun owners challenged the city in court. Section 22 of the Illinois Constitution provides that "subject only to the police power, the right to bear arms shall not be infringed." Handgun owners raised issues of the right to bear arms as put forth in state and federal constitutions and further contended that if Morton Grove were allowed to pass such laws in contradiction to other towns and cities, a "patchwork quilt" situation would result. Handgun owners felt a gun owner would never know if he or she were violating a law when traveling through the town.

Morton Grove defended itself, claiming it was within the police power of the town to limit or ban the possession of handguns if city officials believed handgun possession was a threat to peace and stability. They further claimed that their ordinance did not violate Section 22 of the Illinois Constitution because it guaranteed the right to keep "some guns" and because the Morton Grove law did not ban all guns, only handguns.

LEGAL PROCEEDINGS. The cases of Victor Quilici, Robert Stengl, George Reichert, and Robert Metler were combined and brought to the Federal District Court of Northern Illinois. In *Quilici v. Village of Morton Grove* (532 F.Supp. 1169, 1981) the court upheld the town's right to ban handguns. The U.S. Court of Appeals, Seventh District, also upheld the findings of the district court, saying "the right to keep and bear handguns is not guaranteed by the Second Amendment." In 1983 the case was appealed to the U.S. Supreme Court, which denied *certiorari* (to hear the case), and the ruling of the lower Court of Appeals was upheld.

A NEW ROUTE. The Morton Grove handgun owners then went to the Circuit Court of Cook County to get an injunction to prevent Morton Grove from instituting the ordinance banning handguns. The county circuit court upheld the validity of the ordinance. The handgun owners then appealed to the Appellate Court of Illinois, First District, Third Division. In *Kalodimos v. Village of Morton Grove* (447 NE.2d 849, 1983) the court upheld the lower courts. While the court agreed with the handgun owners that "gun control legislation could vary from municipality to municipality, we find that the framers [of the Illinois Constitution] envisioned this kind of local control."

The case was again appealed, and on October 19, 1984, the Illinois Supreme Court, in *Kalodimos v. Village of Morton Grove* (53 LW 2233), upheld the lower courts. Agreeing with earlier observations, the state's highest court noted that "while the right to possess firearms for the purposes of self-defense may be necessary to protect important personal liberties from encroachment by others, it does not lie at the heart of the relationship between individuals and their government." Thus, Morton Grove needed only have had a "rational basis" for instituting its ban on handguns.

Consequently, the Illinois Supreme Court concluded that

> Because of the comparative ease with which handguns can be concealed and handled, a ban on handguns could rationally have been viewed as a way of reducing the frequency of premeditated violent attacks as well as unplanned criminal shootings in the heat of passion or an overreaction to fears of assault, accidental shootings by children or by adults who are unaware that a handgun is loaded, or suicides. The ordinance is a proper exercise of the police power.

Chicago Limits Handgun Possession

On March 19, 1982, the Chicago City Council passed an ordinance prohibiting the registration of any handgun after April 10, 1982, the effective date of the ordinance, unless it was "validly registered to a current owner in the City of Chicago" before April 10, 1982 (*Municipal Code of the City of Chicago,* Chapter 11.1-3(c)). Jerome Sklar had lived in neighboring Skokie, Illinois, when the law was passed. He owned a handgun and had a valid, current Illinois Firearms Identification Card. On April 15, 1982, after the ordinance had gone into effect, he moved to Chicago. He could not register the weapon and, therefore, was unable to bring it into the city.

Sklar went to court, claiming that the city of Chicago had violated the equal protection clause of the U.S. Constitution because he was unable to register the gun that he owned, while owners of firearms who resided in Chicago before the effective date of the ordinance had an opportunity to take advantage of the law's registration requirements. By this time, *Quilici v. Village of Morton Grove* (see above) had been decided in the Seventh Circuit Court of Appeals, a decision that applied to this judicial region.

The U.S. District Court for the Northern District of Illinois therefore indicated that "*Quilici* compels this court to conclude that the Chicago firearms ordinance does not infringe on a constitutionally protected right." The court concluded that the city of Chicago had legitimately and rationally used its police power to promote the health and safety of its citizens. Sklar's argument that Chicago could have chosen better ways to protect its citizens from the negative effects of firearms was irrelevant.

The court concluded that the ordinance did not violate the equal protection clause of the federal Constitution by limiting new registrations instead of banning handguns altogether. The city was under no legal requirement to go all or nothing on limiting handguns.

Sklar appealed the district court's decision to the U.S. Court of Appeals, Seventh Circuit, the same court that had so recently ruled on *Quilici v. Village of Morton Grove*. In his appeal, Sklar also claimed that this violated his constitutionally guaranteed right to travel, since he could not move into Chicago without giving up his gun. Not surprisingly, in *Sklar v. Byrne* (727 F.2d 633, 1984), the court upheld the lower court, citing the precedent of *Quilici*. The court did not believe that a fundamental constitutional issue was involved. Therefore, the city of Chicago had a right to institute local regulations as long as it did not go overboard:

> The Chicago handgun ordinance as a whole promotes legitimate government goals. . . . The council found that handguns and other firearms play a major role in crimes and accidental deaths and injuries, and that the "convenient availability" of firearms and ammunition contributed to deaths and injuries in Chicago. The council therefore enacted the ordinance to restrict the availability of firearms and thereby to prevent some deaths and injuries among Chicago citizens. The city's primary goals are thus classic examples of the city's police power to protect the health and safety of its citizens.

Sklar argued it was irrational and "inconsistent with the overall purposes of the ordinance" to allow some people to have handguns and others not to and not to classify gun owners on the basis of their ability to handle handguns safely. "That argument," said the court in dismissing his claim,

> . . . essentially asks this court to second-guess the judgment of the city council. The Constitution does not require the city council to act with a single purpose or to be entirely consistent. Indeed, the council is a political body for the accommodation of many conflicting interests. . . . The Constitution does not require the city council to enact the perfect law. The council may proceed step by step "adopting regulations that only partially ameliorate a perceived evil and deferring complete elimination of the evil to future regulations."

In both *Quilici* and *Sklar,* the courts were not saying that handgun control is or is not a good decision for any local authority to make. They did not see the possession of a handgun as a fundamental right protected by either the federal or the state constitution. The courts stated that a local town or city, under the police powers granted it by American tradition and the Constitution of the state of Illinois, has the right to make a decision and implement such an ordinance for its people. A local ordinance does not have to be consistent, or even fair, as long as the city council can prove that it rationally thought out its decision.

West Hollywood, California—Saturday Night Specials

In late 1998 the Supreme Court of California let stand a ruling by the California Court of Appeals upholding the city of West Hollywood's municipal ban on the sale of so-called Saturday night special handguns. Most of the manufacturers of these inexpensive and often shoddily constructed weapon are located within 50 miles of the city. In its opinion, the court rejected the gun lobby's claim that California state law preempted the ordinance and found that the ban did not violate the principles of equal protection or due process.

RESPONSIBILITY FOR HANDGUN DEATHS

While the cases presented above center on the right to bear arms, the following cases probe the responsibilities and liabilities associated with the use of those arms. Victims of certain weapons have tried to place that responsibility and liability on the manufacturer or seller of the weapons, while others fault family members who made weapons available to criminals. Each of the following decisions was based upon individual state laws, so interpretations may differ greatly.

Gun Dealers Can Be Liable for Gun Injuries

Jeff Randa, a 19-year-old minor, had informed a gun dealership on several occasions that he wanted to buy a handgun and ammunition. The dealer told the youth that he could not buy a gun until he was 21 years old. Randa asked if his grandmother could purchase the weapon. The dealer replied that if she were a qualified buyer she could but that the dealer could not sell her the weapon "just so she could give the gun to her grandson."

Subsequently, Randa's grandmother came into the store with him and purchased the handgun the youth had been wanting. Twelve days later, Randa went to a party with the gun. Bryan Hoosier, who was also at the party, told Randa to point the gun and shoot. Randa did so, killing Hoosier, and was later convicted of voluntary manslaughter.

Hoosier's father sued the gun dealership for negligence, accusing the dealership of selling the gun to an adult, knowing that it would be given to a minor. The dealership argued that it could not be liable and that the state laws imposed only criminal penalties on violators.

In 1993, in *Hoosier v. Randa,* the California Court of Appeals ruled that the dealer was indeed liable for injuries. The state gun control laws were passed not only to establish criminal penalties but also to protect the public. If a dealer violated the law, he also violated his responsibility of care owed to the public. Consequently, any person harmed by such a violation may sue the violator.

Ohio—the Responsibilities of Gun Show Promoters

In 1992 four youths under age 18 entered a gun show promoted by Niles Gun Show, Inc., and stole several handguns. The corporation from which the vendors rented space had no policy that required the dealers to protect their wares from being stolen, although it had an unenforced policy barring minors from entering the show.

After leaving the show, one of the youths stole a car. While driving around, the juveniles confronted two men, Greg L. Pavlides and Thomas E. Snedeker. One of the boys, Edward A. Tilley III, shot Pavlides in the chest and Snedeker in the head with one of the stolen guns. Tilley was arrested, charged, and convicted of two counts of attempted murder and one count of unauthorized use of a motor vehicle.

Pavlides and Snedeker sued the Niles Gun Show for negligence for not protecting the public from criminal acts by third parties who stole weapons that had not been properly secured. The trial court dismissed the case, stating that the promoters had no such responsibility, but on appeal, the Ohio Court of Appeals reversed the lower court's decision, sending the case back to be tried. The court of appeals ruled that the promoters of gun shows may have a duty to provide adequate security to protect the public from criminal acts that might occur if the guns were stolen.

The plaintiffs showed a report from a gun show operator in which safeguards, such as hiring security guards to keep out minors, had been used to prevent theft. This promoter also had required vendors to keep weapons in display cases or tied down. The court ruled that the gun show operators should be expected to make a reasonable effort to bar minors from shows where unsecured firearms are displayed and to prevent juveniles from stealing or purchasing weapons. The court further stated that it is "common knowledge" that minors possessing guns can create dangerous situations, and so gun show promoters should have been aware that minors stealing guns might use them in criminal activity.

Filing Suit against a Manufacturer

Olen J. Kelley was injured in 1981 when he was shot in the chest during an armed robbery of the grocery store where he worked. The gun used was a Rohm revolver handgun model GR-38S, designed and marketed by Rohm Gesellschaft, a West German corporation. The handgun was assembled and initially sold by R. G. Industries, Inc., a Miami-based subsidiary of the West German corporation. Kelley and his wife filed suits against Rohm Gesellschaft and R. G. Industries in the Circuit Court of Montgomery County, Maryland.

Two counts charged that the handgun was "abnormally dangerous" and the company was defective in its "marketing, promotion, distribution and design." A third count charged negligence. The case revolved around whether or not the gun in question was a Saturday night special, which has been banned from import by the Bureau of Alcohol, Tobacco and Firearms. The Federal District Court of Baltimore, where the case was first brought, asked the state court for a ruling on whether the manufacturer could be held liable under Maryland law.

In *Kelley v. R. G. Industries, Inc.* (497 A.2d 1143, 1985) the Maryland Court of Appeals ruled that the manufacturer or marketers could not be held strictly liable because handguns are "abnormally dangerous products" and their manufacturing and marketing are "abnormally dangerous activit[ies]." In its decision, the court noted,

> Contrary to Kelley's argument, a handgun is not defective merely because it is capable of being used during criminal activity to inflict harm. A consumer would expect a handgun to be dangerous, by its very nature, and to have the capacity to fire a bullet with deadly force.

The Maryland Court of Appeals continued that Kelley confused a product's normal function, which may be dangerous by its very nature, with a defect in its design and function. He cited as an example the fact that a car is dangerous if it is used to run down pedestrians. The injury that results is from the nature of the product—the ability to be propelled to great speeds at great force. However, if the gas tank of the car leaked in such a way as to cause an explosion in the event of a rear-end collision, then the design of the product would be defective, and the manufacturer would be liable. The court concluded that to impose "strict liability upon the manufacturers or marketers of handguns for gunshot injuries resulting from the misuse of handguns by others would be contrary to Maryland public policy."

However, the Maryland court's opinion differed on Saturday night specials, guns "characterized by short barrels, light weight, easy concealability, low cost, [and] use of cheap materials." The court considered these guns

> . . . largely unfit for any of the recognized legitimate uses sanctioned by the Maryland gun control legislation. They are too inaccurate, unreliable and poorly made for use by law enforcement personnel, sportsmen, homeowners or businessmen. . . . The chief "value" a Saturday Night Special handgun has is in criminal activity because of its easy concealability and low price.

Manufacturers or marketers are liable because they should know this type of gun is made primarily for criminal activity. Judge Eldridge quoted an R. G. Industries salesman as telling a prospective handgun marketer, "If your store is anywhere near a ghetto area, these ought to sell real well. This is most assuredly a ghetto gun." The salesman allegedly went on to say that although the gun sold well, it was virtually useless, and he would be afraid to fire it.

The Maryland Court of Appeals did not rule on whether the gun in question fell within the category of a Saturday night special but referred that decision to the United States District Court. It did, however, indicate that strong evidence had been presented that the gun fit many of the qualifications, and if it were found to be a Saturday night special, liability against manufacturer and marketer could be imposed. This decision applied only in Maryland, and the Maryland legislature soon passed a law overriding this decision.

Few courts have accepted this interpretation. Following are two typical cases in which the court refused to apply the findings in *Kelley v. R. G. Industries, Inc.*

Not Right to Single Out Saturday Night Specials

DOES NOT APPLY IN NEW MEXICO. Dolores Armijo's brother, Steven Armijo, shot and killed James Salusberry, Ms. Armijo's husband, in front of Ms. Armijo and her daughter. He then tried to shoot them, but the gun would not go off. Ms. Armijo, claiming the gun used was a Saturday night special, sued Ex Cam, Inc., the importer and distributor of the weapon.

She sued on the basis of four theories: strict product liability (the product was defective and unreasonably dangerous; therefore, the manufacturer was responsible for the actions of the product); liability under an "ultra-hazardous activity" theory (a gun is a dangerous product and the manufacturer is accountable for the results of its use); negligence liability (the manufacturer did not somehow show reasonable care while marketing a product that carried some degree of risk that it might be used to commit a crime); and a narrow form of strict product liability for Saturday night specials put forth in *Kelley v. R. G. Industries, Inc.* (see above).

A U.S. District Court in New Mexico, in *Armijo v. Ex Cam, Inc.* (656 F.Supp. 771, 1987), did not believe that any court in New Mexico, using New Mexican law, would ever recognize any of these theories as the basis of a court case. Basically, the court said,

> It would be evident to any potential consumer that a gun could be used as a murder weapon. So could a knife, an axe, a bow and arrows, a length of chain. The mere fact that a product is capable of being misused to criminal ends does not render the product defective.

[Based on New Mexican law, any case] would not result in liability for a manufacturer of guns, as guns are commonly distributed and the dangers . . . are so obvious as to not require any manufacturers' warnings.

The court showed little respect for *Kelley v. R. G. Industries, Inc.,* indicating that it went against common law in the state of New Mexico. Therefore, it would not be considered. Furthermore, the court concluded,

All firearms are capable of being used for criminal activity. Merely to impose liability upon the manufacturers of the cheapest types of handguns will not avoid that basic fact. Instead, claims against gun manufacturers will have the anomalous (unusual) result that only persons shot with cheap guns will be able to recover, while those shot with expensive guns, admitted by the *Kelley* court to be more accurate and therefore deadlier, would take nothing.

A CASE RESULTING FROM THE ATTEMPTED ASSASSINATION OF THE PRESIDENT. In 1981 John Hinckley tried to assassinate President Ronald Reagan. An individual injured during the assassination attempt sued to hold the gun manufacturer liable based upon negligence, strict product liability, and a "social utility" claim based upon strict liability for unusually dangerous products.

The Washington, D.C., court, in *Delahanty v. Hinckley* (D.C., No 88-488, 10/11/89), rejected the plaintiff's claims. There was no issue that the gun did not work properly. Furthermore, a manufacturer had no duty to warn a buyer "when the danger, or potentiality of danger is generally known and recognized."

The court did not believe the marketing of a handgun was in and of itself dangerous. Rather, the danger resulted from the action of a third party. The plaintiff had shown no connection between the gun manufacturer and John Hinckley, nor had the plaintiff shown a reasonable way in which the gun manufacturer could have prevented John Hinckley from using the weapon to try to kill President Reagan. Referring to *Kelley* (see above), the court dismissed the argument, not accepting a ruling that categorizes one type of product as liable for negligence simply because it was inexpensive and/or poorly made.

Filing Suit against a Seller

A WRONGFUL-DEATH LAWSUIT. In December 1980, James J. Robertson purchased a handgun. Eighteen months later, he used that gun to kill himself. Robertson's family brought a wrongful-death suit against the seller of the handgun before the 298th Judicial District Court, Dallas County, Texas. In *Robertson v. Grogan Investment Company* (710 SW.2d 678, 1986) the district court found in favor of the defendant, Grogan Investments, because the plaintiff's claim that

The sale of handguns . . . to the general public is an abnormally dangerous and ultrahazardous activity . . .

does not state a cause for strict liability under Texas law. In fact, Texas courts, when confronted with the opportunity to apply strict liability for ultrahazardous activities, have declined to do so and have consistently required some other showing, such as negligence or trespass, for recovery.

Filing Suit against a Retail Establishment

In July 1998 the Florida Supreme Court, in *Wal-Mart Stores, Inc., v. Coker* (1998 Fla. Lexis 861), upheld a $2.6 million verdict against Wal-Mart for negligence in selling handgun ammunition to underaged buyers in January 1991. A Florida Wal-Mart store employee sold the ammunition to two teenagers without asking about age or requesting information, a violation of federal law. Several hours later, the teenagers used the ammunition in a robbery of an auto parts store, during which they shot and killed Billy Wayne Coker. Coker's wife filed suit against Wal-Mart.

Though acknowledging that the sale was illegal, Wal-Mart argued that the perpetrators' intervening act of murder was not foreseeable and, therefore, the illegal sale was not the legal cause of Coker's death. The Florida Court of Appeals, however, ruled that an ammunition vendor's illegal sale could be the legal cause of an injury or death caused by the buyer's intentional or criminal act.

Filing Suit against a Wife

In 1988 Joseph Andrade, while working at a business in New Bedford, Massachusetts, was told that a disturbance was going on outside the store and that another store employee was trying to resolve the problem. Andrade left the store and noticed Robert Baptiste entering a house on the same street that Baptiste occupied with his wife. When Andrade began to return to the store, he heard what he described as "popping sounds." Andrade turned and saw Baptiste in front of his residence repeatedly firing a two-and-a-half-foot-long Japanese AKA 752 assault rifle with a banana clip capable of holding 30 rounds of ammunition. Baptiste's wife later reported that her husband had consumed nine cans of beer that day. Baptiste fired 20 shots, at least one of which hit and seriously injured Joseph Andrade.

Mrs. Baptiste was the sole owner of the home, though Baptiste also lived there. He had purchased the gun about a year before the incident and stored it, sometimes loaded, in the living-room closet. Andrade brought suit against Mrs. Baptiste, claiming that she was at fault because she had not tried to exercise control over the closets where the ammunition or weapons were stored, never required that Baptiste store the weapon in a locked closet, and never told the neighbors about the weapons despite her knowledge of his drinking problem and the fact that police had been called to the residence for domestic disturbances on two prior occasions. Andrade's attorney argued that Mrs. Baptiste owed a duty to him (Andrade) to prevent Baptiste from storing the rifle and ammunition on her property.

In *Andrade v. Baptiste* (583 NE.2d 837, Mass. 1992) the Supreme Judicial Court of Massachusetts found that the wife of the assailant could not be held liable on the theory of premises liability or negligent entrustment. The fact that the wife was the sole owner of the property did not give her the ability or the duty to control her husband's misuse of the gun, which was his property, on the premises, nor could she be held liable under a theory of premises liability for her husband's shooting the victim. The court stated,

> The defendant entrusted or sold nothing to her husband; the injury was caused by Baptiste's own weapon which was under his control. . . . The cases cited by the plaintiff . . . concern a dangerous instrument *owned by the defendant,* which is lent to an irresponsible person or left where such a person could find and use it. Other cases cited . . . involve relationships of control between a defendant and the person causing the injury (such as an employer and his employee or a parent and a minor child). None of the cases . . . supports in any way the argument that one can somehow negligently entrust a dangerous instrument to a person who owns the instrument already.

The court further ruled that despite her knowledge of her husband's drinking problem, social policy did not impose the duty of care on the wife to protect Andrade from being shot by a gun that was kept on her property.

A NEW DIRECTION IN FIREARMS SUITS

In the fall of 1998, two major cities filed suits against the gun industry, seeking compensation for costs associated with gun violence. Influenced by the recent successful litigation against tobacco companies in which states received compensation for the cost of treating smoking-related illness under Medicaid, other cities followed with their own suits against the gun manufacturers. According to the Center to Prevent Handgun Violence, as of September 2000 a total of 32 cities and counties plus the state of New York had filed lawsuits against gun manufacturers. Of those, 18 have withstood motions to dismiss by the defendants, and all five of the jurisdictions that have had rulings against them have filed appeals. Most of the city suits focus on either one of two issues: a product-liability claim or a public-nuisance claim.

New Orleans was the first city to sue the gun industry, contending that handguns are "unreasonably dangerous" because manufacturers do not incorporate safety features that would prevent unauthorized people from firing them. The city of New Orleans and the New Orleans Police Department, in their suit against 15 major handgun manufacturers, three industry trade associations, and several New Orleans gun dealers, contend that the industry is liable for a defective product.

Chicago's suit is based on a claim of public nuisance. City officials maintain that the suburbs of Chicago, where gun-control laws are more lax than in the city, are being flooded with guns by the industry. Suburban gun shops sell quantities of guns to single purchasers, known as "straw buyers." A straw buyer is a person who can legally purchase a gun and who then sells that gun to someone who either cannot legally obtain a gun or who does not want to be traced to it. These weapons from the suburbs end up in the city, often in the hands of criminals, creating a "public nuisance." The city of Chicago is asking $433 million to cover police and hospital costs caused by handgun violence since 1994.

Other cities and counties that have filed lawsuits against gun manufacturers include Miami–Dade County, Florida; Bridgeport, Connecticut; Atlanta, Georgia; Cleveland and Cincinnati, Ohio; Wayne County and Detroit, Michigan; St. Louis, Missouri; Boston, Massachusetts; Gary, Indiana; Newark and Camden, New Jersey; and, in California, Los Angeles City and County and San Francisco.

Some observers think antigun suits are more political than legal. They believe these issues should be decided in the legislature, not the courts. Others, however, believe the gun industry and the National Rifle Association have too much influence over state legislatures and Congress. Most suits brought by individuals against gun manufacturers have been defeated, but some observers feel this is the result of juries who have tended to place the responsibility on a criminal or a negligent owner, not on the gun industry. They believe that jurors who hear the cities' suits will agree that the entire public is burdened by the costs resulting from the use of a dangerous product.

Georgia Law Blocks Antigun Suits

In February 1999 the city of Atlanta, Georgia, filed a lawsuit against 17 gun manufacturers, accusing the companies of failing to install safety devices or provide adequate warnings of the dangers of guns. After heavy lobbying by the National Rifle Association, the Georgia legislature approved a law to prevent a city or county from filing product-liability suits against gun makers. The law reserves that right for the state. Georgia was the first state to pass legislation barring its cities from gun litigation.

Brooklyn Jury Finds Gun Manufacturers Liable

In early 1999, in *Hamilton v. Accu-Tek,* a jury in Brooklyn, New York, found gun manufacturers liable for shootings with illegally obtained handguns. Legal experts have called this decision a test case for the wave of lawsuits filed against the gun industry by a number of large cities, including New Orleans, Louisiana; Chicago, Illinois; Boston, Massachusetts; Bridgeport, Connecticut; Los Angeles, California; Miami, Florida; and Philadelphia, Pennsylvania. The lawsuit, filed in federal district court in Brooklyn, charged 25 gun manufacturers with liability for seven New York City shootings, six of them fatal. The suit claimed that the manufacturers had been negligent in their marketing and distribution practices by oversupplying southern states that have weak gun laws, knowing that the guns would travel to states with strict regulations, like New York, and end up in the hands of criminals.

The Brooklyn jury found 9 of the 25 manufacturers collectively liable for three of the shootings but awarded no damages to relatives of the homicide victims. Though it found that the surviving victim was entitled to $3.95 million, given the intricacies of the case, he will collect only about $500,000 under the verdict. Gun control advocates claimed victory because, for the first time, a jury had found gun manufacturers liable for deaths and injuries caused by guns; gun manufacturers also claimed victory because no damages were awarded for six of the seven shootings involved in the suit.

In Boston, a Precedent-Setting Agreement

On December 11, 2000, gun maker Smith & Wesson agreed to settle a lawsuit with the city of Boston, Massachusetts, and pledged to substantially improve its firearms safety features throughout the country and to initiate special steps to better ensure guns don't end up in the hands of criminals (*Chicago Tribune,* Tribune News Services, December 12, 2000). William McQuillen (Bloomberg. com, December 16, 2000) reported that because Smith & Wesson has, in effect, stated that it is possible to make a safer gun, some observers feel that it has become more difficult for the gun industry to claim that it currently makes the safest guns possible. Other cities around the country are expected to duplicate the agreement, which came in the wake of a similar agreement between Smith & Wesson and the U.S. Department of Housing and Urban Development.

THE RIGHT TO MAKE OR OWN A MACHINE GUN

In 1986 J. D. Farmer, Jr., filed an application with the Bureau of Alcohol, Tobacco and Firearms (ATF) to legally make and register a machine gun for his personal col-

lection. The bureau turned his request down, claiming that the Firearms Owners' Protection Act of 1986 had banned such a weapon from private ownership unless the applicant had owned it before May 19, 1986. Farmer went to court, claiming that the ATF had misread the law. The law had said that such weapons could be produced "under the authority" of a government entity. Since Farmer was making application under the National Firearms Act, he was "under the authority" of a government law and, therefore, should be given permission to make a machine gun.

The federal district court agreed with Farmer, but the U.S. Court of Appeals, Eleventh Circuit, in *Farmer v. Higgins* (907 F.2d 1041, 1990), did not. The court thought this to be a relatively simple case. The Firearms Owners' Protection Act of 1986 stated,

1. Except as provided in paragraph (2), it shall be unlawful for any person to transfer or possess a machine gun.

2. This subsection does not apply with respect to: (A) a transfer to or by, or possession by or under the authority of, the United States or any department or agency thereof or a State, or a department, agency, or political subdivision thereof; or (B) any lawful transfer or lawful possession of a machine gun that was lawfully possessed before the date this subsection takes effect.

The court studied the history of the case and found that Congress clearly intended to ban the private ownership of machine guns. After all,

> If Congress did not intend to change prior law by prohibiting the private possession of machine guns, then Section 922(o)(2)(B)'s "grandfather" clause (which exempts from the general prohibition those machine guns lawfully possessed before May 19, 1986) becomes meaningless.

When the law speaks about production "under the authority" of a government entity, it means a machine gun made for the military, for a police force, or one being made under government authority for sale to a foreign country. The U.S. Supreme Court agreed with the court of appeals and, in 1991, denied review of the case, accepting the lower court's finding that Farmer did not have a right to make a machine gun.

CHAPTER 5

FIREARMS AND CRIME

Guns and crime are often linked. Guns are frequently used to commit robbery and murder, crimes in which human life is either threatened or taken. The misuse of guns places most Americans at some risk. This chapter deals with the frequency and ways in which guns are used to commit crimes.

MURDER

The Federal Bureau of Investigation (FBI) of the U.S. Department of Justice collects crime statistics through its Uniform Crime Reports program. Its annual *Crime in the United States* is considered a primary source for statistical information on crime. The crime statistics are based solely on police investigation reports and arrests; other authorities may later classify a killing initially classified as a murder as justifiable homicide, self-defense, suicide, or accident. A person arrested may be innocent and later released. The FBI defines murder as "the willful [non-negligent] killing of one human being by another."

Murders, Weapons, and Circumstances

In 1999 the estimated number of persons murdered in the United States was 15,533, down by 8 percent from 1998, by 28 percent from 1995, and by 34 percent from 1990. The decline from 1998 was most apparent in the nation's cities, where the volume of murders fell by some 7 percent. Small cities with populations of 25,000 or less fared the best, with an overall 13 percent decline, while the figure for cities with populations greater than 250,000 declined by 3 percent. Suburban counties (12 percent) and rural counties (10 percent) also saw a decline from 1998.

As in previous years, firearms were the weapons most frequently used to commit murders, accounting for approximately 7 in every 10 murders committed in the United States. Handguns were used in 51 percent of all murders. Shotguns were used in 4 percent and rifles, 3 percent. A knife or other cutting instrument was used in 13 percent of murders; personal weapons such as fists, hands, or feet in 7 percent; blunt instruments in 6 percent; and other weapons, such as poisons and explosives, in the remainder. (See Table 5.1.)

Data from the Uniform Crime Reports supports the FBI belief that "murder is primarily a societal problem over which law enforcement has little or no control." In 1999 almost half of all murders were committed by a family member (13.8 percent) or an acquaintance (33.9 percent) of the victim. About 32 percent of all female victims in 1999 were slain by husbands or boyfriends. Arguments precipitated 30 percent of the murders, while 17 percent resulted from felonies such as robbery and arson. Five percent were juvenile gang killings. (See Table 5.2.)

The Violence Policy Center, a national nonprofit educational foundation that conducts research on violence in America, reported that the most common homicides involving one female victim and one male attacker are the result of domestic violence and most often involve a gun. In its study *When Men Kill Women: An Analysis of Homicide Data* (Violence Policy Center, Washington, D.C., November 1998) the center found that more female homicides in 1996 were committed with firearms (56 percent) than all other weapons combined. Of the homicides committed with firearms, three-quarters (74 percent) were committed with handguns.

The Criminal Advantages of Guns

A gun offers several advantages over other weapons. The offender can physically keep a greater distance from the victim to ensure his own safety by avoiding physical contact and increasing the chances of escaping. A gun also allows the offender to maintain a psychological distance, keeping the confrontation more impersonal and minimizing the emotional involvement. Many offenders also understand that control over potential victims can be easier to maintain with a gun. Some victims are less likely

TABLE 5.1

Murder circumstances by weapon, 1999

Circumstances	Total murder victims	Total firearms	Hand-guns	Rifles	Shot-guns	Other guns or type not stated	Knives or cutting instru-ments	Blunt objects (clubs, hammers, etc.)	Personal weapons (hands, fists, feet, etc.)	Poison	Pushed or thrown out window	Explo-sives	Fire	Narcotics	Drown-ing	Strangu-lation	Asphyxia-tion	Other
Total¹	12,658	8,259	6,498	387	503	871	1,667	736	851	11	4	–	125	23	26	190	103	663
Felony type total:	2,137	1,453	1,216	59	60	118	197	142	135	2	–	–	63	4	4	37	22	78
Rape	46	2	2	–	–	–	9	7	11	–	–	–	1	–	–	12	1	3
Robbery	1,010	738	627	24	18	69	105	80	49	–	–	–	–	1	–	11	6	20
Burglary	79	35	23	7	2	3	17	9	9	–	–	–	–	–	–	2	–	7
Larceny-theft	14	6	4	–	2	2	5	1	2	–	–	–	–	–	–	–	–	–
Motor vehicle theft	13	10	5	2	2	1	2	1	–	–	–	–	–	–	–	–	–	3
Arson	63	1	–	1	–	–	–	–	1	–	–	–	56	–	–	–	2	3
Prostitution and commercialized vice	7	4	–	–	–	4	2	–	–	–	–	–	1	–	–	–	1	–
Other sex offenses	19	2	1	–	–	1	2	4	7	–	–	–	1	–	–	2	1	2
Narcotic drug laws	564	482	423	17	21	21	31	16	14	–	–	–	1	3	–	4	2	11
Gambling	17	16	12	–	–	4	–	–	1	–	–	–	–	–	–	–	–	–
Other - not specified	305	157	119	8	17	13	26	24	41	2	–	–	4	–	4	6	9	32
Suspected felony type	64	55	48	1	1	5	3	1	–	–	–	–	–	–	–	1	2	2
Other than felony type total:	6,678	4,220	3,321	252	331	316	1,067	359	554	8	3	–	42	15	18	78	57	257
Romantic triangle	133	100	77	6	12	5	15	9	4	1	–	–	1	–	1	1	1	1
Child killed by babysitter	32	–	–	–	–	–	1	4	22	–	–	–	–	–	–	1	–	4
Brawl due to influence of alcohol	187	89	67	5	12	5	44	13	27	–	–	–	2	–	–	1	–	11
Brawl due to influence of narcotics	111	84	73	1	7	3	12	3	4	2	–	–	1	1	–	–	2	2
Argument over money or property	211	145	109	7	11	18	30	13	18	–	–	–	2	–	–	2	1	–
Other arguments	3,391	2,071	1,669	127	155	120	766	190	212	–	1	–	14	2	2	48	9	76
Gangland killings	116	102	87	2	2	11	7	2	1	–	–	–	–	–	–	–	–	4
Juvenile gang killings	579	539	471	24	16	28	26	8	6	–	–	–	–	1	–	–	–	6
Institutional killings	11	1	1	–	–	–	1	1	6	–	–	–	–	–	–	–	1	–
Sniper attack	4	4	4	–	–	–	–	–	–	–	–	–	–	–	–	–	–	–
Other - not specified	1,903	1,085	763	80	116	126	165	116	260	5	2	–	22	11	15	26	43	153
Unknown	3,779	2,531	1,913	75	111	432	400	234	162	1	1	–	20	4	4	74	22	326

¹ Total murder victims for whom supplemental homicide data were received.

SOURCE: *Crime in the United States, 1999*, Federal Bureau of Investigation, Washington, D.C., 2000

TABLE 5.2

Murder circumstances by victim sex, 1999

Circumstances	Total murder victims[1]	Male	Female	Unknown
Total[1]	12,658	9,558	3,085	15
Felony type total:	2,137	1,710	425	2
Rape	46	1	45	–
Robbery	1,010	872	138	–
Burglary	79	46	33	–
Larceny-theft	14	10	4	–
Motor vehicle theft	13	12	1	–
Arson	63	37	26	–
Prostitution and commercialized vice	7	6	1	–
Other sex offenses	19	8	11	–
Narcotic drug laws	564	519	45	–
Gambling	17	17	–	–
Other - not specified	305	182	121	2
Suspected felony type	64	52	12	–
Other than felony type total:	6,678	4,879	1,796	3
Romantic triangle	133	97	36	–
Child killed by babysitter	32	18	14	–
Brawl due to influence of alcohol	187	169	18	–
Brawl due to influence of narcotics	111	85	26	–
Argument over money or property	211	176	35	–
Other arguments	3,391	2,450	940	1
Gangland killings	116	111	5	–
Juvenile gang killings	579	548	31	–
Institutional killings	11	11	–	–
Sniper attack	4	3	1	–
Other - not specified	1,903	1,211	690	2
Unknown	3,779	2,917	852	10

[1] Total number of murder victims for whom supplemental homicide data were received.

SOURCE: *Crime in the United States, 1999,* Federal Bureau of Investigation, Washington, D.C., 2000

to run from a gun-carrying offender for fear they will be shot, although other victims run, hoping the armed criminal will miss the target.

Mass murders are easier to accomplish with a firearm because, depending on the firearm, an armed person can kill a number of people in a very limited amount of time. Because people with guns can kill from a great distance, they are also most effective against well-guarded targets. Perhaps the best example of this phenomenon is the heavy use of firearms in political assassinations or assassination attempts. It is impossible to conceive of a felon holding a club or knife to rob a large bank with many people and many exits or trying to kill dozens of customers at a fast-food restaurant with multiple exits.

Shootings in the Workplace

On December 26, 2000, 42-year-old software tester Michael McDermott allegedly opened fire on his coworkers at an Internet consulting company in Wakefield, Massachusetts, killing seven. The victims, four women and three men, were shot multiple times. Police recovered an AK-47, a shotgun, and a semiautomatic pistol they say were used in the deadly assault. News reports by ABC, the *Los Angeles Times,* and others cited McDermott's anger over an impending garnishment of his wages by the IRS as a possible motive.

Other businesses have been the scene of similar shootings. On March 20, 2000, Robert Harris, 28, fatally shot five people at a car wash near Dallas, Texas, after he had been fired from his job there. On December 30, 1999, Silvio Izquierdo-Leyva, 36, allegedly gunned down five of his coworkers at a Tampa, Florida, hotel. The previous month, copier technician Bryan Uyesugi, 40, fatally shot seven people at the Xerox Corporation in Honolulu.

Table 5.3 shows that, for roughly the past decade, firearms have been the predominant weapon used in massacres in the United States. The stories of note from 1999 and 2000 all involved the use of firearms, often multiple firearms. In April 1999 Dylan Klebold and Eric Harris killed 13 and wounded 23 at Columbine High School in Littleton, Colorado, using a TEC-DC9 handgun, a sawed-off double-barreled shotgun, a pump-action shotgun, and a 9mm semiautomatic rifle. (See Chapter 7, "School Shootings.") In April 2000 Richard Glassel shot and killed two and injured three others at a homeowners association meeting in Arizona. He was armed with three handguns, an AR-15 assault rifle, and hundreds of rounds of ammunition.

LAW ENFORCEMENT OFFICERS' DEATHS AND INJURIES

In 1998, 61 law enforcement officers were killed in the line of duty. Fifty-five were male and six were female. Their average age was 35, although 7 of the victims were between 18 and 25 and 18 victims were between 25 and 30. Handguns were the murder weapons in 40 of the felonious killings, rifles in 17, and a shotgun in one. The predominance of handguns in officers' deaths is borne out over the period from 1989 to 1998. (See Table 5.4.) The total number of officers murdered in 1998 was down by 23 percent from 1993 and down by 8 percent from 1989.

Patrol officers accounted for 38 of the 61 victims in 1999. This is consistent with the 10-year figures from 1989 through 1998. During that period, 48 percent of the vehicle patrol officers were alone and unassisted at the time of their deaths. Another 32 percent were on other types of assignments but also alone at the time of their killings. In 1998, 16 officers were killed while responding to disturbance calls, 10 were ambushed, 9 were killed while enforcing traffic laws (usually during the course of a traffic stop), 6 were slain while investigating suspicious persons or circumstances, and 4 were killed during the handling or transporting of prisoners. See Table 5.5 for a breakdown by circumstances at the scene from 1989 through 1998.

TABLE 5.3

Recent massacres

2000 In Queens, New York, two young gunmen bound, gagged, and shot seven employees with a .380-caliber gun in a Wendy's restaurant. Five of the workers were killed.

2000 Richard Glassel—armed with three handguns, an AR-15 assault rifle, and hundreds of rounds of ammunition—shot and killed two women, and injured three, during a homeowners association meeting.

1999 In Los Angeles, five were wounded, and a postal worker was fatally shot, at the North Valley Jewish Community Center. Buford O. Furrow Jr. was charged with murder and attempted murder.

1999 In Atlanta, Georgia, Mark Barton killed nine people, and wounded 13, at two brokerage firms, before killing himself.

1999 Twenty-one-year-old Benjamin Nathaniel Smith killed two people, and injured nine, in a three-day rampage through Indiana and Illinois, before shooting himself.

1999 At Colombine High School, in Littleton, Colorado, Dylan Klebold and Eric Harris killed 12 fellow students and a teacher, and wounded 23 others, before shooting and killing themselves. Weapons used: TEC-DC9 handgun; sawed-off double-barreled shotgun; pump-action shotgun; 9mm semi-automatic rifle.

1998 In Springfield, Oregon, a 15-year-old student fired more than 50 rounds from a .22-caliber semiautomatic rifle into a high-school cafeteria. Two male students died, and 23 other students were injured. The boy also shot and killed his parents.

1998 Four middle-school students and a teacher in Jonesboro, Arkansas, were killed, and 10 other students were injured, when a 13-year-old and an 11-year-old shot at the school from a nearby wooded area.

1997 Using a gun, Ali Hassan Abu Kamal killed one person, and injured six others, before taking his own life on the observation deck of the Empire State Building in Manhattan.

1993 Two people were shot and killed, and three wounded, outside the headquarters of the Central Intelligence Agency in Langley, Virginia.

1993 Using an assault weapon, Gian Ferri killed eight people, and wounded six others, in a San Francisco office tower.

1991 Twenty-three people were fatally shot in a cafeteria in Killeen, Texas, by George Hennard Jr., who then shot himself.

1991 Six monks, a nun, and two male followers were slain at a Buddhist temple near Phoenix, Arizona, by Jonathan Dooly, a robber wanting not to be identified.

1990 In Florida, ten people were fatally shot, and seven wounded, by gunman James Pough.

1989 Seven people were killed, and 13 others wounded, at Standard-Gravure Co. in Louisville, Kentucky, by Joseph Wesbecker, a former employee, who then shot himself.

1989 Wielding a semiautomatic AK-47, Patrick Edward Purdy killed five children, and wounded 30, including a teacher, in Stockton, California.

SOURCE: From various sources, compiled by Gale Group, 2000

Accidental deaths claimed a total of 78 law enforcement officers during 1998, and a total of 636 from 1989 through 1998. (See Table 5.6.) In 1998 well over half of the accidental deaths of officers resulted from automobile accidents, a proportion that is seen over the years 1989–98. Being struck by a vehicle while directing traffic, assisting motorists, or during a roadblock or traffic stop accounted for 14 of the 78 deaths in 1998 and 102 of the 636 deaths from 1989 through 1998.

Officers Assaulted

In 1998 more than 59,000 law enforcement officers were assaulted. A large majority (82.5 percent) were attacked with personal weapons such as fists and feet, followed by attacks using weapons other than guns or knives (12.2 percent), firearms (3.5 percent), or knives (1.8 percent). Roughly 3 in 10 of the circumstances in which officers were assaulted with firearms involved disturbance calls. More than two-fifths (41.9 percent) of all ambush assaults (attacks made with no warning) on officers involved firearms. One-fifth (20.6 percent) of assaults that occurred during robberies in progress or while pursuing burglary suspects involved firearms. (See Table 5.7.)

ARMED ROBBERY

Crime in the United States defines robbery as "the taking or attempting to take anything of value from the care, custody, or control of a person or persons by force or threat of force or violence and/or by putting the victim in fear." As in the case of murder, armed robberies are recorded from police investigations and do not involve actual convictions.

Second only to murder, armed robbery (along with rape for women) is perhaps the most feared crime in America. Though crimes of "home invasion," in which criminals force their way into homes when the residents are in the house, do occur, many Americans believe they are safer at home. Many people fear that leaving the safety of their own houses could subject them to being robbed

TABLE 5.4

Law enforcement officers feloniously killed, by type of weapon, by region, 1989–98

Type of weapon	Total	Northeast	Midwest	South	West	U.S. Territories
Total	**682**	**80**	**121**	**292**	**125**	**64**
Handgun	**480**	59	77	205	80	59
Rifle	**112**	82	7	42	31	4
Shotgun	**34**	3	4	21	6	0
Total firearms	**626**	**70**	**108**	**268**	**117**	**63**
Knife	**12**	4	1	4	2	1
Bomb	**11**	1	0	10	0	0
Personal weapons	**6**	1	1	1	3	0
Other	**27**	41	1	9	3	0

SOURCE: *Crime in the United States, 1999*, Federal Bureau of Investigation, Washington, D.C., 2000

TABLE 5.5

Law enforcement officers feloniously killed, circumstance at scene of incident, 1989–98

Circumstance at scene	Total	1989	1990	1991	1992	1993	1994	1995	1996	1997	1998
Total	682	66	66	71	64	70	79	74	61	70	61
Disturbance calls	111	13	10	17	11	10	8	8	4	14	16
Bar fights, man with gun, etc.	42	5	5	8	2	5	4	2	1	3	7
Family quarrels	69	8	5	9	9	5	4	6	3	11	9
Arrest situations	239	24	30	14	27	28	33	21	25	21	16
Burglaries in progress/ pursuing burglary suspects	26	0	1	3	5	1	4	4	3	5	0
Robberies in progress/ pursuing robbery suspects	93	8	13	4	11	9	17	7	11	10	3
Drug-related matters	40	7	5	3	3	3	4	4	3	1	7
Attempting other arrests	80	9	11	4	8	15	8	6	8	5	6
Civil disorders (mass disobedience, riot, etc.)	0	0	0	0	0	0	0	0	0	0	0
Handling, transporting, custody of prisoners	30	6	2	6	2	1	1	4	0	4	4
Investigating suspicious persons/circumstances	112	10	9	10	7	15	15	17	13	10	6
Ambush situations	86	4	8	11	7	5	8	14	7	12	10
Entrapment/premeditation	35	2	2	5	5	3	1	6	2	5	4
Unprovoked attack	51	2	6	6	2	2	7	8	5	7	6
Mentally deranged	11	2	1	0	0	1	4	1	1	1	0
Traffic pursuits/stops	93	7	6	13	10	10	10	9	11	8	9

SOURCE: *Crime in the United States, 1999*, Federal Bureau of Investigation, Washington, D.C., 2000

TABLE 5.6

Law enforcement officers accidentally killed, circumstance at scene of incident, 1989–98

Circumstance at scene	Total	1989	1990	1991	1992	1993	1994	1995	1996	1997	1998
Total	636	79	67	53	66	59	62	59	51	62	78
Automobile accident	343	43	27	24	34	38	32	33	33	33	46
Motorcycle accident	48	5	10	6	5	1	8	3	4	4	2
Aircraft accident	64	10	7	7	5	9	10	8	0	4	4
Struck by vehicle (traffic stops, roadblocks, etc.)	42	8	6	5	6	1	3	1	4	4	4
Struck by vehicle (directing traffic, assisting motorists, etc.)	60	4	9	3	5	3	4	9	3	10	10
Accidental shooting (crossfires, mistaken identities, firearm mishaps)	23	4	4	1	3	3	1	2	1	1	3
Accidental shooting (training sessions)	5	0	1	0	0	2	1	0	1	0	0
Accidental shooting (self-inflicted)	0	0	0	0	0	0	0	0	0	0	0
Other (falls, drownings, etc.)	51	5	3	7	8	2	3	3	5	6	9

SOURCE: *Crime in the United States, 1999*, Federal Bureau of Investigation, Washington, D.C., 2000

on the street and result in personal injury, loss of property, or death.

Weapons Used During Robberies

The impact of robbery on its victims cannot be measured only in terms of monetary loss. The goal of robbing someone is usually to obtain money or property, but the crime always involves force of some kind, and many victims suffer serious personal injury. In addition, the psychological trauma can be extremely serious and affect the victim for the rest of his or her life. Firearms were used in 39.9 percent of all robberies in 1999. The use of strong-arm tactics (bullying) occurred in another 41.8 percent of the robberies; knives or cutting instruments were involved in 8.4 percent; and other weapons were used in the remaining 9.9 percent. (See Table 5.8.)

TABLE 5.7

Law enforcement officers assaulted, circumstance at scene of incident, by type of weapon, percent distribution, 1998

Circumstance at scene	Total	Firearm	Knife or cutting instrument	Other dangerous weapon	Personal weapons
			Type of weapon		
Total	**59,545**	**2,073**	**1,077**	**7,266**	**49,129**
Percent distribution	**100.0**	3.5	1.8	12.2	82.5
Disturbance calls (family quarrels, man with gun, etc.)	**17,769**	602	450	1,466	15,251
Percent distribution	**100.0**	3.4	2.5	8.3	85.8
Burglaries in progress pursuing burglary suspects	**744**	41	16	132	555
Percent distribution	**100.0**	5.5	2.2	17.7	74.6
Robberies in progress/ pursuing robbery suspects	**642**	132	12	107	391
Percent distribution	**100.0**	20.6	1.9	16.7	60.9
Attempting other arrests	**10,997**	305	170	1,060	9,462
Percent distribution	**100.0**	2.8	1.5	9.6	86.0
Civil disorders (mass disobedience, riot, etc.)	**812**	6	8	106	692
Percent distribution	**100.0**	.7	1.0	13.1	85.2
Handling, transporting, custody of prisoners	**6,881**	27	54	429	6,371
Percent distribution	**100.0**	.4	.8	6.2	92.6
Investigating suspicious persons/circumstances	**6,275**	291	144	765	5,075
Percent distribution	**100.0**	4.6	2.3	12.2	80.9
Ambush (no warning)	**236**	99	7	61	69
Percent distribution	**100.0**	41.9	3.0	25.8	29.2
Mentally deranged	**943**	31	65	96	751
Percent distribution	**100.0**	3.3	6.9	10.2	79.6
Traffic pursuits and stops	**6,242**	184	41	1,819	4,198
Percent distribution	**100.0**	2.9	.7	29.1	67.3
All other	**8,004**	355	110	1,225	6,314
Percent distribution	**100.0**	4.4	1.4	15.3	78.9

SOURCE: *Crime in the United States, 1999*, Federal Bureau of Investigation, Washington, D.C., 2000

TABLE 5.8

Robbery, types of weapons used, 1999
Percent distribution by region

Region	Total all weapons	Firearms	Knives or cutting instruments	Other weapons	Strong-arm
			Armed		
Total	**100.0**	**39.9**	**8.4**	**9.9**	**41.8**
Northeastern states	100.0	33.9	9.8	7.9	48.4
Midwestern states	100.0	43.2	6.4	11.2	39.3
Southern states	100.0	45.0	7.5	10.1	37.4
Western states	100.0	34.0	10.1	10.1	45.8

SOURCE: *Crime in the United States,* 1999, Federal Bureau of Investigation, Washington, D.C., 2000

TABLE 5.9

Aggravated assault, types of weapons used, 1999
Percent distribution by region

Region	Total all weapons	Firearms	Knives or cutting instruments	Other weapons (clubs, blunt objects, etc.)	Personal weapons
Total	**100.0**	**18.0**	**17.8**	**35.3**	**28.9**
Northeastern states	100.0	12.1	17.0	33.5	37.4
Midwestern states	100.0	20.8	18.0	34.7	26.4
Southern states	100.0	20.0	19.9	38.2	21.8
Western states	100.0	15.9	14.7	31.7	37.8

SOURCE: *Crime in the United States, 1999*, Federal Bureau of Investigation, Washington, D.C., 2000

AGGRAVATED ASSAULT

Crime in the United States defines aggravated assault as:

> an unlawful attack by one person upon another for the purpose of inflicting severe or aggravated bodily injury.

This type of assault is usually accompanied by the use of a weapon or by means likely to produce death or great bodily harm. Attempts are included since it is not necessary that an injury result when a gun, knife, or other weapon is used that could and probably would result in serious personal injury if the crime were successfully completed.

In 1999, 916,383 aggravated assault offenses occurred nationwide, for a rate of 336 reported victims for every 100,000 population, the lowest rate since 1989, and lower over 1998 by 7 percent. The rate is far higher in metropolitan areas (363 per 100,000 people) and cities outside metropolitan areas (307 per 100,000) than in rural areas (177 per 100,000).

Weapons Used in Aggravated Assaults

About 35 percent of all aggravated assaults were committed with blunt weapons or other dangerous objects in 1999. In the remaining weapons categories, personal weapons, such as hands or feet, were used in 28.9 percent of the assaults; firearms in 18 percent; and knives or cutting instruments in the remainder (17.8 percent). (See Table 5.9.)

VICTIMIZATION

The second major resource for crime statistics, *Criminal Victimization in the United States,* is prepared annually by the Bureau of Justice Statistics (BJS) of the U.S. Department of Justice.

As in all surveys based on interviewing only a representative sample, sampling errors can occur. The BJS indicates that its findings are accurate to a "90 percent confidence level or more." The advantage of this survey method is that it counts both crimes reported to the police and crimes not reported to the authorities.

The definitions of crimes measured by the BJS do not necessarily conform to any federal or state statutes, which vary considerably. However, the BJS definitions of offenses are "generally compatible with conventional usage and with the definitions used by the FBI" in *Crime in the United States,* its annual publication of data from the Uniform Crime Reports.

Number of Victimizations

In 1998 the BJS counted some 15 million crimes, approximately 8 million of which involved violence. Blacks (43 victimizations per 1,000) were more likely than whites (37.5 per 1,000) to suffer from violent crime, while other races had an even lower rate of 29.1 per 1,000. (See Table 5.10.)

In 1998 the offender was armed in about one-fourth (22.5 percent) of the crimes of violence. In 7.5 percent of those crimes of violence, the offender was armed with a gun. Among these, over 80 percent were committed with a handgun. Firearms were used in 18 percent of the robberies and 27 percent of the aggravated assaults in which the criminal had a weapon. Firearms were often used in the threat of assault (34.8 percent). Felons were more likely to use firearms against strangers (11.1 percent) than against nonstrangers (4.52 percent). (See Table 5.11.)

Self-Defense

Many people who buy firearms for protection take training courses on the safe storage and handling of guns, although many people do not follow through on the safety techniques they have learned. The Harvard School of Public Health, in the January 1995 *Journal of the American Medical Association,* found that people who had such training were more likely to keep a gun loaded and unlocked at home, which David Hemenway, deputy director of the school's Injury Control Center, described as a potentially dangerous practice. However, people who buy guns for protection would naturally be more likely to have the weapon ready for use against an intruder.

In response to the study, Gary Kleck, a professor of criminology and criminal justice at Florida State University, observed that the study ignores the fact that people who own guns for self-protection could get hurt if they have the gun locked and unloaded should their home be invaded by a violent or armed intruder. A spokesperson for the National Rifle Association (NRA) said that while the study drew no statistical link between keeping firearms loaded and unlocked at home and firearm accidents, he agreed that it is a dangerous way to keep a gun.

In *Crime, Deterrence, and Right-to-Carry Concealed Handguns* (University of Chicago, August 1996), John R. Lott, Jr., and David B. Mustard reviewed a number of studies and surveys conducted between 1987 and 1992. The researchers concluded that firearms were used for self-defense up to 2.5 million times each year, with 400,000 of these defenders believing that use of the gun almost certainly saved a life. The authors pointed out that cases like the 1992 Louisiana incident involving a Japanese student are rare. The student, on his way to a Halloween party, approached the wrong house and was shot and killed by the homeowner, who claimed he feared for his family's safety. Lott and Mustard further noted that, in this case, the shooting was found lawful.

In most cases, according to the authors, victims who used firearms to defend themselves or their property were confronted by offenders who were either unarmed or armed with weapons other than firearms. Between 1987 and 1992 an average of 62,200 victims of violent crimes, about 7 percent of all victims of violence involving handguns, used firearms to defend themselves. Another 20,300 used firearms to defend their property during a theft, household burglary, or motor vehicle theft. Thirty-eight percent of the victims defending themselves with firearms (30,600 of 82,500 victims) attacked the offenders, and the rest threatened the offenders with the weapons.

MORE GUNS, LESS CRIME? In 1998 Lott published *More Guns, Less Crime* (The University of Chicago Press, Chicago, IL, 1998), a book based on his 1996 study. He

TABLE 5.10

Number of victimizations and victimization rates for persons age 12 and over, by race, gender, age of victims, and type of crime

Race, gender, and age	Total population	Crimes of violence[a]		Robbery		Aggravated assault		Simple assault	
		Number	Rate	Number	Rate	Number	Rate	Number	Rate
White									
Male									
12-15	6,339,700	698,950	110.2	54,250	8.6	133,910	21.1	510,790	80.6
16-19	6,450,640	740,640	114.8	105,420	16.3	183,410	28.4	451,810	70.0
20-24	7,213,130	539,950	74.9	53,620	7.4	139,660	19.4	340,670	47.2
25-34	16,066,250	800,180	49.8	79,120	4.9	151,670	9.4	566,820	35.3
35-49	26,542,400	814,060	30.7	59,190	2.2	213,930	8.1	534,900	20.2
50-64	15,954,420	275,980	17.3	29,220	1.8	48,700	3.1	198,060	12.4
65 and over	12,217,170	47,190	3.9	8,710*	0.7*	9,880*	0.8*	28,600	2.3
Female									
12-15	6,052,250	380,020	62.8	50,950	8.4	38,420	6.3	243,730	40.3
16-19	6,077,860	436,310	71.8	20,000*	3.3*	48,810	8.0	311,250	51.2
20-24	7,071,470	385,630	54.5	44,640	6.3	46,730	6.6	233,650	33.0
25-34	15,887,580	554,590	34.9	44,960	2.8	86,870	5.5	371,350	23.4
35-49	26,475,860	803,980	30.4	102,880	3.9	138,200	5.2	529,670	20.0
50-64	16,899,070	234,900	13.9	28,460	1.7	50,270	3.0	148,330	8.8
65 and over	16,583,620	28,770	1.7	6,160*	0.4*	1,990*	0.1*	20,620*	1.2*
Black									
Male									
12-15	1,291,760	93,190	72.1	12,190*	9.4*	12,220*	9.5*	68,790	53.2
16-19	1,215,920	110,980	91.3	27,190*	22.4*	42,750	35.2	38,030	31.3
20-24	1,049,580	70,180	66.9	4,360*	4.2*	38,470	36.7	27,350*	26.1*
25-34	2,459,000	113,930	46.3	8,630*	3.5*	45,830	18.6	56,200	22.9
35-49	3,567,150	135,130	37.9	16,260*	4.6*	56,750	15.9	62,120	17.4
50-64	1,696,290	45,010	26.5	5,550*	3.3*	21,030*	12.4*	18,430*	10.9*
65 and over	1,027,470	4,900*	4.8*	2,360*	2.3*	0*	0.0*	2,530*	2.5*
Female									
12-15	1,345,420	82,210	61.1	0*	0.0*	3,530*	2.6*	71,090	52.8
16-19	1,151,550	109,550	95.1	16,540*	14.4*	18,490*	16.1*	54,940	47.7
20-24	1,359,440	120,840	88.9	25,390*	18.7*	33,380	24.6	52,250	38.4
25-34	2,910,040	115,690	39.8	28,520	9.8	26,950*	9.3*	52,020	17.9
35-49	4,187,350	103,820	24.8	12,220*	2.9*	15,410*	3.7*	72,760	17.4
50-64	2,131,150	9,920*	4.7*	0*	0.0*	3,080*	1.4*	6,840*	3.2*
65 and over	1,628,480	10,090*	6.2*	0*	0.0*	4,020*	2.5*	6,070*	3.7*

Rate per 1,000 persons in each age group

Note: Excludes data on persons of "other" races.

* Estimate is based on about 10 or fewer sample cases.

[a] Includes data on rape and sexual assault, not shown separately.

SOURCE: *Criminal Victimization in the United States, 1998, Statistical Tables*, U.S. Bureau of Justice Statistics, Washington, D.C., 1999

included data from the *Uniform Crime Report* for 1993 and 1994, allowing him to evaluate the impact of the Brady Law and to double-check his earlier results. Lott found an even larger drop in murder rates related to concealed handgun laws, a 10 percent decline compared with the 7.7 percent decrease in his earlier study. Lott claims that evidence from 1994 indicates that the Brady Law has been associated with significant increases in rapes and aggravated assaults and that declines in murder and robbery have been statistically insignificant. He maintains, as he did in the earlier study, that concealed handgun laws reduce violent crime and that higher arrest rates deter all types of crime.

CRITICISM OF LOTT'S CONCLUSIONS. Reviewing *Crime, Deterrence, and Right-to-Carry Concealed Handguns,* several researchers found Lott and Mustard's claims unsubstantiated. Researchers from the John Hopkins Center for Gun Policy and Research, for example, found the following problems with the study:

- The study uses incorrect and discredited methodology. The techniques used in most of Lott and Mustard's analyses are inappropriate for this type of study, using arrest rates to predict crime rates is problematic, and "shall issue" laws (see below for Lott and Mustard's definition) tend to be approved when violent crime has recently increased (and is, therefore, expected to decrease back to average level).

- The study's results depart from well-established criminological theory and facts about crime. Lott and Mustard found the strongest deterrent effects for the crimes of rape, aggravated assault, and murder. Most rapes and aggravated assaults, however, are committed by an intimate or acquaintance, situations in which carrying a concealed gun in public is less relevant. Also, only 17 percent of murders are the result of predatory crimes, such as robbery by a stranger. "Shall issue" laws were adopted primarily to deter

TABLE 5.11

Estimated percent distribution of type of weapon used by offenders in violent victimization incidents

By type of crime and victim-offender relationship, 1998[a]

All incidents	Total incidents Number	Percent	No weapon used	Weapon used Total	Total firearm	Hand gun	Other gun	Gun type unknown	Knife	Sharp object	Blunt object	Other weapon	Weapon type unknown	Don't know if weapon present
Crimes of violence	7,433,670	100%	68.6%	22.5%	7.5%	6.4%	1.1%	0.0%[b]	4.9%	0.7%	2.9%	4.7%	1.8%	8.9%
Completed violence	2,350,550	100	67.8	24.7	7.5	6.6	0.9[b]	0.0[b]	4.5	0.8[b]	4.0	5.9	2.0	7.5
Attempted/threatened violence	5,083,120	100	68.9	21.5	7.5	6.3	1.2	0.0[b]	5.1	0.7	2.5	4.1	1.6	9.6
Rape/sexual assault[c]	328,130	100	87.7	8.3[b]	3.9[b]	3.9[b]	0.0[b]	0.0[b]	2.9[b]	0.0[b]	0.0[b]	0.0[b]	1.5	4.0[b]
Robbery	833,050	100	50.4	36.5	18.0	16.4	1.6[b]	0.0[b]	10.4	0.0[b]	2.5[b]	4.1	1.5	13.1
Completed/property taken	572,270	100	49.6	37.0	20.5	18.3	2.1[b]	0.0[b]	8.6	0.0[b]	2.5[b]	3.7[b]	1.8	13.4
With injury	159,090	100	54.6	35.1	14.8[b]	13.0[b]	1.8[b]	0.0[b]	10.3[b]	0.0[b]	3.7[b]	4.9[b]	1.4	10.3[b]
Without injury	413,180	100	47.7	37.8	22.6	20.4	2.3[b]	0.0[b]	7.9	0.0[b]	2.0[b]	3.2[b]	2.0	14.6
Attempted to take property	260,770	100	52.0	35.5	12.7	12.2	0.6[b]	0.0[b]	14.2	0.0[b]	2.5[b]	5.0[b]	1.0	12.5
With injury	64,880	100	69.7	26.3[b]	4.0[b]	4.0[b]	0.0[b]	0.0[b]	16.7[b]	0.0[b]	5.6[b]	0.0[b]	0.0	4.0[b]
Without injury	195,900	100	46.1	38.6	15.6	14.9	0.7[b]	0.0[b]	13.4[b]	0.0[b]	1.5[b]	6.7[b]	1.3	15.3
Assault	6,272,490	100	70.0	21.4	6.3	5.2	1.1	0.0[b]	4.3	0.8	3.1	5.0	1.8	8.6
Aggravated	1,457,800	100	7.1	92.1	27.0	22.2	4.8	0.0[b]	18.5	3.6	13.6	21.6	7.8	0.8[b]
With injury	474,320	100	21.8	75.6	10.9	8.8	2.1[b]	0.0[b]	11.3	4.0[b]	16.7	24.9	7.8	2.5[b]
Threatened with weapon	983,480	100	X	100.0	34.8	28.7	6.1	0.0[b]	22.0	3.4	12.0	20.0	7.7	0.0[b]
Simple[d]	4,814,690	100	89.0	X	X	X	X	X	X	X	X	X	X	11.0
With minor injury	1,073,810	100	92.7	X	X	X	X	X	X	X	X	X	X	7.3
Without injury	3,740,870	100	88.0	X	X	X	X	X	X	X	X	X	X	12.0
Involving strangers														
Crimes of violence	3,524,740	100	58.2	28.3	11.1	9.4	1.7	0.0[b]	5.6	0.8[b]	4.1	4.8	1.9	13.5
Rape/sexual assault[c]	89,360	100	81.9	12.9[b]	2.4[b]	2.4[b]	0.0[b]	0.0[b]	4.9[b]	0.0[b]	0.0[b]	0.0[b]	5.6	5.2[b]
Robbery	528,920	100	32.4	50.9	26.0	23.4	2.6[b]	0.0[b]	14.9	0.0[b]	3.5[b]	4.7[b]	1.9	16.7
Aggravated assault	752,590	100	4.0	95.2	33.5	27.3	6.2	0.0[b]	15.3	3.7[b]	16.8	19.2	6.9	0.7[b]
Simple assault[d]	2,153,880	100	82.5	X	X	X	X	X	X	X	X	X	X	17.5
Involving nonstrangers														
Crimes of violence	3,908,920	100	77.9	17.3	4.2	3.6	0.6[b]	0.0[b]	4.3	0.6[b]	1.9	4.6	1.6	4.8[b]
Rape/sexual assault[c]	238,770	100	89.9	6.6[b]	4.5[b]	4.5[b]	0.0[b]	0.0[b]	2.1[b]	0.0[b]	0.0[b]	0.0[b]	0.0	3.6[b]
Robbery	304,130	100	81.6	11.5	4.2[b]	4.2[b]	0.0[b]	0.0[b]	2.5[b]	0.0[b]	0.8[b]	3.0[b]	1.0	6.9[b]
Aggravated assault	705,210	100	10.4	88.7	20.1	16.8	3.3[b]	0.0[b]	22.0	3.5[b]	10.1	24.2	8.7	0.9[b]
Simple assault[d]	2,660,810	100	94.3	X	X	X	X	X	X	X	X	X	X	5.7

[a] Detail may not add to total because of rounding.
[b] Estimate is based on about 10 or fewer sample cases.
[c] Includes verbal threats of rape and threats of sexual assault.
[d] Simple assault, by definition, does not involve the use of a weapon.

SOURCE: *Sourcebook of Criminal Justice Statistics, 1999*, U.S. Bureau of Justice Statistics, Washington, D.C., 1999

predatory street crimes. Lott and Mustard's results indicate that "shall issue" laws had little or no effect on robbery rates.

- The study does not account for the effects of other important gun laws. Other gun laws, such as background checks and waiting periods, were enacted during the time period of the study, but Lott and Mustard did not consider their effects.

- Knowing the exact date that each "shall issue" law took effect is critically important to measuring its impact—yet the study includes some error in these dates. For example, the authors say that Virginia adopted its "shall issue" law in 1988. But that law continued to give courts considerable discretion over when to issue a concealed weapon-carrying permit. Some populous counties issued very few permits.

- The study does not consistently define what it is evaluating. Lott and Mustard's definition for a "shall issue" law is one that requires permit requests to be granted unless the individual has a criminal record or a history of significant mental illness. However, some states they classify as having "shall issue" laws do not fit that definition.

Because of the claim of errors in the study, these researchers found little support for Lott and Mustard's conclusion that concealed handgun laws reduce violent crime. In fact, critics of the study suggest that the laws may even increase homicide rates.

Theft of Firearms

As of July 1995 the FBI's National Crime Information Center (NCIC) had received over two million reports of stolen guns, ammunition, cannons, and grenades. Created in 1967, the NCIC retains all such reports indefinitely until a gun is recovered. The file's reports contain information on approximately 1.25 million handguns (almost 60 percent of all guns reported stolen), 470,000 rifles (24 percent), 356,000 shotguns (18 percent), and 7,700 machine and submachine guns (less than 1 percent).

More than 340,000 crimes annually involved firearm thefts. Almost two-thirds of such losses occurred during household burglaries and almost one-third in larcenies. (Burglary is the "unlawful entry of a structure to commit a felony or theft," and larceny is the "unlawful taking . . . of property from the possession of . . . another.") Loss of firearms through larceny was as likely to occur away from the victim's home as at or near the home. In over half (53 percent) of the firearm thefts, handguns were stolen. (These statistics do not include thefts or burglaries from stores or other businesses.)

A study conducted in the late 1990s found that a large proportion of guns used in crimes were bought, not stolen. Using data compiled by the Bureau of Alcohol, Tobacco, and Firearms (ATF), a study was prepared for the plaintiffs in a New York suit filed against a gun manufacturer by relatives of victims of gun violence (*Hamilton v. Accu-Tek,* 1998). The study showed that nearly 40 percent of the handguns used in crimes had been purchased from licensed dealers within the preceding three years. Based on a study of all handguns seized by the police in 17 cities during 1996 and 1997, the ATF reported that 48.8 percent of the traceable handguns confiscated in crimes had been purchased from dealers within the previous three years, passing far more quickly from manufacturer to dealer to criminal than previously believed.

Gun-control advocates say this shows that many handguns enter the black market (illegal trade) as they leave the store. The gun industry disputes this data. It does not believe short "time to crime" means that the gun is purchased by the criminal rather than stolen. In addition, they point out that large numbers of guns cannot be traced to either the manufacturer or the licensed dealer because of factors such as the age of the gun or the erasure of the serial number. The ATF counters that its data was carefully weighted to include those guns that could not be traced.

GUNS AND THE LOCAL POLICE

A Tool to Detect Gunfire

Some officers, especially those who work in cities with many gangs and random shootings, have spoken of the frustration they feel when responding to reports of gunfire. Not only does it take too long to respond, but also once police arrive on the scene, it is difficult to determine the source of the gunfire, and the person with the gun is already gone.

In June 1996 Redwood City, California, began using acoustic sensors—devices similar to those used to detect earthquake epicenters—to help locate the source of gunfire to within 20 feet. Mounted on buildings and telephone poles throughout the city, the sensors transmit the time of the gunshots to a central computer that displays the location. Police can respond to gunfire before the police dispatchers begin getting phone calls. According to field tests conducted by the Redwood City Police Department, the sensors identified gunfire locations within seconds.

Police Are "Outarmed"

In March 1997, after a failed bank robbery in Los Angeles, the bank robbers faced off against police officers near the bank. The robbers were armed with fully automatic weapons, which are illegal, and protected with full-body armor. The police had their standard service revolvers; some were not wearing any bulletproof garments. The suspects shot indiscriminately toward the officers and into the air, threatening pedestrians, drivers, and homeowners in the area. Both robbers were killed by gunshots to the head by police officers, and 16 officers and bystanders were injured.

The Los Angeles incident is only one of many in which police officers have expressed concern about finding themselves in situations where they are "outarmed" by offenders. Through the illegal gun market, criminals often have access to weapons not available legally, making them better armed than the police. As a result, in 1992 many police officers in both New York City and Chicago, two of the nation's largest cities, began using the Glock 9mm pistol. Police departments in Miami, Houston, and Washington, D.C., among others, used the Glock 9mm. New York State Police and New York City Transit Police also used them. Officers noted that the Glock is more accurate than a .38-caliber revolver, holds about three times as many bullets, and can be loaded faster. Many police believed this weapon put them on somewhat of an equal footing with drug dealers and other criminals.

John Dineen, president of Chicago's Fraternal Order of Police, observed that the city's police officers regularly confiscate Uzis and .45-caliber machine guns, and that, although the officers don't have to fire their guns frequently, when they are in such unequal situations, they face greater danger.

However, some department officials resisted using high-powered pistols, saying the guns are more advanced than the average officer's ability to handle them and could present serious safety problems in crowded areas. Furthermore, LeRoy Martin, Chicago's police superintendent, noted that they now always have sufficient firepower and that 9mm guns are less an issue of public safety than a trend or moral issue.

In May 1992 the Chicago Police Department determined that the Glock was "too dangerous" and banned its use. By the end of 1996 at least 35 suits had been filed against Glock, alleging the 9mm pistol discharged too easi-

TABLE 5.12

Total arrest trends, 1998–99

(7,396 agencies; 1999 estimated population 155,791,000; 1998 estimated population 153,620,000)

	Number of persons arrested											
	Total all ages			Under 15 years of age			Under 18 years of age			18 years of age and over		
Offense charged	1998	1999	Percent change	1998	1999	Percent change	1998	1999	Percent change	1998	1999	Percent change
TOTAL[1]	8,743,442	8,312,163	-4.9	493,014	459,105	-6.9	1,575,963	1,445,517	-8.3	7,167,479	6,866,646	-4.2
Murder and nonnegligent manslaughter	8,890	7,864	-11.5	111	110	-.9	1,175	806	-31.4	7,715	7,058	-8.5
Forcible rape	17,834	16,406	-8.0	1,113	1,075	-3.4	3,108	2,827	-9.0	14,726	13,579	-7.8
Robbery	74,059	67,133	-9.4	5,032	4,562	-9.3	20,155	17,398	-13.7	53,904	49,735	-7.7
Aggravated assault	307,960	291,794	-5.2	14,445	14,890	+3.1	43,676	41,627	-4.7	264,284	250,167	-5.3
Burglary	196,553	174,770	-11.1	25,787	22,388	-13.2	69,399	59,001	-15.0	127,154	115,769	-9.0
Larceny-theft	802,410	728,223	-9.2	104,429	92,083	-11.8	254,582	228,134	-10.4	547,828	500,089	-8.7
Motor vehicle theft	93,226	87,796	-5.8	8,273	7,797	-5.8	32,427	30,873	-4.8	60,799	56,923	-6.4
Arson	9,591	9,286	-3.2	3,412	3,430	+.5	5,091	5,123	+.6	4,500	4,163	-7.5
Violent crime[2]	408,743	383,197	-6.2	20,701	20,637	-.3	68,114	62,658	-8.0	340,629	320,539	-5.9
Property crime[3]	1,101,780	1,000,075	-9.2	141,901	125,698	-11.4	361,499	323,131	-10.6	740,281	676,944	-8.6
Crime Index total[4]	1,510,523	1,383,272	-8.4	162,602	146,335	-10.0	429,613	385,789	-10.2	1,080,910	997,483	-7.7
Other assaults	797,858	763,707	-4.3	57,949	58,748	+1.4	142,256	137,687	-3.2	655,602	626,020	-4.5
Forgery and counterfeiting	67,645	62,305	-7.9	543	510	-6.1	4,257	4,037	-5.2	63,388	58,268	-8.1
Fraud	212,890	202,165	-5.0	1,157	1,644	+42.1	6,787	7,526	+10.9	206,103	194,639	-5.6
Embezzlement	9,653	10,004	+3.6	39	48	+23.1	873	963	+10.3	8,780	9,041	+3.0
Stolen property; buying, receiving, possessing	78,673	68,103	-13.4	5,359	4,611	-14.0	20,264	16,789	-17.1	58,409	51,314	-12.1
Vandalism	182,058	165,948	-8.8	33,872	30,970	-8.6	77,381	70,307	-9.1	104,677	95,641	-8.6
Weapons; carrying, possessing, etc.	112,998	102,737	-9.1	8,733	8,297	-5.0	27,460	25,565	-6.9	85,538	77,172	-9.8
Prostitution and commercialized vice	63,334	60,502	-4.5	132	103	-22.0	932	785	-15.8	62,402	59,717	-4.3
Sex offenses (except forcible rape and prostitution)	57,920	56,158	-3.0	4,899	4,894	-.1	9,683	9,735	+.5	48,237	46,423	-3.8
Drug abuse violations	944,577	924,871	-2.1	19,446	19,020	-2.2	123,764	118,640	-4.1	820,813	806,231	-1.8
Gambling	7,534	6,664	-11.5	147	93	-36.7	1,006	783	-22.2	6,528	5,881	-9.9
Offenses against the family and children	84,136	79,557	-5.4	2,003	1,790	-10.6	5,686	4,933	-13.2	78,450	74,624	-4.9
Driving under the influence	846,273	834,880	-1.3	331	319	-3.6	12,361	12,211	-1.2	833,912	822,669	-1.3
Liquor laws	388,400	388,084	-.1	9,810	9,653	-1.6	97,362	94,094	-3.4	291,038	293,990	+1.0
Drunkenness	423,108	410,713	-2.9	1,857	1,785	-3.9	14,667	13,380	-8.8	408,441	397,333	-2.7
Disorderly conduct	417,158	381,647	-8.5	39,948	38,268	-4.2	112,835	102,935	-8.8	304,323	278,712	-8.4
Vagrancy	20,633	19,001	-7.9	475	284	-40.2	1,838	1,425	-22.5	18,795	17,576	-6.5
All other offenses (except traffic)	2,302,066	2,204,476	-4.2	72,967	70,177	-3.8	270,933	250,564	-7.5	2,031,133	1,953,912	-3.8
Suspicion	3,348	4,265	+27.4	231	285	+23.4	901	1,051	+16.6	2,447	3,214	+31.3
Curfew and loitering law violations	118,896	102,131	-14.1	31,681	27,704	-12.6	118,896	102,131	-14.1	–	–	–
Runaways	97,109	85,238	-12.2	39,064	33,852	-13.3	97,109	85,238	-12.2	–	–	–

[1] Does not include suspicion.
[2] Violent crimes are offenses of murder, forcible rape, robbery, and aggravated assault.
[3] Property crimes are offenses of burglary, larceny-theft, motor vehicle theft, and arson.
[4] Includes arson.

SOURCE: *Crime in the United States, 1999,* Federal Bureau of Investigation, Washington, D.C., 2000

ly. Instead, officers who wished to trade in their .38-caliber revolvers were offered four other brands with mechanisms and heavy trigger pulls that were similar to revolvers. Most police are now armed with high-powered weaponry.

The American Civil Liberties Union (ACLU) and gun control groups are concerned that the use of semiautomatic pistols by local authorities will encourage criminals to acquire even more sophisticated weapons. However, the possibility of weapons escalation, alternating between criminals and police departments, has played no role in police department selection of weapons. Some observers believe that making bulletproof vests mandatory and requiring more training on the shooting range might be more beneficial.

WEAPONS OFFENSES

Weapons offenses are violations of statutes or regulations controlling deadly weapons, which include firearms and their ammunition, silencers, explosives, and certain knives. All 50 states, many cities and towns, and the federal government have laws concerning deadly weapons, including restrictions on their possession, carrying, use, sales, manufacturing, importing, and exporting (see Chapter 3).

According to *Crime in the United States, 1999,* out of a total of 6,846,667 charged offenses during 1999, weapons offenses accounted for 102,737. Of those, 94,740 were committed by males, and only 7,997 by females. These rates are down from 1998 by 9.2 percent

TABLE 5.13

Total arrests, 1999, by race

(8,545 agencies; 1999 estimated population 171,823,000)

Offense charged	Total arrests					Percent distribution[1]				
	Total	White	Black	American Indian or Alaskan Native	Asian or Pacific Islander	Total	White	Black	American Indian or Alaskan Native	Asian or Pacific Islander
TOTAL	9,100,050	6,283,294	2,600,510	113,705	102,541	100.0	69.0	28.6	1.2	1.1
Murder and nonnegligent manslaughter	9,716	4,460	5,029	105	122	100.0	45.9	51.8	1.1	1.3
Forcible rape	18,716	11,510	6,775	214	217	100.0	61.5	36.2	1.1	1.2
Robbery	73,542	32,257	40,040	442	803	100.0	43.9	54.4	.6	1.1
Aggravated assault	317,499	199,893	110,420	3,281	3,905	100.0	63.0	34.8	1.0	1.2
Burglary	192,246	131,832	56,119	1,805	2,490	100.0	68.6	29.2	.9	1.3
Larceny-theft	792,386	524,128	244,085	10,472	13,701	100.0	66.1	30.8	1.3	1.7
Motor vehicle theft	94,161	51,726	39,694	1,015	1,726	100.0	54.9	42.2	1.1	1.8
Arson	10,774	8,019	2,553	108	94	100.0	74.4	23.7	1.0	.9
Violent crime[2]	419,473	248,120	162,264	4,042	5,047	100.0	59.2	38.7	1.0	1.2
Property crime[3]	1,089,567	715,705	342,451	13,400	18,011	100.0	65.7	31.4	1.2	1.7
Crime Index total[4]	1,509,040	963,825	504,715	17,442	23,058	100.0	63.9	33.4	1.2	1.5
Other assaults	842,882	546,873	275,406	11,609	8,994	100.0	64.9	32.7	1.4	1.1
Forgery and counterfeiting	69,679	46,050	22,373	372	884	100.0	66.1	32.1	.5	1.3
Fraud	225,404	148,024	74,868	999	1,513	100.0	65.7	33.2	.4	.7
Embezzlement	11,180	7,199	3,790	32	159	100.0	64.4	33.9	.3	1.4
Stolen property; buying, receiving, possessing	80,263	44,435	34,339	615	874	100.0	55.4	42.8	.8	1.1
Vandalism	181,750	136,624	40,357	2,799	1,970	100.0	75.2	22.2	1.5	1.1
Weapons; carrying, possessing, etc.	113,683	68,556	43,076	807	1,244	100.0	60.3	37.9	.7	1.1
Prostitution and commercialized vice	63,844	37,872	24,496	460	1,016	100.0	59.3	38.4	.7	1.6
Sex offenses (except forcible rape and prostitution)	60,029	45,907	12,676	735	711	100.0	76.5	21.1	1.2	1.2
Drug abuse violations	1,005,385	639,277	353,851	5,438	6,819	100.0	63.6	35.2	.5	.7
Gambling	7,017	2,168	4,471	6	372	100.0	30.9	63.7	.1	5.3
Offenses against the family and children	88,517	58,790	27,227	880	1,620	100.0	66.4	30.8	1.0	1.8
Driving under the influence	913,920	798,570	93,163	12,384	9,803	100.0	87.4	10.2	1.4	1.1
Liquor laws	425,716	363,892	45,074	13,034	3,716	100.0	85.5	10.6	3.1	.9
Drunkenness	436,205	364,328	64,777	5,225	1,875	100.0	83.5	14.9	1.2	.4
Disorderly conduct	420,740	276,772	134,628	6,405	2,935	100.0	65.8	32.0	1.5	.7
Vagrancy	20,203	11,331	8,140	605	127	100.0	56.1	40.3	3.0	.6
All other offenses (except traffic)	2,409,449	1,562,423	785,691	31,546	29,789	100.0	64.8	32.6	1.3	1.2
Suspicion	4,903	3,380	1,462	34	27	100.0	68.9	29.8	.7	.6
Curfew and loitering law violations	114,027	82,617	28,753	1,244	1,413	100.0	72.5	25.2	1.1	1.2
Runaways	96,214	74,381	17,177	1,034	3,622	100.0	77.3	17.9	1.1	3.8

for males and 7.4 percent for females. (See Table 5.12.) Males under 18 accounted for 23,185 weapons offenses, down by 7.3 percent from 1998, and females under 18 accounted for 2,380 weapons offenses, down by 3.3 percent from 1998. (For more information on youths and guns, see Chapter 7.)

Characteristics of Weapons Offenses

In 1999 those most likely to be arrested for weapons offenses were white (60.3 percent). Blacks accounted for 37.9 percent of weapons offenses charged, although that number becomes proportionally higher when factored against the overall percentage of blacks in the population. Asians or Pacific Islanders accounted for 1.1 percent of all weapons offenses charged, while American Indians or Alaskan Natives comprised the smallest segment, 0.7 percent. (See Table 5.13.)

TRACING GUNS USED IN CRIME

On the request of police agencies, the National Tracing Center of the Bureau of Alcohol, Tobacco, and Firearms (ATF) traces firearms to their original point of sale. This information can be used to help identify suspects, provide evidence for possible prosecution, and establish whether a gun has been stolen. The ATF is not able to trace guns manufactured prior to 1968, most surplus military weapons, imported guns without the importer's name, stolen guns, and guns missing a legible serial number. Research by the ATF shows that a high percentage of crime guns with obliterated serial numbers were originally purchased as part of a multiple sale by a licensed dealer and then illegally trafficked.

The ATF traces about 70,000 guns each year at the request of local law enforcement agencies. Almost 50,000

TABLE 5.13

Total arrests, 1999, by race [CONTINUED]

(8,545 agencies; 1999 estimated population 171,823,000)

Offense charged	Total arrests					Percent distribution[1]				
	Total	White	Black	American Indian or Alaskan Native	Asian or Pacific Islander	Total	White	Black	American Indian or Alaskan Native	Asian or Pacific Islander
TOTAL	1,584,718	1,140,123	398,010	20,295	26,290	100.0	71.9	25.1	1.3	1.7
Murder and nonnegligent manslaughter	923	434	452	16	21	100.0	47.0	49.0	1.7	2.3
Forcible rape	3,176	2,001	1,096	35	44	100.0	63.0	34.5	1.1	1.4
Robbery	18,709	8,101	10,184	133	291	100.0	43.3	54.4	.7	1.6
Aggravated assault	45,003	27,993	15,819	486	705	100.0	62.2	35.2	1.1	1.6
Burglary	64,360	46,736	15,749	773	1,102	100.0	72.6	24.5	1.2	1.7
Larceny-theft	248,523	173,430	65,645	3,787	5,661	100.0	69.8	26.4	1.5	2.3
Motor vehicle theft	33,202	18,998	12,901	441	862	100.0	57.2	38.9	1.3	2.6
Arson	5,759	4,595	1,049	56	59	100.0	79.8	18.2	1.0	1.0
Violent crime[2]	67,811	38,529	27,551	670	1,061	100.0	56.8	40.6	1.0	1.6
Property crime[3]	351,844	243,759	95,344	5,057	7,684	100.0	69.3	27.1	1.4	2.2
Crime Index total[4]	419,655	282,288	122,895	5,727	8,745	100.0	67.3	29.3	1.4	2.1
Other assaults	151,413	98,452	49,132	1,826	2,003	100.0	65.0	32.4	1.2	1.3
Forgery and counterfeiting	4,471	3,473	881	34	83	100.0	77.7	19.7	.8	1.9
Fraud	7,926	4,533	3,223	48	122	100.0	57.2	40.7	.6	1.5
Embezzlement	1,099	695	377	2	25	100.0	63.2	34.3	.2	2.3
Stolen property; buying, receiving, possessing	18,817	11,099	7,173	201	344	100.0	59.0	38.1	1.1	1.8
Vandalism	76,175	62,330	11,838	1,035	972	100.0	81.8	15.5	1.4	1.3
Weapons; carrying, possessing, etc.	27,548	18,658	8,148	263	479	100.0	67.7	29.6	1.0	1.7
Prostitution and commercialized vice	877	506	347	9	15	100.0	57.7	39.6	1.0	1.7
Sex offenses (except forcible rape and prostitution)	10,621	7,722	2,720	81	98	100.0	72.7	25.6	.8	.9
Drug abuse violations	128,055	88,564	37,079	1,113	1,299	100.0	69.2	29.0	.9	1.0
Gambling	835	135	680	1	19	100.0	16.2	81.4	.1	2.3
Offenses against the family and children	5,586	4,239	1,162	42	143	100.0	75.9	20.8	.8	2.6
Driving under the influence	13,641	12,531	708	242	160	100.0	91.9	5.2	1.8	1.2
Liquor laws	103,311	94,639	4,707	3,012	953	100.0	91.6	4.6	2.9	.9
Drunkenness	14,055	12,781	1,091	95	88	100.0	90.9	7.8	.7	.6
Disorderly conduct	113,171	75,600	35,380	1,269	922	100.0	66.8	31.3	1.1	.8
Vagrancy	1,592	1,191	361	26	14	100.0	74.8	22.7	1.6	.9
All other offenses (except traffic)	274,478	202,858	63,870	2,990	4,760	100.0	73.9	23.3	1.1	1.7
Suspicion	1,151	831	308	1	11	100.0	72.2	26.8	.1	1.0
Curfew and loitering law violations	114,027	82,617	28,753	1,244	1,413	100.0	72.5	25.2	1.1	1.2
Runaways	96,214	74,381	17,177	1,034	3,622	100.0	77.3	17.9	1.1	3.8

of these involve weapons offenses, many of which are never prosecuted. The rest of the guns are recovered during crime investigations: about 5,000 in homicides, 5,000 in assaults, 2,000 in burglaries, nearly 2,000 in robberies, and 10,000 in drug-related offenses. One out of 10 firearms the police recover is from a juvenile (17 and under). When ages 18 to 24 are included, the number changes to 4 out of 10. Almost one-half (48.8 percent) of the guns traced had been sold by a dealer within the previous three years.

In 1999, the top 10 crime guns traced by the ATF were:

- Smith & Wesson .38 revolver
- Lorcin .380 semiautomatic pistol
- Ruger 9mm semiautomatic pistol
- Raven .25 semiautomatic pistol
- Smith & Wesson 9mm semiautomatic pistol
- Smith & Wesson .357 revolver
- Mossberg 12-gauge shotgun
- Bryco .389 semiautomatic pistol
- Davis .380 semiautomatic pistol
- Bryco 9mm semiautomatic pistol

Nine of the top 10 were handguns. Over half of all crime guns recovered were semiautomatic pistols. Four of the top crime guns were manufactured by well-established domestic gun companies: Smith & Wesson, Ruger, and Mossberg. The Raven, the Lorcin, and the Davis are small, cheap handguns, often called "junk guns" or "Saturday night specials."

TABLE 5.13

Total arrests, 1999, by race [CONTINUED]

(8,545 agencies; 1999 estimated population 171,823,000)

Offense charged	Total arrests					Percent distribution[1]				
	Total	White	Black	American Indian or Alaskan Native	Asian or Pacific Islander	Total	White	Black	American Indian or Alaskan Native	Asian or Pacific Islander
TOTAL	**7,515,332**	**5,143,171**	**2,202,500**	**93,410**	**76,251**	**100.0**	**68.4**	**29.3**	**1.2**	**1.0**
Murder and nonnegligent manslaughter	8,793	4,026	4,577	89	101	100.0	45.8	52.1	1.0	1.1
Forcible rape	15,540	9,509	5,679	179	173	100.0	61.2	36.5	1.2	1.1
Robbery	54,833	24,156	29,856	309	512	100.0	44.1	54.4	.6	.9
Aggravated assault	272,496	171,900	94,601	2,795	3,200	100.0	63.1	34.7	1.0	1.2
Burglary	127,886	85,096	40,370	1,032	1,388	100.0	66.5	31.6	.8	1.1
Larceny-theft	543,863	350,698	178,440	6,685	8,040	100.0	64.5	32.8	1.2	1.5
Motor vehicle theft	60,959	32,728	26,793	574	864	100.0	53.7	44.0	.9	1.4
Arson	5,015	3,424	1,504	52	35	100.0	68.3	30.0	1.0	.7
Violent crime[2]	351,662	209,591	134,713	3,372	3,986	100.0	59.6	38.3	1.0	1.1
Property crime[3]	737,723	471,946	247,107	8,343	10,327	100.0	64.0	33.5	1.1	1.4
Crime Index total[4]	1,089,385	681,537	381,820	11,715	14,313	100.0	62.6	35.0	1.1	1.3
Other assaults	691,469	448,421	226,274	9,783	6,991	100.0	64.9	32.7	1.4	1.0
Forgery and counterfeiting	65,208	42,577	21,492	338	801	100.0	65.3	33.0	.5	1.2
Fraud	217,478	143,491	71,645	951	1,391	100.0	66.0	32.9	.4	.6
Embezzlement	10,081	6,504	3,413	30	134	100.0	64.5	33.9	.3	1.3
Stolen property; buying, receiving, possessing	61,446	33,336	27,166	414	530	100.0	54.3	44.2	.7	.9
Vandalism	105,575	74,294	28,519	1,764	998	100.0	70.4	27.0	1.7	.9
Weapons; carrying, possessing, etc.	86,135	49,898	34,928	544	765	100.0	57.9	40.6	.6	.9
Prostitution and commercialized vice	62,967	37,366	24,149	451	1,001	100.0	59.3	38.4	.7	1.6
Sex offenses (except forcible rape and prostitution)	49,408	38,185	9,956	654	613	100.0	77.3	20.2	1.3	1.2
Drug abuse violations	877,330	550,713	316,772	4,325	5,520	100.0	62.8	36.1	.5	.6
Gambling	6,182	2,033	3,791	5	353	100.0	32.9	61.3	.1	5.7
Offenses against the family and children	82,931	54,551	26,065	838	1,477	100.0	65.8	31.4	1.0	1.8
Driving under the influence	900,279	786,039	92,455	12,142	9,643	100.0	87.3	10.3	1.3	1.1
Liquor laws	322,405	269,253	40,367	10,022	2,763	100.0	83.5	12.5	3.1	.9
Drunkenness	422,150	351,547	63,686	5,130	1,787	100.0	83.3	15.1	1.2	.4
Disorderly conduct	307,569	201,172	99,248	5,136	2,013	100.0	65.4	32.3	1.7	.7
Vagrancy	18,611	10,140	7,779	579	113	100.0	54.5	41.8	3.1	.6
All other offenses (except traffic)	2,134,971	1,359,565	721,821	28,556	25,029	100.0	63.7	33.8	1.3	1.2
Suspicion	3,752	2,549	1,154	33	16	100.0	67.9	30.8	.9	.4
Curfew and loitering law violations	–	–	–	–	–	–	–	–	–	–
Runaways	–	–	–	–	–	–	–	–	–	–

[1] Because of rounding, the percentages may not add to total.
[2] Violent crimes are offenses of murder, forcible rape, robbery, and aggravated assault.
[3] Property crimes are offenses of burglary, larceny-theft, motor vehicle theft, and arson.
[4] Includes arson.

SOURCE: *Crime in the United States, 1999*, Federal Bureau of Investigation, Washington, D.C., 2000

In 1994 the type of crime most likely to lead to a request for tracing was a weapons offense (72 percent). In all categories of crime in which police asked for gun tracings, handguns predominated as the type of gun used. (See Table 5.14.)

GUNRUNNING ACROSS STATE LINES

Some states have enacted strict gun control laws to keep prohibited buyers, such as felons and children, from purchasing firearms. However, gunrunners are allegedly making firearms easily available by legally buying guns in states with relaxed purchasing regulations and transporting them to states with tougher gun laws. Although only state residents can buy guns, gunrunners get around this by obtaining false identification or hiring someone (often called a "straw purchaser") to purchase multiple guns for them. Gunrunners can then sell those guns on the black market for four to five times their legal purchase price. These guns often end up being used in crimes.

States with weak gun laws are far more often the source of guns used in crimes committed in states with strong laws than the reverse. In 1996, for instance, 702

TABLE 5.14

What crimes are most likely to result in a gun-tracing request?

| | | Percent of traces by crime type | | | | | | |
| | | Handgun | | | | | | |
Crime type	Percent of all 1994 traces	Total	Total	Pistol	Pistol Derringer	Pistol Revolver	Rifle	Shotgun
Weapons offenses	72%	100%	81%	55%	1%	25%	10%	9%
Drug offenses	12	100	75	50	2	23	14	11
Homicide	6	100	79	49	1	29	11	10
Assault	5	100	80	50	1	28	10	11
Burglary	2	100	57	34	1	22	24	19
Robbery	2	100	84	53	1	29	7	10
Other	2	100	76	54	1	21	14	10

SOURCE: Marianne W. Zawitz, *Guns Used in Crime*, U.S. Bureau of Justice Statistics, Washington, D.C., 1995

guns bought in South Carolina, Georgia, or Florida (states with weak gun laws) were traced to crimes committed in New York or New Jersey (states with strong gun laws). On the other hand, just 11 guns bought in New York or New Jersey were traced to crimes in South Carolina, Georgia, or Florida. More than three-quarters of the guns traced from crimes in South Carolina, Mississippi, Georgia, Florida, Kansas, Ohio, and Texas (states with weak gun laws) led back to dealers in the same state. Less than one-quarter of the guns used in crimes in New York and New Jersey (states with strong gun laws) were bought in those states. In fact, 90 percent of the guns found at crime scenes in New York City in 1996 and traced by the ATF came from other states.

"The War Between the States: How Gunrunners Smuggle Weapons Across America" (April 1997), a report released by Congressman Charles Schumer (D-Brooklyn and Queens), Senator Robert Torricelli (D-NJ), and Senator Dick Durbin (D-IL), analyzed the 47,068 guns traced by the ATF in 1996. Florida, Texas, South Carolina, and Georgia provided the most crime guns traced to other states, one-quarter of the total number (16,684) used in crimes outside of the state where they were bought.

Table 5.15 adjusts for population and shows the number of guns per capita crossing state lines. The "export rate" is the number of guns per 100,000 state residents traced from out-of-state crimes. For example, for every 100,000 Mississippi residents, 29 guns were sold in Mississippi and traced to crimes in other states. For every 100,000 residents in New York, 1.19 crime guns were traced to other states. Although New York's population is seven times larger than Mississippi's, in 1996 Mississippi had three times more out-of-state traces than New York (782 vs. 215).

Each state was rated on how strongly its laws reduced the gunrunners' easy access to firearms. According to this rating system, 27 states were rated "very weak" because they have no significant restrictions beyond what is required under federal regulation such as the Brady Law. Four states were rated "weak," four "moderate," six "strong," and 10 "very strong." None of the top 10 states in Table 5.15 had either a "strong" or "very strong" rating.

Gun control advocates want to combat the problem of gunrunning with a law limiting gun buyers to one gun a month. They point to the success of such a law in Virginia. For years, most of the guns that arrived in New York came from Virginia. Since passing the one-gun-a-month law, Virginia is no longer a top supplier of guns used in crimes in northeastern states.

TABLE 5.15

Crime guns crossing state lines, per capita 1996

(Number of guns used in out-of state crimes by
place of origination per 100,000 residents)

Rank	State	Rating	Export rate
1	Mississippi	Very weak	29.00
2	South Carolina	Moderate	27.01
3	West Virginia	Very weak	15.65
4	Nevada	Very weak	15.03
5	Kansas	Very weak	14.19
6	Virginia	Weak	13.96
7	Georgia	Very weak	13.04
8	Alabama	Moderate	12.13
9	Arizona	Very weak	11.55
10	Indiana	Moderate	11.45
11	Alaska	Very weak	11.26
12	Arkansas	Very weak	11.23
13	Kentucky	Very weak	11.09
14	North Carolina	Very strong	10.45
15	Delaware	Very weak	10.32
16	Maryland	Strong	9.06
17	New Mexico	Very weak	9.02
18	Florida	Very weak	8.65
19	Idaho	Very weak	8.08
20	Oklahoma	Very weak	7.99
21	Vermont	Very weak	7.86
22	Louisiana	Very weak	7.61
23	Ohio	Very weak	7.38
24	New Hampshire	Weak	6.88
25	Montana	Very weak	6.67
26	Wyoming	Very weak	6.49
27	South Dakota	Very weak	6.17
28	Tennessee	Weak	6.03
29	Colorado	Very weak	5.76
30	Texas	Very weak	5.70
31	Maine	Very weak	5.00
32	Pennsylvania	Moderate	4.41
33	Wisconsin	Very weak	4.37
34	Washington	Weak	4.11
35	Connecticut	Very strong	4.09
36	Oregon	Very weak	3.69
37	Utah	Very weak	3.54
38	Iowa	Strong	3.48
39	Illinois	Very strong	3.37
40	Nebraska	Strong	3.30
41	District of Columbia	Very strong	3.25
42	Missouri	Strong	2.91
43	California	Strong	2.62
44	North Dakota	Very weak	2.34
45	Minnesota	Very strong	2.30
46	Michigan	Very strong	2.09
47	Rhode Island	Strong	1.82
48	Massachusetts	Very strong	1.48
49	Hawaii	Very strong	1.26
50	New York	Very strong	1.19
51	New Jersey	Very strong	0.94

SOURCE: *The War between the States: How Gunrunners Smuggle Weapons across America,* Congressional Study based on data from the Bureau of Alcohol, Tobacco and Firearms, Washington, D.C., 1997

CHAPTER 6
GUNS—INJURIES AND FATALITIES

In their report *Firearm Injury and Death from Crime, 1993–97* (U.S. Department of Justice, Bureau of Justice Statistics, Selected Findings, October 2000) BJS statisticians Marianne W. Zawitz and Kevin J. Strom culled firearm injury and death data from a wide range of sources, including *Vital Statistics of the United States,* the FBI's *Supplemental Homicide Reports,* the Centers for Disease Control and Prevention's *Firearms Injury Surveillance Study,* as well as victim surveys and hospital emergency room surveillance. From among their findings they report the following highlights:

- Twenty-eight percent of serious nonfatal violent victimizations were committed with a firearm, and 4 percent resulted in serious injury.

- Assault accounted for 62 percent of all nonfatal firearm-related injuries treated in emergency departments. Of firearm-related fatalities, 44 percent were homicides.

- Gunshot wounds from assaults treated in emergency departments fell by 39 percent, from 64,100 in 1993 to 39,400 in 1997. Homicides committed with a firearm declined by 27 percent, from 18,353 in 1993 to 13,252 in 1997. (See Table 6.1.)

TABLE 6.1

Nonfatal gunshot injuries and firearm-related deaths, 1993–97

	Total	Assault or homicide	Legal intervention	Suicide attempts/Suicide	Unintentional	Undetermined
Nonfatal gunshot injury						
1993–97	411,800	257,200	5,100 *	23,400	70,900	55,200
1993	104,200	64,100	1,300 *	5,600	18,200	15,100
1994	89,600	61,200	1,100 *	5,700	13,600	8,000
1995	84,200	53,400	1,000 *	5,000	14,300	10,400
1996	69,600	39,200	700 *	4,000	13,600	12,000
1997	64,200	39,400	900 *	3,100	11,100	9,700
Percent change	-38%	-39%	-31% *	-45%	-39%	-36%
Firearm-related deaths						
1993–97	180,533	78,620	1,501	91,940	6,217	2,255
1993	39,595	18,253	318	18,940	1,521	563
1994	38,505	17,527	339	18,765	1,356	518
1995	35,957	15,551	284	18,503	1,225	394
1996	34,040	14,037	290	18,166	1,134	413
1997	32,436	13,252	270	17,566	981	367
Percent change	-18%	-27%	-15%	-7%	-36%	-35%
Injury deaths**						
1993–97	737,650	112,877	1,770	154,966	450,778	17,259

*Annual estimates for legal intervention injuries are presented for completeness but may be statistically unreliable because they are based on a small number of cases.
**Injury deaths include firearm-related deaths. The total represents only the categories presented here.

SOURCE: Marianne W. Zawitz and Kevin J. Strom, *Firearm Injury and Death from Crime, 1993–97,* U.S. Bureau of Justice Statistics, Washington, D.C., 2000

- Eighty percent of victims for both fatal and nonfatal gunshot wounds from crime were male. About half were black males, and about half of those were between the ages of 15 and 24. About one in five victims of nonfatal gunshot wounds from crime were Hispanic.

- More than 50 percent of victims of nonfatal gunshot wounds from crime were younger than 25, while older victims were more frequent in gun-related homicides.

- Of all victims of nonfatal firearm injury who were treated in emergency departments, more than half were hospitalized overnight. (See Tables 6.2 and 6.3 for a year-by-year breakdown of the above information.)

Of the 412,312 nonfatal firearm injuries reported from 1993 to 1997, nearly three-quarters (302,972) were assaults or a result of legal intervention (police or self-defense incidents). Firearm injuries whose cause was unintentional or undetermined accounted for nearly one-fourth of that total (82,307).

While suicide attempts amounted to only about 5 percent (27,033) of nonfatal gunshot injuries, suicides comprised over half of the 180,533 firearm-related deaths reported between 1993 to 1997. Next highest among gun fatalities were homicides or legal interventions at about 45 percent (81,139), followed by unintentional or undetermined (6,296).

Of assaults resulting in gunshot wounds treated in emergency departments, the location of the assault was unknown in about half of the cases. Of known locations, 23 percent were on streets or highways, 14 percent were at residences, and 13 percent occurred in schools, recreation areas, or other locations. In over half the cases the victim's relationship to the offender was not reported to hospital personnel. Where the relationship was reported, 49 percent of victims were injured by strangers, and 28 percent did not see who shot them.

REPORTING INJURIES

According to a recent report (see below) from Handgun Epidemic Lowering Plan (HELP), a coalition of doctors and public health and policy professionals, state and local health departments lack the funding to conduct firearms surveillance. As a result, information on individual gun incidents, such as who was shot, under what circumstances, and with what kind of weapon, is lacking. Without a collection of comprehensive data on firearms injuries and deaths, public health remedies to reduce these injuries and deaths will be inadequate. Referring to the number of gun fatalities each year, Dr. Katherine Kaufer Christoffel, one of the authors of the report, stated that good health-policy decisions designed to fight the handgun epidemic cannot be formulated without good local data, which thus far is unavailable.

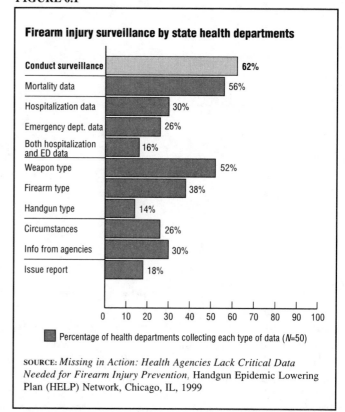

FIGURE 6.1

Firearm injury surveillance by state health departments

SOURCE: *Missing in Action: Health Agencies Lack Critical Data Needed for Firearm Injury Prevention*, Handgun Epidemic Lowering Plan (HELP) Network, Chicago, IL, 1999

Roger Hayes, Emile LeBrun, and Katherine Kaufer Christoffel, in *Missing in Action: Health Agencies Lack Critical Data Needed for Firearm Injury Prevention* (HELP Network, Chicago, IL, 1999), surveyed all 50 state health departments and the city and county health departments of the 50 largest urban areas in the country. Thirty-one states (62 percent) do maintain some type of firearm injury surveillance, while 19 (38 percent) do not. Of the 31 states that collect some type of data, more than one-half of the states track mortality and hospital data and 38 percent track the type of firearm. Twenty-six percent track circumstances, and 18 percent issue a report. (See Figure 6.1.) According to the report, the main obstacles to adequate surveillance were funding and staffing.

The city and county health department survey found that 25 states conducted firearm injury surveillance. About one-half of all city and county health departments collected data on both firearm deaths and injuries. Less than one-quarter collected information on firearm types involved in injuries. Twenty-two percent gathered information on the circumstances, and 35 percent issued a report. (See Figure 6.2.) Those health departments without surveillance, like the state departments, identified funding and staffing as the reasons they did not collect data.

HELP plans to ask for federal funding to enhance the national reporting system. According to the report, the

TABLE 6.2

Nonfatal firearm-related injuries in the United States: overall and by selected populations, 1993–97

Characteristic	Number*					Rate†					% Change from 1993 to 1997	(95% CI§)
	1993	1994	1995	1996	1997	1993	1994	1995	1996	1997		
Sex												
Male	92,375	79,904	75,766	61,903	57,004	73.4	62.8	58.9	47.7	43.5	−40.7%	(−77.3, −4.1)
Female	11,998	9,840	8,556	7,746	7,203	9.1	7.4	6.4	5.7	5.3	−42.1%	(−77.3, −6.8)
Unknown**	17	0	0	0	0							
Race/Ethnicity												
White, non-Hispanic	24,951	23,889	22,827	18,787	17,016	13.0	12.4	11.8	9.7	8.7	−32.8%	(−67.2, 1.5)
Black	56,852¶	46,473	40,676	34,002	29,717	176.7¶	142.4	122.9	101.5	87.5	−50.5%	(−91.2, −9.7)
Hispanic	14,543¶	13,412¶	14,922¶	10,562¶	11,440¶	60.8¶	54.0¶	58.0¶	39.6¶	41.3¶	−32.1%	(−123.7, 59.6)
Other/unknown**	8,044	5,970	5,897	6,298	6,034							
Age (yrs)												
0–14	4,346	3,696	2,996	3,390	2,514	7.7	6.5	5.2	5.9	4.3	−43.5%	(−73.0, 14.0)
15–24	50,086	42,421	40,638	32,470	30,225	138.4	117.3	112.2	89.6	82.6	−40.3%	(−79.9, −0.7)
25–34	25,968	22,200	21,077	16,758	16,510	62.1	53.8	51.6	41.5	41.7	−32.8%	(−73.8, 8.1)
35–44	14,065	11,471	10,426	9,001	7,990	34.5	27.5	24.5	20.7	18.2	−47.3%	(−78.9, 15.8)
≥45	9,153	9,649	9,134	7,945	6,835	11.1	11.5	10.7	9.1	7.6	−31.3%	(−74.4, 11.8)
Unknown**	772	307	51	85	133							
Intent of injury												
Assault/legal intervention	76,491	68,491	62,206	48,331	47,453	29.7	26.3	23.7	18.2	17.7	−40.2%	(−82.4, 2.0)
Intentionally self-inflicted	6,514	6,302	5,669	4,849	3,699	2.5	2.4	2.2	1.8	1.4	−45.3%	(−85.9, −4.7)
Unintentional	21,385	14,951	16,447	16,469	13,055	8.3	5.7	6.3	6.2	4.9	−41.2%	(−65.0, −17.3)
Disposition at discharge from ED												
Hospitalized	51,298	44,497	38,658	31,894	27,393¶	19.9	17.1	14.7	12.0	10.2¶	−48.6%	(−92.4, −4.7)
Treated and released	47,559	40,349	40,341	33,229	31,628	18.5	15.5	15.4	12.5	11.8	−35.9%	(−67.5, −4.4)
Transferred	5,448	4,786	5,154	4,391	4,933	2.1	1.8	2.0	1.7	1.8	−12.8%	(−59.4, 33.8)
Unknown**	85	112	169	135	253							
Overall	**104,390**	**89,744**	**84,322**	**69,649**	**64,207**	**40.5**	**34.5**	**32.1**	**26.3**	**24.0**	**−40.8%**	**(−77.0, −4.5)**

*Estimated number of nonfatal injuries treated in U.S. hospital emergency departments (EDs) based on data from CDC's Firearm Injury Surveillance Study using National Electronic Injury Surveillance System; rates were calculated using postcensal population estimates from the Bureau of the Census. The unweighted sample sizes of weighted cases used to calculate annual national estimates and rates were 3,491 for 1993; 2,860 for 1994; 2,639 for 1995; 2,231 for 1996; and 2,181 for 1997. The unweighted sample size of weighted cases used to calculate national estimates and rates within subgroups (excluding unknowns) ranged from 74 for transferred at ED discharge in 1994 to 3,099 for males in 1993.

†Per 100,000 population.

§Confidence interval; statistically significant at the 0.05 level if the confidence interval does not include zero.

¶Estimate has a coefficient of variation ≥30% and, therefore, may be unstable.

**Rates, percentage change, CIs, and coefficients of variation were not computed.

SOURCE: "Nonfatal and Fatal Firearm-Related Injuries—United States, 1993–97," *Morbidity and Mortality Weekly Report*, vol. 48, no. 45, November 19, 1999, Centers for Disease Control and Prevention, Atlanta, GA, 1999

TABLE 6.3

Fatal firearm-related injuries in the United States: overall and by selected populations, 1993–97

Characteristic	Number*					Rate[†]					Percent change from 1993 to 1997	(95% CI[§])
	1993	1994	1995	1996	1997	1993	1994	1995	1996	1997		
Sex												
Male	33,711	33,021	30,724	29,183	27,756	26.8	25.9	23.9	22.5	21.2	−20.9%	(−22.1, −19.6)
Female	5,884	5,484	5,233	4,857	4,680	4.5	4.1	3.9	3.6	3.4	−23.2%	(−26.1, −20.2)
Race/ethnicity												
White, non-Hispanic[¶]	21,960	21,549	20,764	20,004	19,507	11.6	11.3	10.9	10.5	10.2	−12.5%	(−14.2, −10.8)
Black[¶]	11,763	11,223	9,643	9,175	8,389	36.6	34.4	29.1	27.4	24.7	−32.4%	(−34.3, −30.5)
Hispanic[¶]	4,300	4,302	4,108	3,561	3,246	18.0	17.4	16.0	13.4	11.8	−34.8%	(−37.7, −31.7)
Other/unknown**	1,572	1,431	1,442	1,300	1,294							
Age (yrs)												
0–14	957	872	853	693	630	1.7	1.5	1.5	1.2	1.1	−35.7%	(−41.8, −28.9)
15–24	11,204	11,056	9,778	8,766	8,173	31.0	30.6	27.0	24.2	22.3	−27.8%	(−29.8, −25.7)
25–34	9,391	9,074	8,225	7,403	7,045	22.4	22.0	20.1	18.3	17.8	−20.8%	(−23.2, −18.3)
35–44	6,526	6,519	6,120	6,064	5,802	16.0	15.6	14.4	14.0	13.2	−17.5%	(−20.4, −14.6)
≥45	11,483	10,954	10,951	11,086	10,759	13.9	13.0	12.8	12.7	12.0	−13.8%	(−16.0, −11.5)
Unknown**	34	30	30	28	27							
Intent/manner of death												
Homicide/legal intervention	18,839	18,110	16,010	14,503	13,677	7.3	7.0	6.1	5.5	5.1	−30.1%	(−31.6, −28.5)
Suicide	19,213	19,021	18,708	18,389	17,767	7.5	7.3	7.1	6.9	6.6	−10.9%	(−12.7, −9.1)
Unintentional	1,543	1,374	1,239	1,148	992	0.6	0.5	0.5	0.4	0.4	−38.1%	(−42.8, −32.9)
Overall	**39,595**	**38,505**	**35,957**	**34,040**	**32,436**	**15.4**	**14.8**	**13.7**	**12.8**	**12.1**	**−21.1%**	**(−22.2, −19.9)**

*Number of fatal injuries from CDC's National Vital Statistics System; rates were calculated using postcensal population estimate from the Bureau of the Census.
[†]Per 100,000 population.
[§]Confidence interval; statistically significant at the 0.05 level if the confidence interval does not include zero.
[¶]Number of fatalities and death rates do not include data from Oklahoma because Hispanic origin was not recorded on state death certificates from 1993 through 1996.
**Rates, percentage change, and CIs were not computed.

SOURCE: "Nonfatal and Fatal Firearm-Related Injuries—United States, 1993–97," *Morbidity and Mortality Weekly Report*, vol. 48, no. 45, November 19, 1999, Centers for Disease Control and Prevention, Atlanta, GA, 1999

FIGURE 6.2

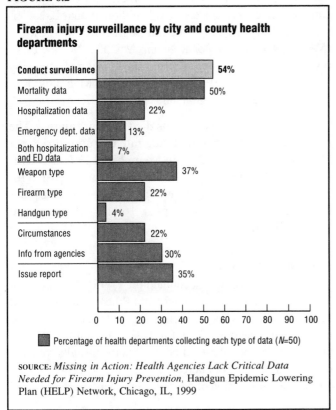

Firearm injury surveillance by city and county health departments

Conduct surveillance	54%
Mortality data	50%
Hospitalization data	22%
Emergency dept. data	13%
Both hospitalization and ED data	7%
Weapon type	37%
Firearm type	22%
Handgun type	4%
Circumstances	22%
Info from agencies	30%
Issue report	35%

0 10 20 30 40 50 60 70 80 90 100

◼ Percentage of health departments collecting each type of data (*N*=50)

SOURCE: *Missing in Action: Health Agencies Lack Critical Data Needed for Firearm Injury Prevention,* Handgun Epidemic Lowering Plan (HELP) Network, Chicago, IL, 1999

federal cost of instituting tracking of firearms deaths and injuries at the state and local levels would be about $4 million.

There are several federally funded national data collection systems, such as the National Electronic Injury Surveillance System (NEISS), established by the Centers for Disease Control and Prevention (CDC). However, the samples of firearm injuries are relatively small, and the NEISS collects little information about the circumstances of the injuries. The NEISS collects data on firearm-related injuries from a population-based sample of 91 hospital emergency departments. However, no system currently exists for the comprehensive and routine collection of information about firearm injuries that are seen in emergency departments, clinics, physician offices, or other health service providers.

Massachusetts's Weapons-Related Injury Surveillance System

In 1994, as injuries and deaths from the use of guns and other weapons increasingly became a public health issue, the Massachusetts Department of Public Health (MDPH) designed a system to track those injuries and deaths. Catherine W. Barber et al. ("When Bullets Don't Kill," *Public Health Reports,* Vol. 3, No. 6, November/ December 1996) reviewed that state's Weapon-Related Injury Surveillance System (WRISS) program. Created in 1990 with help from the CDC, it was the first of its kind in

the nation to track fatal and nonfatal weapons injuries. According to the authors, WRISS data indicated that self-inflicted injuries (generally suicide) were the most lethal, violence-related injuries were far less lethal, and accidental injuries rarely ended in death.

In an effort to standardize existing reporting systems so that all states can provide the same kinds of information to a national database, the CDC is helping other states develop tracking methods similar to WRISS. As of October 1996, the National Center for Injury Prevention and Control (NCIPC), the agency that coordinates the reporting programs for the CDC, funded such systems in seven other states. CDC officials hope that, because similar data has been used to reduce death and injury rates related to automobile accidents, information on weapons-related injuries will eventually reduce deaths and injuries from firearms and other weapons.

COLLECTING INFORMATION. WRISS uses hospital emergency departments as its primary source for weapons-related injuries. Physicians in Massachusetts are required to report stabbings and shootings to police, but according to a review of WRISS records, reporting compliance is only about 75 percent.

WRISS also uses death certificates to identify firearm victims who did not go to physicians for medical care and those who may have sought help but later died. This data enables researchers to determine fatality and injury rates, the proportion of cases ending in death among all cases, and what type of incident precipitated the use of firearms.

CHARACTERISTICS OF VICTIMS. In 1994, 1,239 firearm-related injuries were reported to WRISS, for a rate of 20.6 per 100,000 residents. Males (38.7 per 100,000 men), blacks (182.1 per 100,000 blacks), and young people between the ages of 15 and 24 (69 per 100,000) were far more likely to incur firearms injuries than females (3 per 100,000 women), whites (7.3 per 100,000 whites), and people of all other age groups.

Firearms injuries were predominantly related to violence (70.5 percent), followed by those that were self-inflicted (13.9 percent); the rest were unintended. While 15- to 24-year-olds were most likely to have suffered injuries related to violence (56.2 per 100,000) and unintentional injuries (3.0 per 100,000), people older than 45 (3.8 per 100,000) were most likely to incur self-inflicted injuries (usually from suicide attempts). Males and whites made up the majority of all self-inflicted injuries (91 percent and 87 percent, respectively).

CHARACTERISTICS OF SHOOTINGS. Eighty percent of the people who intentionally shot themselves died. All of those who did not die suffered serious harm and required hospitalization. While the rates for completed suicides were higher among whites than blacks, the rates for nonfatal suicide attempts were higher among blacks than whites. The majority of those who survived wounded themselves. Barber reports that medical narratives on the reporting forms suggest some self-inflicted shootings may have not been suicide attempts but acts of self-mutilation resulting from self-directed anger or delusional thoughts.

Among all shootings, accidents were least likely to cause death; almost all (96 percent) of the victims survived. In 1994 unintentional shootings were fairly evenly spread across the state, while violence-related shootings clustered in urban areas such as Boston, where illegal gun ownership is higher and, according to the authors, more guns are thought to be in the hands of teenagers. WRISS also indicates, however, that weapons-related injuries are more likely to involve knives than guns. From 1992 through 1993 Massachusetts had an overall incidence rate of 14.5 gun assaults and 42 knife assaults for every 100,000 residents.

WHO IS AT RISK? A review of injuries to Boston residents from 1992 to 1993 indicated that people 15–19 years old were at the greatest risk of injury from gun violence. Within this group, non-Hispanic black males were 41 times more likely to suffer gunshot wounds than non-Hispanic white males and up to 5 times more likely to be shot than Hispanic males. The dramatic difference between black males and white males prompted a violence researcher to ask WRISS officials to recalculate the numbers, which were found to be accurate. WRISS also indicated that one of every 38 black male teenagers was shot or stabbed in one year's time in Boston.

Officials with the MDPH find it difficult to explain these hugely disproportionate ratios. Barber et al. speculate that there is a high correlation between violence and urban poverty and point to studies finding that, once differences in socioeconomic status are considered, the ratio between black and white males evens out. They add that it might help to know not only who the victims are but also who the offenders are.

WRISS, however, does not obtain information concerning offenders who use guns in violent crime. For 63 percent of the gun-related cases reported to WRISS in 1994, the relationship between the victim and the attacker was unknown. Information supplied by the FBI, however, generally indicates that offenders mirror their victims (for example, blacks usually attack blacks, whites attack whites, young people attack other young people). The opposite is true for women, who are primarily attacked by men; older people, who are attacked by people younger than them; and children, who are attacked by people older than them.

THE OUTCOME OF GUN-RELATED SHOOTINGS

Death and injury from weapons have become major public health issues. In the study described below, a team of researchers found that the cost of emergency and inpatient care in three cities exceeded $16.5 million. Arthur L. Kellermann et al., in "Injuries Due to Firearms in Three Cities" (*New England Journal of Medicine,* Vol. 335, No. 19, 1996) reviewed 1,915 cases of firearm-related injuries occurring between November 1992 and May 1994 in Memphis, Tennessee; Seattle, Washington; and Galveston, Texas.

Five percent of the victims died of their injuries. The researchers found that the crude rate of gun injuries per 100,000 people was 222.6 in Memphis, 143.6 in Galveston, and 54.1 in Seattle. When the rates were adjusted for age, gender, and race or ethnic group, the rates per 100,000 were 155.6 in Memphis, 160 in Galveston, and 110.2 in Seattle.

Confirmed Assaults

Confirmed assaults accounted for 1,496 (78 percent) of the 1,915 shootings and 65 percent of the deaths. Age- and sex-adjusted rates for assaults were 15.6 per 100,000 for non-Hispanic whites, 42.8 for Hispanics, and 308.3 for blacks. Almost one-third (31 percent) of the assaults were the result of arguments or altercations. Twenty percent occurred during the commission of a robbery or other felony.

Fifteen percent were "drive-by" shootings; 3 percent were drug-related; and in 25 percent of the incidents, the victim claimed the shooting was unprovoked. In those cases in which the relationship between the victim and offender was known, 42 percent were strangers, 38 percent were "nonintimate acquaintances," 8 percent were criminal or romantic rivals, and 7 percent were relatives or friends.

More than half of all gun assaults took place at a distance of less than 10 feet, and 15 percent of the victims sustained multiple gunshot wounds. Forty-two percent were discharged from the hospital, while 39 percent were treated and released from emergency rooms. Sixteen percent died at the scene or in emergency rooms or hospitals. (See Table 6.4.)

Suicides and Attempted Suicides

Suicides accounted for 7 percent of all shootings but 33 percent of all deaths. Most suicide attempts (86 percent) were successful. In the three cities studied, males attempted suicide with guns 6.5 times as often as females. Seventy-seven percent of all suicide attempts took place in the home of the victim. The shooter killed someone else before shooting himself or herself in five of the suicide cases, four of which were the result of domestic violence, while one involved an argument between acquaintances.

Almost three-quarters (72 percent) of those who attempted suicide shot themselves in the head, compared to 17 percent who shot themselves in the chest and 3 percent who shot themselves in the face or neck. A handgun was used in 85 percent of the cases, while a rifle or

TABLE 6.4

Firearm-related assault in three cities

Variable	Value
Incidence — no./100,000 person-yr.	
Race or ethnic group	
Non-Hispanic white	15.6
Black	308.3
Hispanic	42.8
Asian	49.9
Other	51.7
City	
Memphis	122.5
Seattle	84.1
Galveston	127.2
Circumstances (1,346 cases) — no. (%)	
Argument or altercation	412 (31)
"Unprovoked"	334 (25)
Felony-related (e.g., robbery)	274 (20)
Drive-by shooting	208 (15)
Drug-related activity	43 (3)
Legal intervention	13 (1)
Other	62 (5)
Shooter's relationship to victim (1,063 cases) — no. (%)	
Stranger	445 (42)
Nonintimate acquaintance	408 (38)
Rival or adversary	86 (8)
Spouse, intimate friend, or family member	78 (7)
Other	46 (4)
Location of shooting (1,423 cases) — no. (%)	
Victim's home	266 (19)
Shooter's home	36 (3)
Another person's home	136 (10)
Street or parking lot	663 (47)
Motor vehicle	99 (7)
Bar or nightclub	79 (6)
Store or place of work	68 (5)
Other	76 (5)
Legally justifiable shooting or self-defense (1,475 cases) — no. (%)	
Yes	
Police	13 (1)
Citizen	21 (1)
No	1441 (98)
Type of firearm (1,089 cases) — no. (%)	
Handgun	972 (89)
Rifle	19 (2)
Shotgun	96 (9)
Other	2 (<1)
Site of injury (1,443 cases) — no. (%)	
Head	159 (11)
Face	81 (6)
Neck	66 (5)
Chest	223 (15)
Abdomen	160 (11)
Back	111 (8)
Pelvis or perineum	25 (2)
Arm	261 (18)
Leg	477 (33)
Hand or fingers	90 (6)
Foot or toes	67 (5)
Back or buttocks	84 (6)
Outcome (1,496 cases) — no. (%)	
Died at scene	114 (8)
Died in emergency department or hospital	124 (8)
Treated and released from emergency department	582 (39)
Discharged from hospital alive	632 (42)
Unknown or refused care	44 (3)

There as a total of 1,496 cases. Rates for racial or ethnic groups have been adjusted for age and sex; rates for the three cities have been adjusted for age, sex, and race or ethnic group. Percentages in each category are based on the total number of cases with available data.

† Individual wounds exceed the total number of cases.

SOURCE: Arthur L. Kellerman et al., "Injuries Due to Firearms in Three Cities," *New England Journal of Medicine*, vol. 335, no. 19, November 7, 1996

TABLE 6.5

Firearm-related suicide and attempted suicide in three cities

Variable	Value
Incidence — no./100,000 person-yr.	
Race or ethnic group	
Non-Hispanic white	9.3
Black	10.0
Hispanic	11.6
Asian	3.1
Other	9.2
City	
Memphis	10.6
Seattle	9.2
Galveston	7.1
Location of shooting (136 cases) — no. (%)	
Victim's home	105 (77)
Another person's home	13 (10)
Motor vehicle	8 (6)
Other	10 (7)
Type of firearm involved (130 cases) — no. (%)	
Handgun	111 (85)
Rifle	13 (10)
Shotgun	6 (5)
Site of injury (134 cases) — no. (%)†	
Head	97 (72)
Face	1 (1)
Neck	3 (2)
Chest	23 (17)
Abdomen	3 (2)
Other	11 (8)
Outcome (138 cases) — no. (%)	
Died at scene	93 (67)
Died in emergency department or hospital	26 (19)
Treated and released from emergency department	5 (4)
Discharged from hospital alive	14 (10)

There was a total of 138 cases. Rates for racial or ethnic groups have been adjusted for age and sex; rates for the three cities have been adjusted for age, sex, and race or ethnic group. Percentages in each category are based on the total number of cases with available data (shown in parentheses).

† Individual wounds exceeded the total number of cases.

SOURCE: Arthur L. Kellerman et al., "Injuries Due to Firearms in Three Cities," *New England Journal of Medicine*, vol. 335, no. 19, November 7, 1996

shotgun was used in the remaining 15 percent. (See Table 6.5.)

Accidental Shootings

Unintentional shootings made up about 5 percent of all shootings and 2 percent of all shooting deaths. Ninety percent of the victims were males. Most (67 percent) accidentally shot themselves, while the rest were shot by someone else. Most accidents (65 percent) happened in the homes of the victims, and about 1 in 10 (11 percent) happened in an automobile. About one-third (35 percent) of the victims of accidents were shot in the leg. Victims were also shot in the hand or fingers (21 percent), foot or toes (12 percent), head (8 percent), or arm (8 percent). The remaining 16 percent involved the chest, abdomen, face, back, buttocks, pelvis, and neck.

Nonfatal injuries outnumbered deaths 16 to 1. Most victims (59 percent) were treated and released from emergency departments, while 35 percent were admitted to the hospital and later released. Only 6 percent of the victims died. Almost all gun accidents (89 percent) involved handguns. (See Table 6.6.)

Medical Care for Injuries

Of the 1,915 shootings, ambulances were dispatched 63 percent of the time. Of 1,677 victims who received care in emergency rooms, 5 percent died, 52 percent were hospitalized, 42 percent were treated and released, and 1 percent refused medical treatment. Of the 867 patients admitted to the hospital, 8 percent died while in the hospital—most within 24 hours of admission.

For those patients who were released or who died in the emergency room, the median charge was $538, not including physician and other professional fees. Patients admitted to hospitals incurred a median (half were higher; half were lower) charge of $10,050; 28 patients incurred bills of more than $100,000.

FIREARM FATALITIES

Firearm and Car Injury Mortality

The number of deaths attributable to firearms dropped steadily from 1994 to 1998. (See Table 6.7.) As of 1995 firearm injuries continue to be the second leading cause of injury deaths in the United States, surpassed only by motor-vehicle-related injuries. (See Figure 6.3.) According to the CDC, firearms will likely supplant automobile accidents as the leading cause of injury death by 2003. In some states the number of firearm deaths is already greater than the number of deaths from car crashes. As of 1996 firearm death rates were higher than motor vehicle death rates in Alaska, California, Louisiana, Maryland, Nevada, and Virginia.

AGE. From 1996 to 1998 the firearm death rate for persons 15–24 years old fell from 24.2 per 100,000 to 19.9. Likewise, the death rate for motor-vehicle-related injuries in the 15–24 age group declined from 29.2 per 100,000 in 1996 to 26.9 in 1998. That trend also holds true for all other age groups, although the rate of decline was least pronounced in the oldest group of 65 years and over, for whom the rate moved down from 13.9 per 100,000 in 1996 to 13.1 in 1998. Conversely, death rates for motor-vehicle-related injuries in the 65 and older group rose slightly from 23.0 per 100,000 in 1996 to 23.7 in 1998. In all other age groups the death rate for vehicle-related injuries was either stable or in slight decline.

Citing a study by the Los Angeles-based Women Against Gun Violence, the *Los Angeles Times* (December 15, 2000) reported that although gun deaths were down overall in Los Angeles County in 1999 from the previous year, firearm deaths for senior citizens, including suicides, rose 14.6 percent. According to the article, these results did not surprise Dr. David Trader, medical director of geriatric

TABLE 6.6

Accidental firearm-related injuries in three cities

Variable	Value	
Incidence — no./100,000 person-yr.		
Race or ethnic group		
Non-Hispanic white	2.4	
Black	12.7	
Hispanic	6.3	
Asian	1.6	
City		
Memphis	5.5	
Seattle	8.7	
Galveston	13.5	
Shooter's relationship to victim (86 cases) — no. (%)		
Self	67	(78)
Nonintimate acquaintance	8	(9)
Boyfriend	2	(2)
Spouse, family member, or relative	6	(7)
Other or unknown	3	(3)
Location of shooting (74 cases) — no. (%)		
Victim's home	48	(65)
Shooter's or another person's home	6	(8)
Street or parking lot	5	(7)
Motor vehicle	8	(11)
Other or unknown	7	(9)
Type of firearm (71 cases) — no. (%)		
Handgun	63	(89)
Rifle	4	(6)
Shotgun	4	(6)
Site of injury (86 cases) — no. (%)†		
Head	7	(8)
Face	4	(5)
Neck	1	(1)
Chest	6	(7)
Abdomen	5	(6)
Pelvis or perineum	2	(2)
Arm	7	(8)
Leg	30	(35)
Hand or fingers	18	(21)
Foot or toes	10	(12)
Back or buttocks	4	(5)
Outcome (85 cases) — no. (%)		
Died at scene	2	(2)
Died in emergency department or hospital	3	(4)
Treated and released from emergency department	50	(59)
Discharged from hospital alive	30	(35)

There was a total of 86 cases. Rates for racial or ethnic groups have been adjusted for age and sex; rates for the three cities have been adjusted for age, sex, and race or ethnic group. Percentages in each category are based on the total number of cases with available data.

† Individual wounds exceeded the total number of cases.

SOURCE: Arthur L. Kellerman et al., "Injuries Due to Firearms in Three Cities," *New England Journal of Medicine*, vol. 335, no. 19, November 7, 1996

psychiatry services at Cedars-Sinai Medical Center in Los Angeles, who equated old age with loss, including the loss of health, family, occupation, income, and friends. Trader believes the elderly may see guns as a finality, or a sure end.

RACE AND AGE. From 1996 through 1998 the firearm death rate for black males 15–24 years old was twice that for Hispanic males 15–24, and four times higher than that for white non-Hispanics in the same age group. For death rates for motor-vehicle-related injuries from 1996 to 1998, white non-Hispanic males 15–24 years old ranked highest, at 40.5 deaths per 100,000, followed by Hispanic males

TABLE 6.7

Death rates for firearm-related injuries, by sex, race, Hispanic origin, and age, selected years 1970–98
(Data are based on the National Vital Statistics System)

Sex, race, Hispanic origin, and age	1970	1980	1985	1990	1994	1995	1996	1997	1998	1996–98[1]
All persons				Deaths per 100,000 resident population						
All ages, age adjusted	14.0	14.8	12.8	14.6	15.1	13.9	12.9	12.2	11.3	12.1
All ages, crude	13.0	14.9	13.3	14.9	14.8	13.7	12.8	12.1	11.4	12.1
Under 1 year	*	*	*	*	*	*	*	*	*	0.2
1–14 years	1.6	1.4	1.4	1.5	1.6	1.6	1.3	1.1	1.1	1.2
1–4 years	1.0	0.7	0.7	0.6	0.6	0.6	0.5	0.5	0.5	0.5
5–14 years	1.7	1.6	1.8	1.9	2.0	2.0	1.6	1.4	1.4	1.4
15–24 years	15.5	20.6	17.2	25.8	30.8	27.2	24.2	22.3	19.9	22.1
25–44 years	20.9	22.5	17.9	19.3	18.8	17.2	16.1	15.4	14.4	15.3
25–34 years	22.2	24.3	19.3	21.8	21.9	20.1	18.3	17.8	16.3	17.5
35–44 years	19.6	20.0	16.0	16.3	15.6	14.4	14.0	13.2	12.8	13.3
45–64 years	17.6	15.2	14.3	13.6	12.2	11.8	11.9	11.3	10.7	11.3
45–54 years	18.1	16.4	14.7	13.9	12.8	12.1	12.3	11.5	10.9	11.6
55–64 years	17.0	13.9	13.9	13.3	11.4	11.4	11.2	11.0	10.4	10.8
65 years and over	13.8	13.5	15.6	16.0	14.3	14.2	13.9	13.2	13.1	13.4
65–74 years	14.5	13.8	15.1	14.4	12.6	12.9	12.6	11.9	11.3	11.9
75–84 years	13.4	13.4	17.7	19.4	16.9	16.4	15.9	14.9	15.5	15.4
85 years and over	10.2	11.6	12.2	14.7	15.1	14.6	14.5	14.3	14.3	14.4
Male										
All ages, age adjusted	23.8	25.3	21.9	25.4	26.2	24.1	22.4	21.1	19.6	21.0
All ages, crude	22.2	25.7	22.8	26.2	26.0	23.9	22.5	21.2	19.8	21.2
Under 1 year	*	*	*	*	*	*	*	*	*	*
1–14 years	2.3	2.0	2.1	2.2	2.3	2.3	1.8	1.7	1.5	1.7
1–4 years	1.2	0.9	0.8	0.7	0.7	0.8	0.5	0.5	0.6	0.6
5–14 years	2.7	2.5	2.7	2.9	3.0	2.9	2.4	2.1	1.9	2.1
15–24 years	26.4	34.8	29.1	44.7	54.0	47.6	42.2	38.9	34.7	38.6
25–44 years	34.1	38.1	29.7	32.6	31.7	28.9	27.0	25.8	24.2	25.7
25–34 years	36.5	41.4	32.1	37.0	37.4	34.3	31.4	30.5	28.0	30.0
35–44 years	31.6	33.2	26.6	27.4	26.0	23.7	22.9	21.5	20.9	21.8
45–64 years	31.0	25.9	24.5	23.4	21.0	20.2	20.4	19.4	18.4	19.4
45–54 years	30.7	27.3	24.4	23.2	21.3	20.4	20.5	19.3	18.3	19.4
55–64 years	31.3	24.5	24.6	23.7	20.5	20.0	20.2	19.7	18.4	19.4
65 years and over	29.7	29.7	34.2	35.3	31.2	30.9	30.2	28.5	28.5	29.1
65–74 years	29.5	27.8	30.0	28.2	24.6	25.3	24.8	23.1	22.2	23.4
75–84 years	31.0	33.0	42.7	46.9	39.9	37.7	36.4	34.1	35.1	35.2
85 years and over	26.2	34.9	38.2	49.3	49.7	47.4	46.7	45.8	44.9	45.8
Female										
All ages, age adjusted	4.8	4.8	4.2	4.3	4.2	4.0	3.6	3.4	3.3	3.4
All ages, crude	4.4	4.7	4.2	4.3	4.1	3.9	3.6	3.4	3.3	3.4
Under 1 year	*	*	*	*	*	*	*	*	*	*
1–14 years	0.8	0.7	0.7	0.8	0.9	0.8	0.7	0.6	0.7	0.7
1–4 years	0.9	0.5	0.5	0.5	0.5	0.5	0.4	0.5	0.4	0.4
5–14 years	0.8	0.7	0.8	1.0	1.0	0.9	0.8	0.7	0.8	0.8
15–24 years	4.8	6.1	5.0	6.0	6.5	6.0	5.1	4.8	4.5	4.8
25–44 years	8.3	7.4	6.2	6.1	6.0	5.6	5.2	5.0	4.7	5.0
25–34 years	8.4	7.5	6.6	6.7	6.5	5.9	5.2	5.1	4.7	5.0
35–44 years	8.2	7.2	5.8	5.4	5.5	5.3	5.1	4.9	4.7	4.9
45–64 years	5.4	5.4	5.0	4.5	4.1	4.0	3.9	3.7	3.6	3.7
45–54 years	6.4	6.2	5.6	4.9	4.6	4.3	4.4	4.1	3.9	4.1
55–64 years	4.2	4.6	4.5	4.0	3.3	3.5	3.1	3.0	3.1	3.1
65 years and over	2.4	2.5	3.2	3.1	2.7	2.8	2.6	2.5	2.3	2.5
65–74 years	2.8	3.1	3.6	3.6	3.0	3.0	2.8	2.9	2.4	2.7
75–84 years	1.7	1.7	3.0	2.9	2.5	2.8	2.6	2.3	2.5	2.5
85 years and over	*	1.3	1.8	1.3	1.8	1.8	1.7	1.7	1.6	1.6
White male										
All ages, age adjusted	18.2	21.1	19.4	20.5	20.4	19.3	18.0	17.1	16.2	17.1
All ages, crude	17.6	21.8	20.7	21.8	21.1	20.1	19.0	18.1	17.4	18.1
1–14 years	1.8	1.9	2.1	1.9	1.8	1.9	1.5	1.4	1.3	1.4
15–24 years	16.9	28.4	24.1	29.5	34.2	31.4	26.9	24.8	23.1	24.9
25–44 years	24.2	29.5	25.0	25.7	24.9	23.6	22.0	21.2	20.3	21.2
25–34 years	24.3	31.1	26.3	27.8	27.6	26.1	23.6	23.1	21.2	22.7
35–44 years	24.1	27.1	23.3	23.3	22.3	21.2	20.6	19.5	19.5	19.9
45–64 years	27.4	23.3	23.6	22.8	20.6	19.7	20.2	19.4	18.5	19.3
65 years and over	29.9	30.1	35.4	36.8	32.5	32.3	31.8	30.0	30.3	30.7

TABLE 6.7

Death rates for firearm-related injuries, by sex, race, Hispanic origin, and age, selected years 1970–98 [CONTINUED]

(Data are based on the National Vital Statistics System)

Sex, race, Hispanic origin, and age	1970	1980	1985	1990	1994	1995	1996	1997	1998	1996–98[1]
Black male				Deaths per 100,000 resident population						
All ages, age adjusted	73.4	61.8	42.2	61.5	65.1	55.6	52.0	47.4	41.6	47.0
All ages, crude	60.6	57.7	41.3	61.9	63.8	54.0	50.6	46.1	40.3	45.6
1–14 years	5.3	3.0	2.7	4.4	5.2	4.6	3.6	3.1	2.4	3.0
15–24 years	97.3	77.9	61.3	138.0	169.6	140.2	131.6	119.9	101.8	117.6
25–44 years	126.2	114.1	71.8	90.3	84.5	71.2	67.0	61.8	55.3	61.3
25–34 years	145.6	128.4	79.8	108.6	109.0	94.4	88.6	84.0	75.3	82.7
35–44 years	104.2	92.3	59.2	66.1	57.7	46.6	44.7	39.5	35.9	40.0
45–64 years	71.1	55.6	36.9	34.5	29.1	29.1	27.0	23.3	22.1	24.1
65 years and over	30.6	29.7	26.3	23.9	23.2	21.4	19.1	17.8	14.2	17.0
American Indian or Alaska Native male[2]										
All ages, age adjusted	- - -	26.5	24.9	20.8	24.6	23.4	19.4	20.7	19.7	19.9
All ages, crude	- - -	27.5	24.4	20.5	24.1	22.9	19.1	20.1	19.3	19.5
15–24 years	- - -	55.3	39.8	49.1	54.6	45.5	40.0	39.4	43.3	40.9
25–44 years	- - -	43.9	40.3	25.4	33.8	34.1	26.7	29.3	25.6	27.2
45–64 years	- - -	*	21.2	*	13.6	15.6	13.8	13.9	13.4	13.7
65 years and over	- - -	*	*	*	*	*	*	*	*	13.5
Asian or Pacific Islander male[3]										
All ages, age adjusted	- - -	8.1	7.1	9.2	10.9	10.8	8.7	9.0	7.2	8.3
All ages, crude	- - -	8.2	7.3	9.4	10.8	10.4	8.6	8.7	7.0	8.1
15–24 years	- - -	10.8	12.6	21.0	26.9	27.1	19.6	19.7	13.9	17.7
25–44 years	- - -	12.8	9.8	10.9	13.0	11.3	10.0	9.6	8.7	9.4
45–64 years	- - -	10.4	6.7	8.1	7.4	8.6	7.7	8.7	6.1	7.5
65 years and over	- - -	*	*	*	*	*	*	7.7	8.0	7.0
Hispanic male[4]										
All ages, age adjusted	- - -	- - -	25.3	28.9	29.9	28.0	22.5	19.9	18.3	20.2
All ages, crude	- - -	- - -	26.0	29.9	30.0	27.6	22.6	19.9	18.1	20.2
1–14 years	- - -	- - -	1.4	2.6	2.3	2.9	1.9	1.4	1.3	1.5
15–24 years	- - -	- - -	42.0	55.5	72.0	70.7	54.4	47.9	44.9	49.0
25–44 years	- - -	- - -	43.2	42.7	38.8	33.5	27.5	24.5	22.6	24.9
25–34 years	- - -	- - -	47.3	47.3	45.5	39.9	32.8	29.3	28.6	30.2
35–44 years	- - -	- - -	35.9	35.4	29.5	24.9	20.8	18.7	15.6	18.3
45–64 years	- - -	- - -	19.2	21.4	19.2	17.2	16.2	13.7	10.7	13.4
65 years and over	- - -	- - -	12.4	19.1	14.7	15.6	11.7	12.3	14.2	12.8
White, non-Hispanic male[4]										
All ages, age adjusted	- - -	- - -	18.4	18.7	18.1	17.2	16.4	15.9	15.2	15.8
All ages, crude	- - -	- - -	19.9	20.4	19.5	18.6	18.0	17.5	17.0	17.5
1–14 years	- - -	- - -	2.0	1.6	1.6	1.6	1.4	1.4	1.3	1.4
15–24 years	- - -	- - -	22.0	24.1	26.3	23.3	20.4	19.4	18.1	19.3
25–44 years	- - -	- - -	23.0	23.3	22.4	21.6	20.6	20.3	19.6	20.2
25–34 years	- - -	- - -	23.7	24.7	23.9	22.9	21.2	21.4	19.3	20.7
35–44 years	- - -	- - -	22.0	21.6	20.9	20.4	20.1	19.4	19.8	19.7
45–64 years	- - -	- - -	23.0	22.7	20.5	19.7	20.2	19.8	19.0	19.6
65 years and over	- - -	- - -	37.3	37.4	33.2	32.7	32.6	30.8	31.1	31.5
White female										
All ages, age adjusted	4.0	4.2	3.9	3.7	3.6	3.5	3.1	3.1	3.0	3.1
All ages, crude	3.7	4.1	4.0	3.8	3.6	3.5	3.2	3.2	3.0	3.2
15–24 years	3.4	5.1	4.4	4.8	4.9	4.6	3.8	3.8	3.4	3.7
25–44 years	6.9	6.2	5.6	5.3	5.2	5.0	4.6	4.7	4.4	4.5
45–64 years	5.0	5.1	5.0	4.5	4.1	4.0	3.9	3.8	3.7	3.8
65 years and over	2.2	2.5	3.2	3.1	2.7	2.9	2.6	2.6	2.4	2.5
Black female										
All ages, age adjusted	11.4	9.1	6.6	7.8	8.0	6.8	6.5	5.6	5.2	5.7
All ages, crude	10.0	8.8	6.5	7.8	7.8	6.6	6.4	5.4	5.0	5.6
15–24 years	15.2	12.3	8.3	13.3	15.5	13.5	12.0	10.6	10.2	10.9
25–44 years	19.4	16.1	11.4	12.4	11.9	10.0	9.8	8.0	7.5	8.4
45–64 years	10.2	8.2	5.8	4.8	4.6	4.1	4.1	3.4	3.2	3.5
65 years and over	4.3	3.1	3.7	3.1	2.9	2.6	3.0	2.2	1.8	2.3

TABLE 6.7

Death rates for firearm-related injuries, by sex, race, Hispanic origin, and age, selected years 1970–98 [CONTINUED]

(Data are based on the National Vital Statistics System)

Sex, race, Hispanic origin, and age	1970	1980	1985	1990	1994	1995	1996	1997	1998	1996–98[1]
American Indian or Alaska Native female[2]					Deaths per 100,000 resident population					
All ages, age adjusted	- - -	6.1	4.3	3.6	4.5	4.5	3.8	3.2	4.3	3.8
All ages, crude	- - -	5.8	4.1	3.4	4.4	4.4	3.7	3.0	4.2	3.6
15–24 years	- - -	*	*	*	*	*	*	*	*	5.3
25–44 years	- - -	10.2	*	*	7.5	7.7	5.9	*	6.9	5.4
45–64 years	- - -	*	*	*	*	*	*	*	*	4.4
65 years and over	- - -	*	*	*	*	*	*	*	*	*
Asian or Pacific Islander female[3]										
All ages, age adjusted	- - -	2.0	1.7	2.0	2.1	2.2	1.7	1.8	1.8	1.8
All ages, crude	- - -	2.1	1.7	2.1	2.1	2.2	1.7	1.7	1.8	1.7
15–24 years	- - -	*	*	*	4.0	4.2	3.7	3.2	*	3.1
25–44 years	- - -	3.2	2.2	2.7	2.6	2.9	2.1	1.9	2.2	2.1
45–64 years	- - -	*	*	*	*	*	*	*	2.1	1.9
65 years and over	- - -	*	*	*	*	*	*	*	*	*
Hispanic female[4]										
All ages, age adjusted	- - -	- - -	3.2	3.6	3.5	3.5	2.8	2.4	2.3	2.5
All ages, crude	- - -	- - -	3.2	3.6	3.4	3.4	2.7	2.3	2.2	2.4
15–24 years	- - -	- - -	5.1	6.9	6.9	6.6	5.0	4.5	4.0	4.5
25–44 years	- - -	- - -	5.5	5.1	5.0	4.9	4.1	3.3	3.0	3.5
45–64 years	- - -	- - -	2.2	2.4	2.4	2.4	2.3	2.2	1.6	2.0
65 years and over	- - -	- - -	*	*	*	*	*	*	*	1.0
White, non-Hispanic female[4]										
All ages, age adjusted	- - -	- - -	3.9	3.6	3.5	3.4	3.1	3.2	3.0	3.1
All ages, crude	- - -	- - -	4.1	3.7	3.6	3.5	3.2	3.3	3.1	3.2
15–24 years	- - -	- - -	4.5	4.3	4.5	4.1	3.5	3.6	3.3	3.4
25–44 years	- - -	- - -	5.6	5.1	5.1	4.8	4.5	4.8	4.5	4.6
45–64 years	- - -	- - -	5.1	4.6	4.1	4.1	4.0	3.9	3.8	3.9
65 years and over	- - -	- - -	3.4	3.2	2.7	2.9	2.7	2.7	2.5	2.6

* Based on fewer than 20 deaths.

- - - Data not available.

[1]Average annual death rate.

[2]Interpretation of trends should take into account that population estimates for American Indians increased by 45 percent between 1980 and 1990, partly due to better enumeration techniques in the 1990 decennial census and to the increased tendency for people to identify themselves as American Indian in 1990.

[3]Interpretation of trends should take into account that the Asian population in the United States more than doubled between 1980 and 1990, primarily due to immigration.

[4]Excludes data from States lacking an Hispanic-origin item on their death certificates.

Note: Rates are age adjusted to the 1940 U.S. standard million population.

SOURCE: *Health, United States 2000*, National Center for Health Statistics, Hyattsville, MD, 2000

15–24, at 36.3 per 100,000, and by black males in the same age group, at 32.7 per 100,000 resident population. (See Tables 6.7 and 6.8.) Females of all races had far lower death rates for both firearm- and motor-vehicle-related injuries.

INTERNATIONAL COMPARISONS. A report released by the National Center for Health Statistics at the end of 1998 compared injury mortality among 11 of the countries participating in the International Collaborative Effort on Injury Statistics, an international group of researchers who work together to identify and develop issues for research on injury statistics. In 1994 the motor-vehicle-related death rate among males 15–24 years of age was 41 per 100,000 in the United States. Compared with the selected countries, only New Zealand (in 1992–93) had a higher death rate than the United States, at 63 per 100,000. France had a motor vehicle death rate similar to that of the United States. (See Figure 6.4.)

The firearm death rate among males 15–24 years old was 54 per 100,000 in the United States. This was far higher than the rate in 10 other countries. The United States had a firearm death rate 4.5 times the rates of Norway, Israel, and Canada, which averaged 11–12 per 100,000. Death rates in Scotland, the Netherlands, and England and Wales were the lowest, at about 1 per 100,000. (See Figure 6.5.)

The firearm death rate among males 15–24 in the United States was 32 percent higher than the motor vehicle death rate. In no other comparison country did the firearm death rate exceed the motor vehicle death rate.

In the United States, 63 percent of the firearm deaths among males in this age group were homicides, and 30 percent were suicides. In no other country, except the Netherlands, were more than 25 percent of the firearm

FIGURE 6.3

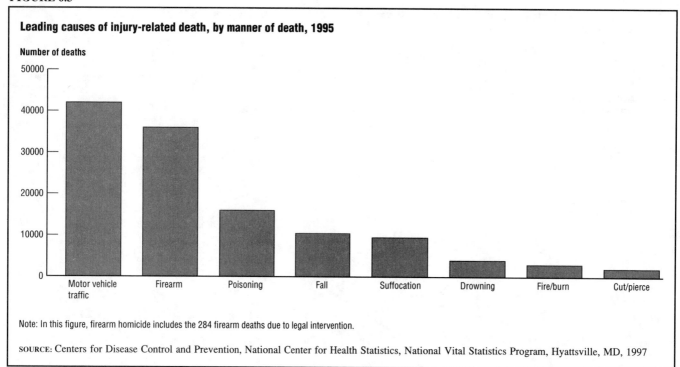

Leading causes of injury-related death, by manner of death, 1995

Number of deaths

Note: In this figure, firearm homicide includes the 284 firearm deaths due to legal intervention.

SOURCE: Centers for Disease Control and Prevention, National Center for Health Statistics, National Vital Statistics Program, Hyattsville, MD, 1997

FIGURE 6.4

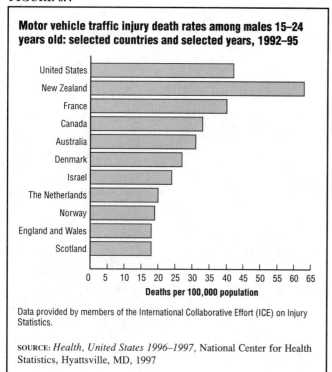

Motor vehicle traffic injury death rates among males 15–24 years old: selected countries and selected years, 1992–95

Data provided by members of the International Collaborative Effort (ICE) on Injury Statistics.

SOURCE: *Health, United States 1996–1997*, National Center for Health Statistics, Hyattsville, MD, 1997

FIGURE 6.5

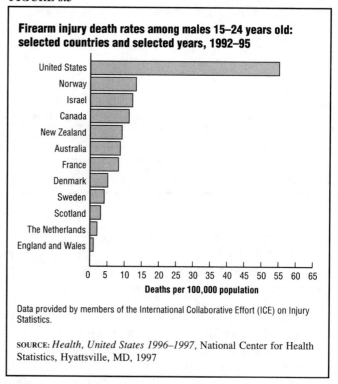

Firearm injury death rates among males 15–24 years old: selected countries and selected years, 1992–95

Data provided by members of the International Collaborative Effort (ICE) on Injury Statistics.

SOURCE: *Health, United States 1996–1997*, National Center for Health Statistics, Hyattsville, MD, 1997

deaths homicides. Firearm suicide accounted for at least 70 percent of firearm deaths in Norway, Sweden, France, Canada, New Zealand, and Australia.

THE COST OF FIREARM INJURIES

As observed earlier, the number of deaths and injuries related to firearms will likely soon surpass the number of deaths and injuries related to automobile accidents. Unlike most car crash victims, who are privately insured, most gunshot victims are on public assistance or uninsured. According to the CDC the cost of firearm fatalities per person is the highest of any injury-related death. Researchers estimate the annual total cost of firearm violence to be about $40 billion in medical

TABLE 6.8

Death rates for motor vehicle–related injuries, by sex, race, Hispanic origin, and age, selected years, 1950–98
(Data are based on the National Vital Statistics System)

Sex, race, Hispanic origin, and age	1950[1]	1960[1]	1970	1980	1985	1990	1995	1996	1997	1998	1996–98
All persons					Deaths per 100,000 resident population						
All ages, age adjusted	23.3	22.5	27.4	22.9	18.8	18.5	16.3	16.2	15.9	15.6	15.9
All ages, crude	23.1	21.3	26.9	23.5	19.3	18.8	16.5	16.5	16.2	16.1	16.3
Under 1 year	8.4	8.1	9.8	7.0	4.9	4.9	4.7	5.7	4.3	4.3	4.8
1–14 years	9.8	8.6	10.5	8.2	7.0	6.0	5.3	5.2	5.1	4.8	5.0
1–4 years	11.5	10.0	11.5	9.2	7.2	6.3	5.2	5.3	5.0	5.0	5.1
5–14 years	8.8	7.9	10.2	7.9	6.9	5.9	5.4	5.2	5.1	4.8	5.0
15–24 years	34.4	38.0	47.2	44.8	35.7	34.1	29.5	29.2	27.9	26.9	28.0
25–34 years	24.6	24.3	30.9	29.1	23.0	23.6	19.8	19.1	18.9	18.4	18.8
35–44 years	20.3	19.3	24.9	20.9	17.2	16.9	15.4	15.6	15.2	15.6	15.5
45–64 years	25.2	23.0	26.5	18.0	15.4	15.7	14.2	14.4	14.7	14.7	14.6
45–54 years	22.2	21.4	25.5	18.6	15.2	15.6	13.9	14.1	14.3	14.4	14.3
55–64 years	29.0	25.1	27.9	17.4	15.6	15.9	14.6	15.0	15.3	15.1	15.1
65 years and over	43.1	34.7	36.2	22.5	21.7	23.1	22.7	23.0	23.6	23.7	23.4
65–74 years	39.1	31.4	32.8	19.2	17.9	18.6	17.6	18.3	18.2	18.5	18.4
75–84 years	52.7	41.8	43.5	28.1	27.4	29.1	28.6	28.3	29.0	28.9	28.7
85 years and over	45.1	37.9	34.2	27.6	26.5	31.2	31.4	30.1	32.7	31.5	31.4
Male											
All ages, age adjusted	36.4	34.5	41.1	34.3	27.3	26.3	22.7	22.3	21.7	21.6	21.9
All ages, crude	35.4	31.8	39.7	35.3	28.0	26.7	22.7	22.4	22.0	22.0	22.1
Under 1 year	9.1	8.6	9.3	7.3	5.0	5.0	4.9	5.7	4.3	4.6	4.8
1–14 years	12.3	10.7	13.0	10.0	8.5	7.0	6.2	5.9	5.7	5.6	5.7
1–4 years	13.0	11.5	12.9	10.2	8.3	6.9	5.6	5.7	5.3	5.4	5.5
5–14 years	11.9	10.4	13.1	9.9	8.6	7.0	6.4	6.0	5.8	5.7	5.8
15–24 years	56.7	61.2	73.2	68.4	52.7	49.5	41.4	40.7	38.1	37.3	38.7
25–34 years	40.8	40.1	49.4	46.3	35.9	35.7	29.1	27.5	27.5	27.0	27.4
35–44 years	32.5	29.9	37.7	31.7	25.2	24.7	21.9	21.8	21.2	21.7	21.6
45–64 years	37.7	33.3	38.9	26.5	22.0	21.9	19.7	19.8	20.0	20.4	20.1
45–54 years	33.6	31.6	37.2	27.6	21.9	22.0	19.6	19.6	19.9	20.3	20.0
55–64 years	43.1	35.6	40.9	25.4	22.1	21.7	19.8	20.1	20.2	20.5	20.3
65 years and over	66.6	52.1	54.4	33.9	30.4	32.1	30.8	31.4	31.9	32.1	31.8
65–74 years	59.1	45.8	47.3	27.3	23.0	24.2	22.3	23.9	23.6	23.5	23.7
75–84 years	85.0	66.0	68.2	44.3	41.3	41.2	39.7	38.7	39.7	39.7	39.4
85 years and over	78.1	62.7	63.1	56.1	55.3	64.5	61.9	59.0	60.4	61.2	60.3
Female											
All ages, age adjusted	10.7	11.0	14.4	11.8	10.5	10.7	10.0	10.2	10.2	9.9	10.1
All ages, crude	10.9	11.0	14.7	12.3	11.0	11.3	10.6	10.7	10.8	10.5	10.7
Under 1 year	7.6	7.5	10.4	6.7	4.7	4.9	4.4	5.8	4.4	4.0	4.7
1–14 years	7.2	6.3	7.9	6.3	5.4	4.9	4.5	4.4	4.4	4.0	4.3
1–4 years	10.0	8.4	10.0	8.1	6.0	5.6	4.8	4.8	4.7	4.6	4.7
5–14 years	5.7	5.4	7.2	5.7	5.1	4.7	4.3	4.2	4.3	3.8	4.1
15–24 years	12.6	15.1	21.6	20.8	18.2	17.9	17.1	17.1	17.1	16.1	16.7
25–34 years	9.3	9.2	13.0	12.2	10.1	11.5	10.4	10.7	10.4	9.9	10.3
35–44 years	8.5	9.1	12.9	10.4	9.4	9.2	9.0	9.4	9.2	9.7	9.4
45–64 years	12.6	13.1	15.3	10.3	9.5	10.1	9.1	9.4	9.6	9.3	9.5
45–54 years	10.9	11.6	14.5	10.2	9.0	9.6	8.5	8.8	8.9	8.8	8.8
55–64 years	14.9	15.2	16.2	10.5	9.9	10.8	9.9	10.3	10.8	10.1	10.4
65 years and over	21.9	20.3	23.1	15.0	15.8	17.2	17.2	17.2	17.8	17.8	17.6
65–74 years	20.6	19.0	21.6	13.0	14.0	14.1	13.8	13.9	13.8	14.5	14.1
75–84 years	25.2	23.0	27.2	18.5	19.2	21.9	21.5	21.5	22.0	21.8	21.8
85 years and over	22.1	22.0	18.0	15.2	15.0	18.3	19.6	18.6	21.5	19.2	19.8
White male											
All ages, age adjusted	35.9	34.0	40.1	34.8	27.6	26.3	22.6	22.2	21.6	21.5	21.8
All ages, crude	35.1	31.5	39.1	35.9	28.3	26.7	22.6	22.4	21.9	21.9	22.1
Under 1 year	9.1	8.8	9.1	7.0	4.6	4.8	4.3	5.2	3.7	4.6	4.5
1–14 years	12.4	10.6	12.5	9.8	8.3	6.6	5.9	5.7	5.4	5.1	5.4
15–24 years	58.3	62.7	75.2	73.8	56.5	52.5	43.2	42.2	39.8	39.4	40.5
25–34 years	39.1	38.6	47.0	46.6	35.8	35.4	28.8	27.0	26.8	26.3	26.7
35–44 years	30.9	28.4	35.2	30.7	24.3	23.7	21.1	21.4	20.7	21.2	21.1
45–64 years	36.2	31.7	36.5	25.2	20.8	20.6	18.9	19.2	19.2	19.6	19.3
65 years and over	67.1	52.1	54.2	32.7	29.9	31.4	30.2	31.1	31.8	31.9	31.6

TABLE 6.8

Death rates for motor vehicle–related injuries, by sex, race, Hispanic origin, and age, selected years, 1950–98

[CONTINUED]

(Data are based on the National Vital Statistics System)

Sex, race, Hispanic origin, and age	1950[1]	1960[1]	1970	1980	1985	1990	1995	1996	1997	1998	1996–98
Black male					Deaths per 100,000 resident population						
All ages, age adjusted	39.8	38.2	50.1	32.9	28.0	28.9	25.3	24.9	24.9	25.0	25.0
All ages, crude	37.2	33.1	44.3	31.1	27.1	28.1	24.6	24.3	24.2	24.5	24.3
Under 1 year	- - -	*	10.6	7.8	*	*	8.3	7.6	7.8	*	6.9
1–14 years	- - -	11.2	16.3	11.4	9.7	8.9	7.8	7.6	7.6	8.5	7.9
15–24 years	41.6	46.4	58.1	34.9	32.0	36.1	34.3	35.2	32.7	30.3	32.7
25–34 years	57.4	51.0	70.4	44.9	37.7	39.5	32.9	32.5	33.2	34.5	33.4
35–44 years	45.9	43.6	59.5	41.2	34.7	33.5	28.9	26.6	27.0	26.9	26.8
45–64 years	54.6	47.8	61.7	39.5	32.9	33.3	26.9	26.8	28.9	29.0	28.3
65 years and over	52.6	48.2	53.4	42.4	35.2	36.3	36.3	35.6	32.3	36.0	34.6
American Indian or Alaska Native male[3]											
All ages, age adjusted	- - -	- - -	- - -	77.4	52.3	49.0	45.4	45.4	43.3	41.0	43.2
All ages, crude	- - -	- - -	- - -	74.6	51.7	47.6	43.8	44.2	42.2	39.9	42.1
1–14 years	- - -	- - -	- - -	15.1	16.2	11.6	8.5	13.5	8.2	10.1	10.6
15–24 years	- - -	- - -	- - -	126.1	77.3	75.2	76.6	69.6	67.6	60.4	65.8
25–34 years	- - -	- - -	- - -	107.0	84.0	78.2	73.1	70.5	64.3	55.9	63.6
35–44 years	- - -	- - -	- - -	82.8	55.8	57.0	50.4	48.8	54.7	51.3	51.6
45–64 years	- - -	- - -	- - -	77.4	52.2	45.9	42.5	39.8	37.8	44.5	40.7
65 years and over	- - -	- - -	- - -	97.0	*	43.0	*	43.5	50.1	36.2	43.2
Asian or Pacific Islander male[4]											
All ages, age adjusted	- - -	- - -	- - -	17.1	16.2	15.8	13.6	11.9	11.7	10.9	11.5
All ages, crude	- - -	- - -	- - -	17.1	16.0	15.8	13.1	11.5	11.4	10.8	11.2
1–14 years	- - -	- - -	- - -	8.2	5.2	6.3	4.3	2.9	2.7	3.2	3.0
15–24 years	- - -	- - -	- - -	27.2	28.1	25.7	20.6	22.4	15.7	16.3	18.1
25–34 years	- - -	- - -	- - -	18.8	18.4	17.0	13.2	13.3	15.7	12.5	13.9
35–44 years	- - -	- - -	- - -	13.1	12.0	12.2	10.4	9.9	8.5	9.3	9.3
45–64 years	- - -	- - -	- - -	13.7	13.4	15.1	15.0	9.7	12.1	12.3	11.4
65 years and over	- - -	- - -	- - -	37.3	37.3	33.6	34.4	23.9	31.0	22.9	25.9
Hispanic male[5]											
All ages, age adjusted	- - -	- - -	- - -	- - -	25.3	29.1	24.5	23.2	21.4	21.7	22.1
All ages, crude	- - -	- - -	- - -	- - -	25.6	29.2	23.5	22.3	20.8	20.8	21.3
1–14 years	- - -	- - -	- - -	- - -	7.7	7.2	5.8	5.6	5.1	5.4	5.3
15–24 years	- - -	- - -	- - -	- - -	44.9	48.2	42.4	37.5	35.3	36.0	36.3
25–34 years	- - -	- - -	- - -	- - -	31.2	41.0	31.6	28.0	27.4	27.4	27.6
35–44 years	- - -	- - -	- - -	- - -	26.3	28.0	23.8	23.9	22.9	21.5	22.7
45–64 years	- - -	- - -	- - -	- - -	25.9	28.9	23.0	23.8	21.3	21.5	22.2
65 years and over	- - -	- - -	- - -	- - -	22.9	35.3	35.1	35.2	28.6	31.3	31.7
White, non-Hispanic male[5]											
All ages, age adjusted	- - -	- - -	- - -	- - -	25.3	25.7	21.9	21.7	21.3	21.2	21.4
All ages, crude	- - -	- - -	- - -	- - -	25.9	26.0	22.0	21.9	21.7	21.7	21.8
1–14 years	- - -	- - -	- - -	- - -	7.8	6.4	5.8	5.5	5.4	5.0	5.3
15–24 years	- - -	- - -	- - -	- - -	53.3	52.3	42.3	42.0	40.1	39.4	40.5
25–34 years	- - -	- - -	- - -	- - -	33.2	34.0	27.5	26.1	26.2	25.5	25.9
35–44 years	- - -	- - -	- - -	- - -	21.6	23.1	20.3	20.5	20.0	20.8	20.4
45–64 years	- - -	- - -	- - -	- - -	18.0	19.8	18.2	18.4	18.8	19.2	18.8
65 years and over	- - -	- - -	- - -	- - -	27.6	31.1	29.6	30.5	31.7	31.8	31.3
White female											
All ages, age adjusted	10.6	11.1	14.4	12.3	10.8	11.0	10.3	10.4	10.3	10.0	10.3
All ages, crude	10.9	11.2	14.8	12.8	11.4	11.6	10.8	11.0	10.9	10.7	10.9
Under 1 year	7.8	7.5	10.2	7.1	3.9	4.7	4.5	5.7	4.3	3.3	4.4
1–14 years	7.2	6.2	7.5	6.2	5.4	4.8	4.3	4.3	4.1	3.9	4.1
15–24 years	12.6	15.6	22.7	23.0	20.0	19.5	18.4	18.1	18.4	17.3	18.0
25–34 years	9.0	9.0	12.7	12.2	10.1	11.6	10.4	10.8	10.3	10.0	10.4
35–44 years	8.1	8.9	12.3	10.6	9.4	9.2	9.0	9.3	9.0	9.6	9.3
45–64 years	12.7	13.1	15.1	10.4	9.5	9.9	8.9	9.3	9.4	9.1	9.3
65 years and over	22.2	20.8	23.7	15.3	16.2	17.4	17.7	17.4	17.9	18.1	17.8

TABLE 6.8

Death rates for motor vehicle–related injuries, by sex, race, Hispanic origin, and age, selected years, 1950–98

[CONTINUED]

(Data are based on the National Vital Statistics System)

Sex, race, Hispanic origin, and age	1950[1]	1960[1]	1970	1980	1985	1990	1995	1996	1997	1998	1996–98
Black male				Deaths per 100,000 resident population							
All ages, age adjusted	10.3	10.0	13.8	8.4	8.2	9.3	8.9	9.4	9.8	9.2	9.5
All ages, crude	10.2	9.7	13.4	8.3	8.3	9.4	9.0	9.5	9.9	9.3	9.6
Under 1 year	- - -	8.1	11.9	*	8.1	7.0	*	7.8	*	9.4	7.6
1–14 years	- - -	6.9	10.2	6.3	5.1	5.3	5.1	4.8	5.6	4.8	5.1
15–24 years	11.5	9.9	13.4	8.0	9.1	9.9	10.7	13.3	11.3	10.3	11.6
25–34 years	10.7	9.8	13.3	10.6	9.3	11.1	10.5	10.9	11.2	8.9	10.4
35–44 years	11.1	11.0	16.1	8.3	9.1	9.4	9.8	9.6	10.2	11.1	10.3
45–64 years	11.8	12.7	16.7	9.2	9.0	10.7	9.4	8.9	11.0	10.6	10.2
65 years and over	14.3	13.2	15.7	9.5	11.2	13.5	11.5	13.1	14.2	13.8	13.7
American Indian or Alaska Native female[3]											
All ages, age adjusted	- - -	- - -	- - -	32.5	20.9	17.8	21.0	22.6	21.3	22.8	22.2
All ages, crude	- - -	- - -	- - -	32.0	20.6	17.3	20.4	21.8	20.9	22.3	21.7
1–14 years	- - -	- - -	- - -	15.0	9.2	8.1	9.1	9.7	10.0	9.4	9.7
15–24 years	- - -	- - -	- - -	42.3	29.5	31.4	32.7	27.1	24.5	30.4	27.4
25–34 years	- - -	- - -	- - -	52.5	30.2	18.8	36.7	31.9	27.6	33.4	31.0
35–44 years	- - -	- - -	- - -	38.1	27.0	18.2	19.4	23.0	21.5	21.7	22.1
45–64 years	- - -	- - -	- - -	32.6	19.5	17.6	17.1	27.1	22.5	24.1	24.5
65 years and over	- - -	- - -	- - -	*	*	*	*	*	35.7	27.7	28.3
Asian or Pacific Islander female[4]											
All ages, age adjusted	- - -	- - -	- - -	8.4	8.0	9.2	8.2	7.2	8.0	6.6	7.2
All ages, crude	- - -	- - -	- - -	8.2	7.9	9.0	8.0	7.4	8.0	6.6	7.3
1–14 years	- - -	- - -	- - -	7.4	5.0	3.6	3.0	2.3	3.2	2.4	2.6
15–24 years	- - -	- - -	- - -	7.4	7.4	11.4	12.4	8.3	11.5	9.4	9.8
25–34 years	- - -	- - -	- - -	7.3	8.4	7.3	5.1	5.6	6.1	6.1	5.9
35–44 years	- - -	- - -	- - -	8.6	7.0	7.5	6.2	7.5	6.9	4.6	6.3
45–64 years	- - -	- - -	- - -	8.5	8.6	11.8	10.8	8.9	8.6	7.5	8.3
65 years and over	- - -	- - -	- - -	18.6	20.5	24.3	19.7	21.3	20.7	16.7	19.5
Hispanic female[5]											
All ages, age adjusted	- - -	- - -	- - -	- - -	8.3	9.2	8.5	8.7	8.5	8.1	8.4
All ages, crude	- - -	- - -	- - -	- - -	7.9	8.9	8.3	8.5	8.3	7.8	8.2
1–14 years	- - -	- - -	- - -	- - -	4.8	4.8	4.4	4.7	3.9	3.8	4.1
15–24 years	- - -	- - -	- - -	- - -	10.1	11.6	12.8	11.8	13.1	11.4	12.1
25–34 years	- - -	- - -	- - -	- - -	7.5	9.4	7.7	9.0	8.3	8.5	8.6
35–44 years	- - -	- - -	- - -	- - -	8.8	8.0	8.1	7.7	8.1	7.4	7.7
45–64 years	- - -	- - -	- - -	- - -	9.4	11.4	9.2	9.7	9.0	9.6	9.4
65 years and over	- - -	- - -	- - -	- - -	14.8	14.9	13.9	13.9	14.1	11.2	13.0

costs and lost productivity. When pain, suffering, and lost quality of life are considered, the figure increases to $112 billion.

Many emergency room staff members report that a growing number of victims of gun-related injuries are incurring multiple wounds. As victims suffer greater damage, the cost of their medical care increases. The following are examples of the complications and costs of gun-related violence:

- A man sitting in his car in Washington, D.C., was shot 13 times. He spent eight months in the hospital and incurred medical costs for the hospital room, blood, intravenous drugs, surgical supplies, nursing care, X rays, lab tests, acute care, and an electric wheelchair that doctors predict he will need for the rest of his life. The cost of these items has been more than $500,000.

- In Newark, New Jersey, a 23-year-old bystander was shot seven times. The perforations from the bullets caused the contents of his bowels to leak into his lacerated vital organs, causing massive infection. His abdominal skin eroded so badly it had to be replaced with a sheet of plastic wrap. He spent 61 days in the hospital, endured 14 surgeries, and received a hospital bill for $270,000.

- A former crack dealer shot in the neck is paralyzed from the neck down. He requires a ventilator and experiences recurring lung and bladder infections. He has spent six years in hospitals, and his medical bills have already exceeded $1 million.

In 1996, Keith Ghezzi, an emergency room physician and former medical director at George Washington University Medical Center in Washington, D.C., reported that medical care for the typical gunshot patient admitted to the hospital cost $101,000, not including

TABLE 6.8

Death rates for motor vehicle–related injuries, by sex, race, Hispanic origin, and age, selected years, 1950–98

[CONTINUED]

(Data are based on the National Vital Statistics System)

Sex, race, Hispanic origin, and age	1950[1]	1960[1]	1970	1980	1985	1990	1995	1996	1997	1998	1996–98
White, non-Hispanic female[5]					Deaths per 100,000 resident population						
All ages, age adjusted	- - -	- - -	- - -	- - -	10.4	11.1	10.3	10.4	10.4	10.2	10.3
All ages, crude	- - -	- - -	- - -	- - -	10.9	11.7	10.9	11.0	11.1	11.0	11.1
1–14 years	- - -	- - -	- - -	- - -	4.9	4.7	4.2	4.2	4.1	3.8	4.0
15–24 years	- - -	- - -	- - -	- - -	20.2	20.4	19.0	18.8	19.2	18.3	18.7
25–34 years	- - -	- - -	- - -	- - -	9.8	11.7	10.6	10.8	10.4	10.1	10.4
35–44 years	- - -	- - -	- - -	- - -	8.6	9.3	8.9	9.3	9.0	9.8	9.3
45–64 years	- - -	- - -	- - -	- - -	8.6	9.7	8.7	9.0	9.4	9.0	9.1
65 years and over	- - -	- - -	- - -	- - -	15.3	17.5	17.7	17.4	18.0	18.4	17.9

- - - Data not available.

* Based on fewer than 20 deaths.

[1] Includes deaths of persons who were not residents of the 50 States and the District of Columbia.

[2] Average annual death rate.

[3] Interpretation of trends should take into account that population estimates for American Indians increased by 45 percent between 1980 and 1990, partly due to better enumeration techniques in the 1990 decennial census and to the increased tendency for people to identify themselves as American Indian in 1990.

[4] Interpretation of trends should take into account that the Asian population in the United States more than doubled between 1980 and 1990, primarily due to immigration.

[5] Excludes data from States lacking an Hispanic-origin item on their death certificates.

Note: Rates are age adjusted to the 1940 U.S. standard million population.

SOURCE: *Health, United States 2000*, National Center for Health Statistics, Hyattsville, MD, 200

physician fees. For those patients who suffer debilitating injuries as a result of gunfire, such as the loss of the use of arms and legs, the costs are much higher.

Kenneth Kizer et al., in "Hospitalization Charges, Costs, and Income for Firearm-Related Injuries at a University Trauma Center" (*The Journal of the American Medical Association,* Vol. 273, No. 22, 1995), revealed a new dimension to the costs by considering how much hospitals are actually reimbursed for those costs. For instance, one hospital studied recovered only 38 percent of the total hospital charges accrued. The hospital had a loss of $2.2 million due to uninsured gunshot victims. However, hospital fee structures are such that charges to insured patients generally cover losses from uninsured patients. The hospital covered its losses through charges to patients covered by Medicare, health maintenance organizations (HMOs), and other insurance plans. The researchers concluded that private health insurance pays for the majority of the treatment for firearm-related injuries even though it may pay only about one-fourth of the actual injuries. As a result, taxpayers and insurance holders pay the costs of firearm violence.

A STUDY OF SELF-DEFENSE CASES

The National Rifle Association (NRA) and Doctors for Integrity in Policy Research, a gun rights group chaired by Dr. Edgar A. Suter, have challenged many of the studies conducted or funded by the CDC. Gun rights advocacy groups generally believe that gun-related deaths and injuries can be reduced in the same way that automobile-related deaths and injuries have been reduced:

through the education of owners, the enforcement of laws, and engineering to increase safety. NRA officials believe that the studies purposely ignore the times a gun may be used to prevent violence.

Gary Kleck, a Florida State University criminologist and researcher, found between 1,527 and 2,819 self-defense homicides yearly. Based on Kleck's research, Larry Pratt, executive director of Gun Owners of America ("Health Care and Firearms," *Journal of the Medical Association of Georgia,* March 1994), concluded that firearms preserved lives and thus saved injury costs. Kleck also concluded that people defend themselves with firearms as often as 2.4 million times a year. Since firearms are used in about 32,000 deaths (murders, suicides, and accidents) every year, the defensive use of firearms might save as many as 75 lives for every life lost to gun-related crime.

Based on an estimated 162,000 gun deaths and injuries annually, Pratt concluded that the use of guns in self-defense saves lives and prevents 15 times more injuries than they cause. According to the FBI, 32 percent of attempted rapes were completed in 1992; however, only 3 percent of attempted rapes were successful when women were armed with knives or guns. Not only did firearms cut the costs of injuries, but they also reduced the crime rate.

In "What Are the Risks and Benefits of Keeping a Gun in the Home?" (*Journal of the American Medical Association,* Vol. 280, No. 5, 1998) Gary Kleck claims that the large number of defensive gun uses (DGUs) has been confirmed in at least 16 surveys. Evidence from the surveys suggested that DGUs are effective in preventing injuries and that the number of defensive uses in the home is about six times higher than the number of criminal/aggressive uses in the same setting.

SAFE STORAGE OF GUNS IN THE HOME

According to the *1999 National Report Series: Kids and Guns* (U.S. Department of Justice, Office of Juvenile Justice and Delinquency Prevention, *Juvenile Justice Bulletin,* March 2000) the number of juveniles killed with firearms increased by 65 percent from 1987 to a peak in 1993, then decreased from 1993 to 1997, although still 20 percent above the level in 1987. According to the report, all of the increase from 1987 to 1993 was firearm-related, as was the subsequent decrease from 1993 to 1997.

Several states have laws making gun owners criminally liable if someone is injured as a result of a child (usually defined as under 15 years of age) gaining unsupervised access to a gun. In "State Gun Safe Storage Laws and Child Mortality Due to Firearms" (*Journal of the American Medical Association,* Vol. 278, No. 13, 1997) Dr. Peter Cummings et al. reported on a study of firearm mortality from 1979 through 1994. The study was designed to discover whether laws making gun owners responsible for storing firearms so that they are inaccessible to children significantly reduced deaths of children under 15 years.

In 12 states with safe-storage laws that had been in effect for at least one year from 1990 through 1994, unintentional shooting deaths were reduced by an average of 23 percent during the years covered by the laws. Gun-related homicides and suicides showed small declines, but these were not statistically significant. The study also showed that safe-storage laws are most effective when the penalty for unsafe storage is a felony rather than a misdemeanor.

AVAILABILITY OF GUNS

Most studies on the reduction of injuries and deaths from firearms focus on the availability of guns, especially handguns and, more recently, assault guns. Many researchers believe that making guns more difficult to get would reduce injuries. On the other hand, many gun owners believe many crimes and injuries are prevented by using a gun for self-defense.

A NATIONAL GOAL

A growing number of public and health policy professionals are trying to reduce both deliberate and unintentional firearm injuries and fatalities. *Healthy People 2000,* the U.S. Public Health Service's health prevention goals for 2000, covered all aspects of life, including several that dealt with firearm-related injuries and deaths:

- Reduce suicides to no more than 10.5 per 100,000 people—Mental disorders, stress reactions, and alcohol and drug abuse are often involved in both attempted and completed suicides. Antisocial personality disorder is also frequently associated with suicidal behavior, especially for young males. Gunshot injuries cause a majority of suicide deaths, and much of the increase in suicide rates since the 1950s corresponds to the rise in firearm-related deaths. However, while most successful suicides involve a firearm, most attempted suicides are caused by taking pills and by inflicting minor lacerations (cuts).

- Reduce weapons-related violent deaths to no more than 12.6 per 100,000 people—The violent and accidental use of firearms is the second most important contributor, after motor vehicles, to injury deaths. Suicides and homicides account for more than 90 percent of all firearm-related deaths and more than 95 percent of knife-related deaths. Of the approximately 21,000 homicides that occur in the United States annually, over 60 percent involve firearms and about 20 percent involve knives. In 1994 firearms caused 38,505 deaths: 49 percent from suicides, 46 percent from homicide, and 4 percent from unintentionally inflicted injuries.

- Reduce by 20 percent the incidence of weapon-carrying by adolescents 14–17 years old—Many experts consider the immediate availability of firearms and other lethal weapons to be the factor most likely to turn a violent disagreement or conflict into a lethal one. Regardless of their views on gun control, few people would argue that adolescents should have ready access to loaded firearms or other lethal weapons at school or on the streets; nonetheless, many adolescents do.

- Reduce by 20 percent the proportion of people who possess weapons that are inappropriately stored and, therefore, dangerously available—Many homicides and suicides are committed on impulse, and a substantial portion of these deaths might have been prevented if lethal weapons had not been immediately available and if guns and ammunition had been properly stored. The impulsive nature of most homicides is reflected in the fact that half of the 20,000 or so homicide victims in the United States each year were killed by persons they knew.

- Reduce immediate access to firearms—The U.S. Public Health Service points out that environmental and behavioral measures that might be effective in reducing the immediate access to loaded firearms are often lost in the controversy over gun control. "Immediate access" is defined as the ability to retrieve a loaded firearm within 10 minutes. Preventive measures could reduce the possibility of immediate access to loaded weapons if fewer people purchased them, if weapons and ammunition were stored in separate locations, or if all parents kept guns and ammunition locked away from children. While parents would have access to weapons and ammunition, their children would not.

- Enact in all 50 states laws requiring that new handguns be designed to minimize the likelihood of discharge by children—While the death rate for children is generally lower than that of young and middle-aged adults, the greatest opportunities to prevent firearm-related deaths probably are among children. Newly manufactured handguns could be modified so that children cannot discharge them. This change in design could reduce both the intentional and unintentional discharges of handguns associated with firearm injuries in children.

CHAPTER 7
GUNS AND YOUTH

Twenty-five or 30 years ago, when teenage boys got into a fight or started feuding, it usually meant a fistfight. Unfortunately, in more and more neighborhoods throughout the country, it can now mean a shoot-out. An increasing number of young people are growing up in neighborhoods with high levels of violence. In 1996 the Children's Defense Fund reported that gunfire was the second leading cause of death among American children between the ages of 10 and 19. (Accidents involving automobiles are the leading cause of children's deaths.)

In 1997 the Centers for Disease Control and Prevention (CDC) reported that American children were 12 times more likely to fall victim to gun-related death than children in the rest of the industrialized world, including Israel and Northern Ireland, two nations noted for internal strife. The death rate involving firearms was 1.66 per 100,000 children in the United States, compared with 0.14 per 100,000 in other countries. (See Table 7.1.) The CDC report also noted that homicide is the fourth leading cause of death among children under age four and the third leading cause of death among 5- to 14-year-olds. (Not all homicides involve firearms.)

MURDERS

In 1998, 12,132 firearms homicides occurred, down from 13,844 the year before and from a high of 19,157 in 1993. (See Table 7.2.) The largest number of gun homicides by age were committed by persons ages 18–24 (5,376), but only by a narrow margin over homicides committed by persons 25 years of age or older (5,269).

TABLE 7.1

Rates of homicide, suicide, and firearm-related death among children 0–14 years old: United States and 25 other industrialized countries*

Age group (yrs)	Total homicide	Total suicide	Firearm-related deaths				
			Homicide	Suicide	Unintentional	Intention undetermined	Total
0–4							
U.S.	4.10	0	0.43	0	0.15	0.01	0.59
Non-U.S.	0.95	0	0.05	0	0.01	0.01	0.07
Ratio U.S.:Non-U.S.	4.3:1		8.6:1		15.0:1	1.0:1	8.4:1
5–14							
U.S.	1.75	0.84	1.22	0.49	0.46	0.06	2.23
Non-U.S.	0.30	0.40	0.07	0.05	0.05	0.01	0.18
Ratio U.S.:Non-U.S.	5.8:1	2.1:1	17.4:1	9.8:1	9.2:1	6.0:1	12.4:1
0–14							
U.S.	2.57	0.55	0.94	0.32	0.36	0.04	1.66
Non-U.S.	0.51	0.27	0.06	0.03	0.04	0.01	0.14
Ratio U.S.:Non-U.S.	5.0:1	2.0:1	15.7:1	10.7:1	9.0:1	4.0:1	11.9:1

* All countries classified in the high-income group with populations ≥1 million that provided complete data (Australia, Austria, Belgium, Canada, Denmark, England and Wales, Finland, France, Germany, Hong Kong, Ireland, Israel, Italy, Japan, Kuwait, Netherlands, New Zealand, Northern Ireland, Norway, Scotland, Singapore, Sweden, Spain, Switzerland, and Taiwan). In this analysis, Hong Kong, Northern Ireland, and Taiwan are considered as countries.

SOURCE: "Rates of Homicide, Suicide, and Firearms-Related Death Among Children—26 Industrialized Countries," *Morbidity and Mortality Weekly Report*, vol. 46, no. 5, February 7, 1997, Centers for Disease Control and Prevention, Atlanta, GA, 1997

Teens ages 14–17 committed 1,433 murders with guns, down from 1,985 in 1997, and 54 were perpetrated by children under age 14, up slightly from 44 the year before. All numbers have declined significantly since 1993–94. (See Figure 7.1.)

Crime in the United States, 2000 (Federal Bureau of Investigation, Washington, D.C., 2000), compiles crime statistics provided by state and local law enforcement agencies. The FBI found that in 1999, of the 12,658 total murder victims, almost two-thirds (8,259) were killed with a firearm. About 11 percent of all murder victims were under 18 years of age. Over 80 percent of all murder victims ages 13–19 were killed with guns. (See Table 7.3.) In 1998, 1,733 teens were fatally shot, down slightly from the 1,802 teens fatally shot in 1997, and down significantly from 4,173 in 1990 and 2,577 in 1995.

Murder Rates by Age, Gender, and Race

With the exception of both white and black female offenders ages 18–24, all 1997 homicide rates for young people decreased significantly from the highest rates in 1993. Figure 7.2 (*Homicide Trends in the U.S.*, Bureau of Justice Statistics, Washington, D.C., December 1998) shows homicide offending rates by age, gender, and race.

Of note from 1976 to 1998:

- Rates for adults 25 and over declined for all racial and gender groups.

- Young adults 18–24 had the highest rate of homicide offenders.

- Homicide offending rates for white males 18–24 did not decline as much as those for young black males and white males ages 14–17.

- Black females teens followed a pattern similar to those of black male teens and white male teens.

Homicide victimization rates also decreased from 1976 to 1998, most significantly for black males and females ages 18–24. The victimization rate for black males of that age dropped most precipitously, while the drop for black males ages 14–17 also saw a dramatic decline. (See Figure 7.3.)

Young males, especially young black males, are disproportionately involved in homicides compared with their proportion of the population. The proportion of young black males has remained at about 1 percent of the population since 1976, while the proportions of homicide victims and offenders who were young black males increased dramatically until 1994. Black males ages 14–24 represented 17.3 percent of all homicide offenders in 1976, compared with one-third (32.8 percent) of the total in 1994. Young black males made up 9.2 percent of all homicide victims in 1976 and 17.5 percent in 1994.

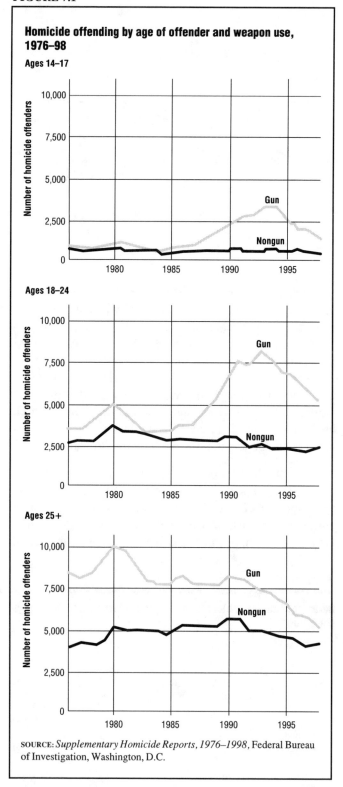

FIGURE 7.1

Homicide offending by age of offender and weapon use, 1976–98

SOURCE: *Supplementary Homicide Reports, 1976–1998*, Federal Bureau of Investigation, Washington, D.C.

Since 1994, the proportions of both homicide offenders and victims began to decline for young black males. (See Figure 7.4.)

The proportion of the population represented by white males 18–24 years of age has declined since 1976, while the proportions of homicide victims and offenders of that same group has risen. White males ages 14–24 rep-

TABLE 7.2

Homicides by weapon type and age of offender

Year	Under 14 Gun	Under 14 Nongun	14-17 Gun	14-17 Nongun	18-24 Gun	18-24 Nongun	25+ Gun	25+ Nongun
1976	53	50	965	809	3,586	2,658	8,413	3,817
1977	49	51	991	669	3,489	2,776	8,144	4,219
1978	77	43	885	760	3,931	2,699	8,513	4,075
1979	49	49	1,032	862	4,506	3,072	9,232	4,383
1980	59	53	1,185	898	5,085	3,620	10,131	5,169
1981	45	32	1,034	759	4,321	3,353	9,911	5,020
1982	42	56	863	753	3,820	3,359	8,927	5,061
1983	35	43	746	690	3,363	3,149	8,051	4,930
1984	35	37	711	555	3,335	2,933	7,805	4,925
1985	54	39	855	581	3,374	2,788	7,864	4,816
1986	60	34	1,004	713	3,752	2,882	8,376	5,357
1987	53	58	1,118	675	3,846	2,850	7,802	5,301
1988	54	47	1,507	733	4,477	2,849	7,858	5,308
1989	86	43	1,963	631	5,309	2,745	7,658	5,269
1990	58	45	2,325	817	6,181	3,007	8,397	5,634
1991	95	37	2,737	839	7,676	3,058	8,165	5,662
1992	91	49	2,869	727	7,492	2,472	7,792	5,056
1993	115	43	3,371	801	8,171	2,627	7,500	5,009
1994	131	49	3,337	778	7,824	2,403	7,147	4,820
1995	98	40	2,692	741	7,049	2,269	6,657	4,643
1996	60	37	2,135	779	6,656	2,273	5,998	4,475
1997	44	48	1,985	563	6,048	2,127	5,767	4,020
1998	54	44	1,433	571	5,376	2,310	5,269	4,196

SOURCE: *Supplementary Homicide Reports, 1976–1998,* Federal Bureau of Investigation, Washington, D.C.

TABLE 7.3

Murder victims by age: types of weapons used, 1999

Age	Total	Firearms	Knives or cutting instruments	Blunt objects (clubs, hammers, etc.)	Personal weapons (hands, fists, feet, etc.)[1]	Poison	Explosives	Fire	Narcotics	Strangulation	Asphyxiation	Other weapon or weapon not stated[2]
Total	12,658	8,259	1,667	736	855	11	–	125	23	190	103	689
Percent distribution[3]	100.0	65.2	13.2	5.8	6.8	.1	–	1.0	.2	1.5	.8	5.4
Under 18[4]	1,449	748	102	72	260	7	–	42	4	27	44	143
Under 22[4]	3,322	2,289	265	120	300	7	–	50	4	44	48	195
18 and over[4]	10,997	7,434	1,546	643	568	4	–	83	18	162	57	482
Infant (under 1)	205	4	6	10	105	–	–	2	2	2	27	47
1 to 4	280	39	10	33	123	2	–	13	–	4	12	44
5 to 8	95	35	6	6	9	3	–	15	1	6	2	12
9 to 12	79	34	8	7	8	2	–	8	–	5	1	6
13 to 16	447	355	38	11	14	–	–	3	1	4	1	20
17 to 19	1,286	1,068	108	29	19	–	–	5	–	13	2	42
20 to 24	2,258	1,812	234	59	49	–	–	8	1	21	4	70
25 to 29	1,793	1,384	193	55	56	–	–	7	3	16	12	67
30 to 34	1,385	937	212	55	73	2	–	13	1	23	10	59
35 to 39	1,289	793	228	92	77	–	–	10	3	25	5	56
40 to 44	1,064	596	200	97	89	1	–	7	–	24	4	46
45 to 49	706	413	124	53	49	–	–	9	3	10	6	39
50 to 54	456	244	77	42	37	–	–	10	2	10	2	32
55 to 59	291	139	63	36	23	–	–	2	1	7	3	17
60 to 64	208	107	36	23	15	1	–	7	–	4	1	14
65 to 69	181	80	33	27	21	–	–	1	1	4	–	14
70 to 74	142	54	27	26	14	–	–	1	–	3	3	14
75 and over	281	88	45	54	47	–	–	4	3	8	6	26
Unknown	212	77	19	21	27	–	–	–	1	1	2	64

[1] Pushing is included in personal weapons.
[2] Includes drowning.
[3] Because of rounding, the percentages may not add to total.
[4] Does not include unknown ages.

SOURCE: *Crime in the United States, 1999,* Federal Bureau of Investigation, Washington, D.C., 2000

FIGURE 7.2

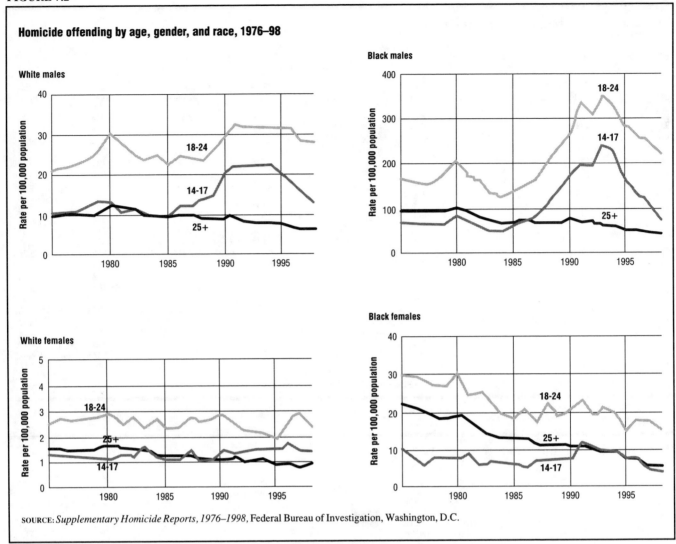

Homicide offending by age, gender, and race, 1976–98

SOURCE: *Supplementary Homicide Reports, 1976–1998,* Federal Bureau of Investigation, Washington, D.C.

resented 8.7 percent of homicide victims in 1976, compared with 10.1 percent in 1997. (See Figure 7.4.)

Gun Injuries from Crime

Not only were black males most susceptible to homicides involving guns, they were at greatest risk of being injured by firearms during the commission of a crime. Between 1993 and 1997 almost half (49 percent) of the victims of nonfatal, crime-related gunshot wounds who were treated in hospitals were black (Table 7.4), while black females made up about 5 percent. Slightly more than one-half of gun injury victims were between 15 and 24 years old. Among that age group, the primary circumstances for nonfatal firearm-related injuries were assaults, about 51 percent.

CARRYING WEAPONS

The Office of Juvenile Justice and Delinquency Programs, an agency of the Department of Justice, reviewed national surveys and studies to provide a comprehensive report on juvenile crime in *Juvenile Offenders and Victims: 1997 Update on Violence* (Washington, D.C., August 1997). The report concluded that the rise in the number of deaths of young people is connected to the increasing number of young people carrying weapons. From 1983 to 1995, the proportion of homicides in which a juvenile used a gun increased from 55 percent to 80 percent. Figure 7.5 shows the rapid rise in juvenile gun homicides since 1987.

Several studies have shown that virtually all the increases in homicides by juveniles were due to crimes committed with handguns, not a change in the nature of teenagers. Many observers attribute the increase to the growth of the crack cocaine market, easy access to guns, and the prevalence of gangs, primarily in poor inner-city neighborhoods. In the early 1990s, hundreds of thousands of unskilled, unemployed young men entered the crack business as sellers, using handguns as protection in an unstable business market.

The end of the 1990s and beginning of 2000 saw a booming economy which provided legitimate jobs to

FIGURE 7.3

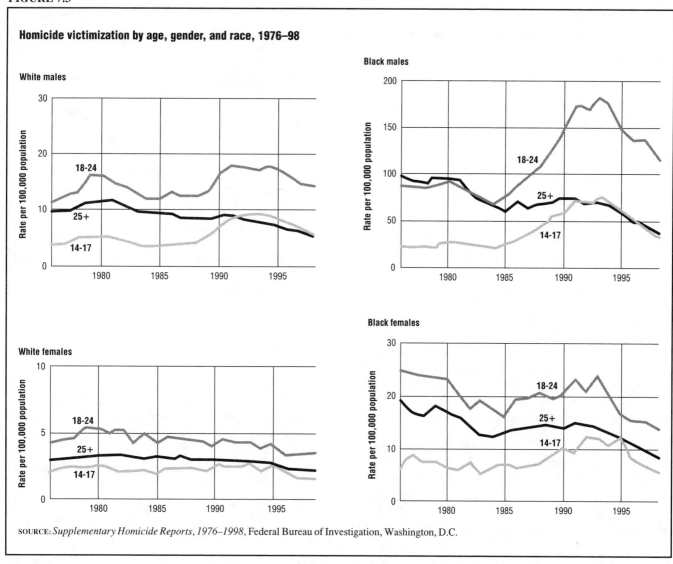

Homicide victimization by age, gender, and race, 1976–98

SOURCE: *Supplementary Homicide Reports, 1976–1998,* Federal Bureau of Investigation, Washington, D.C.

some urban youth who had worked in the drug trade. In addition, there has been a change in attitude toward the use of crack and a resulting decline in the market for it. These factors, plus aggressive programs by the police to take guns away from juveniles, have contributed to the decrease in violent crimes. Though many experts in juvenile crime are optimistic about this decrease, Professor James Alan Fox, dean of the College of Criminal Justice at Northeastern University, warns that the worst may not be over because contributing factors such as easy gun access, media violence, and lack of parental supervision persist.

Juvenile Violence in Boston

Boston, Massachusetts, like other major cities in the United States, has struggled with the problem of youth violence in some of its poor, inner-city neighborhoods. During the first half of the 1990s, the city experienced 155 youth homicides by gun and knife, most of which were gun victimizations of young black men. Gun violence started when the youths started selling crack

cocaine in the 1980s. They began carrying guns as protection and as a part of the dynamics of gang activity.

In an effort to contain gun violence in Boston, the National Institute of Justice launched a problem-solving initiative to create and implement strategic interventions to disrupt the illegal firearms markets and deter serious youth violence. Working together with many groups, including gang outreach and mediation specialists (known as "street workers"), the intervention team first analyzed the supply and demand for guns. Gun traces pointed to the existence of a flow of new guns diverted into the illicit market at points very close to first retail sale. This showed that the majority of guns were not stolen but rather obtained illegally from gun traffickers or straw purchasers (legal buyers who then sell to those who cannot pass background checks) who purchase several guns at a time to sell.

Looking at the demand side, the team found that both homicide victims and offenders were often participants in criminally active neighborhood gangs. Most youths were

FIGURE 7.4

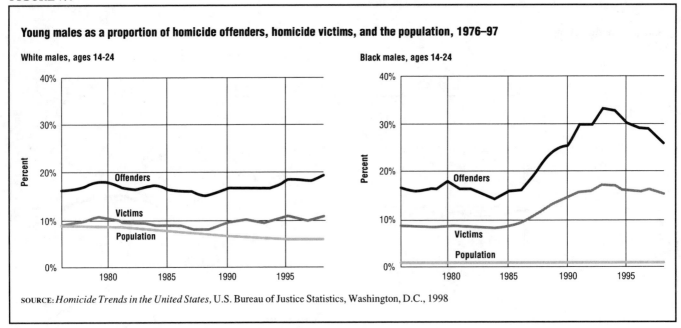

Young males as a proportion of homicide offenders, homicide victims, and the population, 1976–97

White males, ages 14-24

Black males, ages 14-24

SOURCE: *Homicide Trends in the United States,* U.S. Bureau of Justice Statistics, Washington, D.C., 1998

well known to the criminal justice system, having previous arraignments or arrests. Fifty-five percent had been on probation; in fact, 25 percent of the offenders were on probation at the time they committed murder.

The team then crafted intervention strategies to curtail serious youth violence. For instance, in one particularly tough neighborhood, the street workers told the gang members to stop the shootings and relinquish their guns or they would face severe restrictions. They were told that drug markets would shut down, warrants would be served, the streets would swarm with law enforcement officers, bed checks would be performed on probationers, rooms would be searched by parole officers, unregistered cars would be taken away, and disorder offenses such as drinking in public would be pursued.

When the threats were actually carried out, stunned gang members soon turned over their handguns, and the neighborhood became quiet. The intervention team let it be known that shooting people, terrorizing their neighborhoods, and possessing or selling guns would not be tolerated. In addition, gun suppliers discovered that the Bureau of Alcohol, Tobacco, and Firearms (ATF) was tracing recovered firearms, getting information from arrestees, and following up on the results.

Consequently, youth violence in Boston has been substantially reduced. The credit goes to Boston's combination of social outreach and youth programs—and very tough law enforcement.

Tracing Juvenile Crime Guns

The Youth Crime Gun Interdiction Initiative, developed by ATF, is a project designed to reduce youth firearms violence. Guns recovered from crimes, mostly from firearms offenses, are analyzed and traced to their original sources. According to findings reported in *Crime Gun Trace Reports (1999) National Report* (Department of the Treasury, Bureau of Alcohol, Tobacco and Firearms, Washington, D.C., November 2000), there were a total of 64,637 crime gun trace reports from 32 participating cities across the United States. Of the approximately 40,730 gun trace requests for which the possessor's age could be verified, 56.7 percent were 25 or older, 34 percent were 18–24, and 9.3 percent were 17 or younger.

According to the report, the age distribution of crime gun possessors varied considerably from city to city. For example, adults comprised 82 percent of gun possessors in San Jose, California, while in Cleveland, Ohio, and Phoenix, Arizona, the figure was 70 percent. Persons between 18 and 24 comprised 48 percent of gun possessors in Washington, D.C., and Charlotte–Mecklenburg, North Carolina, and 46 percent in Boston.

As to the type of guns recovered, semiautomatic pistols were most prevalent among possessors in the 18–24 age group (60 percent), closely followed by gun possessors 17 and under (57 percent). Of adults 24 and older, semiautomatic pistols accounted for 47 percent of guns recovered. Adults were more than twice as likely to possess long guns (24 percent) than were those 17 and under (13 percent). Once again, there were some significant differences from city to city. For example:

• In Atlanta, Georgia, 97 percent of traced firearms were handguns. Semiautomatic pistols accounted for 79 percent of guns recovered from possessors 18–24; 72 percent in the 17-and-under age group; and 69 percent among adults.

TABLE 7.4

Who are the victims of crime-related gunshot wounds?

| | Firearm homicides, 1993-97 | | |
	Vital statistics*	FBI's Supplementary Homicide Reports	Nonfatal firearm injury from assault
Race and gender			
White male	36 %	34 %	33 %**
White female	9	9	5 **
Black male	46	47	49
Black female	6	7	6
Other	3	2	4
Age			
0-14	3 %	2 %	3 %
15-19	17	17	26
20-24	22	22	25
25-34	29	29	26
35-44	17	16	12
45 and older	13	13	7
Unknown	0	1	0

* Includes legal intervention homicides.
** For comparison, Hispanics who were included in the other racial category in the original data were included in the white racial category. Hispanic origin is not sufficiently reported in the Supplementary Homicide Reports to allow comparison.

SOURCE: Marianne W. Zawitz and Kevin J. Strom, *Firearm Injury and Death from Crime, 1993–97*, U.S. Bureau of Justice Statistics, Washington, D.C., 2000

- Revolvers were the most frequently recovered firearms among gun possessors 17 and under in Houston, Texas (40 percent) and in Tampa, Florida (47 percent).

- Long guns were the weapon of choice among gun possessors 24 and under in San Jose, California; Houston, Texas; and San Antonio, Texas.

Many recovered firearms move rapidly from first retail sales at federally licensed gun dealers to a black market that supplies juveniles with guns. When crime guns are recovered within three years from the time of sale, they can be more easily traced to their illegal sources than older guns, which are more likely to have passed through numerous hands before entering the illegal market. According to the ATF, these "new" crime guns made up nearly one-third of all firearms recovered in 1999.

GUNS IN THE CLASSROOM

According to the 1997–98 Parents' Resource Institute for Drug Education (PRIDE) Survey (PRIDE, Inc., Atlanta, GA, 1998), close to a million students—some as young as 10—carried a gun to school during the 1997–98 school year. Almost half of them (45 percent) claimed they carried a gun to school on six or more occasions. The percentage of students who say they carried guns to school has actually fallen 37 percent, from 6.0 percent of students in grades 6–12 in 1993–94 to 3.8 percent in 1997–98.

FIGURE 7.5

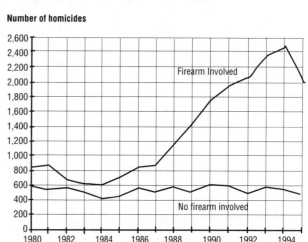

Gun-related homicides by juveniles, 1980–95

- From 1983 through 1995, the proportion of homicides in which a juvenile used a gun increased from 55 to 80 percent.

SOURCE: H. N. Snyder and T. A. Finnegan, *Easy Access to the FBI's Supplementary Homicide Reports: 1980–1995*, Office of Juvenile Justice and Delinquency Prevention, U.S. Department of Justice, Washington, D.C., 1997

FIGURE 7.6

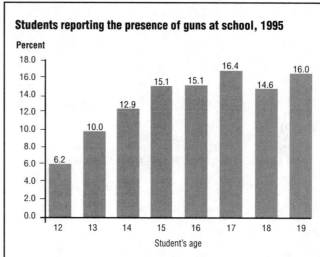

Students reporting the presence of guns at school, 1995

SOURCE: K. A. Chandler, C. D. Chapman, M. R. Rand, and B. M. Taylor, *Students' Reports of School Crime: 1989 and 1995*, U.S. Departments of Education and Justice, Washington, D.C., 1998

Of the total number of students interviewed, 79 percent were white, 10 percent black, 6 percent Hispanic, 3 percent Asian, 1 percent Native American, and 2 percent other. Of the students who said they carried a gun to school, 59 percent were white, 18 percent black, 12 percent Hispanic, 3 percent Asian, and 3 percent Native American.

Students who carried guns to school are more likely to use illegal drugs. Nearly two-thirds (64 percent) said they used drugs, such as marijuana, cocaine, heroin, and

TABLE 7.5

Percentage of high school students who carried weapons or were threatened or injured with a weapon in school in 1997

	Percent reporting they carried a weapon on school property in the past 30 days			Percent reporting they were threatened or injured with a weapon on school property in the past year		
Reporting States	Total	Male	Female	Total	Male	Female
U.S. total*	9%	13%	4%	7%	10%	4%
Alabama	11	17	5	8	10	5
Arkansas	12	18	6	8	11	6
Californiaᵃ	**7**	**12**	**3**	**7**	**11**	**4**
Los Angeles	6	9	3	9	13	5
Colorado	**11**	**19**	**4**	**9**	**11**	**6**
Connecticut	7	10	3	6	8	5
Delaware	**9**	**13**	**4**	**8**	**9**	**6**
Dist. of Columbia	17	19	13	13	18	9
Florida	**8**	**12**	**3**	**8**	**10**	**6**
Hawaii	6	9	3	6	8	5
Iowa	9	14	3	7	10	4
Kentucky	15	27	4	7	10	4
Louisiana	7	11	4	8	9	5
Maine	11	19	3	8	9	5
Massachusetts	8	12	4	8	10	4
Michigan	8	13	4	9	13	5
Mississippi	10	15	5	9	13	6
Missouri	10	16	3	8	11	4
Montana	12	19	5	7	9	6
Nevada	10	15	5	9	11	6
New Hampshire	**7**	**13**	**2**	**7**	**10**	**4**
New Jersey	**8**	**13**	**3**	**7**	**9**	**5**
New York	9	14	4	7	10	4
North Carolina	**8**	**13**	**3**	**8**	**10**	**6**
North Dakota	8	15	2	6	8	4
Ohio	8	13	3	7	9	5
Rhode Island	8	11	4	8	11	6
South Carolina	10	14	5	9	11	7
South Dakota	9	15	2	5	8	3
Tennessee	**11**	**19**	**4**	**7**	**8**	**6**
Utah	11	18	3	8	11	4
Vermont	12	19	5	7	10	4
West Virginia	11	19	3	8	10	6
Wisconsin	5	8	3	8	9	6
Wyoming	13	22	4	7	11	4

	Percent who had carried a weapon on school property in the past 30 days			Percent threatened or injured with a weapon at school in the past year		
	Total	Male	Female	Total	Male	Female
Total	9%	13%	4%	7%	10%	4%
9th grade	10	15	5	10	14	6
10th grade	8	11	4	8	10	5
11th grade	9	15	3	6	9	2
12th grade	7	10	3	6	8	3
White	8	12	2	6	8	4
Black	9	11	8	10	14	6
Hispanic	10	16	4	9	13	5

*U.S. total is based on a national sample.

ᵃData do not include students from the Los Angeles Unified School District.

Note: **Bold** indicates data are unweighted because the overall response rate was less than 60%. Thus, data apply only to respondents.

SOURCE: *Juvenile Offenders and Victims: 1999 National Report,* Office of Juvenile Justice and Delinquency Prevention, Washington, D.C., 2000

TABLE 7.6

Firearm possession among high school males, 1996

Type of firearm	Percentage of respondents (N=730)
Any type of gun	29
Regular rifle	19
Automatic or semiautomatic rifle	8
Regular shotgun	18
Sawed-off shotgun	2
Revolver	7
Automatic or semiautomatic handgun	4
3 or more types of guns	8

Note: Timeframe is past 12 months. Multiple responses permitted.

SOURCE: *High School Youths, Weapons, and Violence: A National Survey,* National Institute of Justice, Washington, D.C., 1998

TABLE 7.7

Youths carrying firearms, 1996

Setting, frequency, and type of firearm	Percentage of respondents	(N)
Carried gun outside home within past 12 months		(731)
Never	94	
Only now and then	4	
Most or all of the time	2	
Carrying vs. keeping guns in a car (for those who reported carrying a gun)		(39)
More likely to carry gun	41	
More likely to keep gun in car	59	
Most common type of firearm carried (for those who reported carrying a gun)		(30)
Regular rifle	3	
Automatic or semiautomatic rifle	3	
Regular shotgun	7	
Sawed-off shotgun	7	
Revolver	30	
Automatic or semiautomatic handgun	50	

SOURCE: *High School Youths, Weapons, and Violence: A National Survey,* National Institute of Justice, Washington, D.C., 1998

hallucinogens, compared with 15 percent of students who did not carry guns. Almost a third (30 percent) reported using cocaine at least once a month, 32 percent used stimulants such as crystal methamphetamine monthly, and 31 percent used hallucinogens monthly. These rates compare to 1.3 percent monthly cocaine use by students who did not carry guns to school, 3 percent use of stimulants, and 1.8 percent use of hallucinogens.

The PRIDE survey also found that involvement in school activities and after-school programs can help prevent violence. Students who said they did not carry guns to school were 53 percent more likely to be involved in community-based after-school programs and 34 percent more likely to be involved in school activities, such as band and athletics, than gun-carrying students. Those who did not carry guns were more likely to live with both parents (62 percent versus 45 percent) and more likely to make good grades (68 percent versus 37 percent). They were less likely to be in gangs and to be in trouble with the police.

Of the 3,370 high school students surveyed in *Who's Who Among American High School Students' 27th Annual Survey of High Achievers* (Educational Communications, Inc., Lake Forest, IL, November 1996), 29 percent reported that they knew someone who had brought a weapon to school, and 17 percent claimed it was not very difficult to obtain weapons at school. The 1995 School Crime Supplement to the *National Crime Victimization Survey* found that 12.7 percent of student respondents knew someone who brought a gun to school. The percentage of students who reported this tended to rise as their age increased. (See Figure 7.6.)

High School Youths and Weapons

According to *Juvenile Offenders and Victims: 1999 National Report* (U.S. Department of Justice, Office of Juvenile Justice and Delinquency Prevention, Washington, D.C., 2000), in 1997 some 9 percent of high school students reported that in the past 30 days they had carried a weapon (gun, knife, or club) on school property. Males were more likely (13 percent) than females (4 percent) to say they carried a weapon at school. The highest rate of weapon carrying to school was reported by 9th and 11th graders (15 percent), while 12th graders were least like to carry a weapon on school property (10 percent). Male Hispanics were most likely to have carried a weapon at school in the past 30 days (16 percent), followed by white males (12 percent) and black males (11 percent), while white females were the least likely, at 2 percent. (See Table 7.5.)

Joseph F. Sheley and James D. Wright, in *High School Youths, Weapons, and Violence: A National Survey* (National Institute of Justice, Washington, D.C., October 1998), reported the results from a 1996 survey of male 10th and 11th graders from 53 high schools nationwide. They found that 29 percent of the respondents possessed at least one firearm. Most owned firearms generally suited to hunting and sporting purposes: rifles (19 percent of the respondents) and shotguns (18 percent). One in 25 owned a handgun and 1 in 50 owned a sawed-off shotgun, the two types of weapons least likely to be used as recreational weapons. Eight percent of the respondents owned three or more types of guns. (See Table 7.6.)

Very few of the young respondents reported carrying a gun outside the home during the 12 months prior to the survey. Only 2 percent said they carried a gun most or all of the time. The gun carriers were more likely to keep a gun in the car (59 percent) than carry it on them (41 percent). Handguns (50 percent) and revolvers (30 percent) were the most common types of firearms carried. (See Table 7.7.)

The survey found that many juveniles have easy access to firearms. Half of the respondents reported that obtaining a gun would be "little" or "no" trouble if they wanted one. Among those who claimed they had carried a

TABLE 7.8

High school students' reasons for carrying a weapon

Reasons	Percentage of gun carriers (N = 40)
I needed protection	43
I was holding it for someone	35
I used the weapon in a crime	10
To scare someone	18
To get back at someone	18
Most of my friends carry them	10
It made me feel important	10
Other	15

Note: Multiple responses permitted

SOURCE: *High School Youths, Weapons, and Violence: A National Survey*, National Institute of Justice, Washington, D.C., 1998

gun outside the home during the past 12 months, nearly half (48 percent) reported they had been given or lent the gun by a family member or friend. Four percent reported sneaking the gun from home, and 6 percent revealed that they had stolen or traded something for the gun. Thirty-five percent said they had bought the gun, most commonly from a family member or friend.

Although gun-related activity is generally associated with crime, drugs, and gangs, criminal behavior characterized only a small number of the respondents. The average 10th and 11th grade male claimed not to be seriously involved in criminal activity. The survey included questions to indicate the presence or absence of a dangerous social environment for the respondents.

A link between dangerous environment and firearm possession is supported by the respondents' reasons for carrying a gun. (See Table 7.8.) The most common reason given by gun carriers was the need for protection (43 percent). Holding a gun for someone was the other commonly cited response (35 percent). Ten percent reported criminal activity. A few juveniles reported that they carried a gun to gain respect from their peers. Possession of handguns and carrying a gun outside the house were related to that perceived need for respect, making the issue of youths and weapons a serious social problem.

According to the authors, the results of the study indicate the need for community policy directed toward reducing the likelihood that youths will become involved in gun possession and carrying rather than confronting already developed gun-related behaviors among youth. The vast majority of students have had little or no experience with weapons.

National Longitudinal Study of Adolescent Health

The *National Longitudinal Study of Adolescent Health, 1997,* the largest survey of teens ever taken in the

United States, questioned 90,000 students in grades 7–12 at 145 schools around the country. This federally funded study, conducted by researchers at the University of North Carolina, Chapel Hill, and the University of Minnesota, found that 24 percent of those surveyed claimed they had easy access to guns at home. Adolescents from homes where guns are kept are more likely to behave violently and are more likely to contemplate or attempt suicide.

More than 10 percent of males and 5 percent of females surveyed said that they had committed a violent act in the previous year. These violent acts included participating in fights, injuring someone with a weapon, using a weapon in a fight, or shooting or stabbing someone. More 7th and 8th graders reported involvement in violence than older teenagers. Urban teens, teens whose families receive welfare, and Native Americans appeared more likely than other teens to have been involved in violent activities. About one in eight students said they carried a weapon to school in the month prior to being surveyed. About the same number said they had been victims of violent behavior by peers.

The survey found that parents—not just peers—play a central role for their adolescent children. Teens less likely to be involved in interpersonal violence were those with strong family ties. Older teens (9th–12th graders) who had a parent present at key times during the day—breakfast, after school, dinner, and bedtime—were less likely to behave violently.

TEEN GUN POSSESSION

The National Institute of Justice (NIJ), with joint funding from the Office of Juvenile Justice and Delinquency Prevention, commissioned a study (*Gun Acquisition and Possession in Selected Juvenile Samples*, Washington, D.C., 1993) to learn about the level and nature of juvenile gun possession in high-risk neighborhoods. The researchers surveyed 835 male serious offenders incarcerated in six juvenile correctional facilities in four states and 758 male students in ten inner-city high school facilities.

Both students and inmates came from environments marked by crime and violence. Because the study focused on serious juvenile offenders and students from schools in high-risk areas, the results cannot be generalized to the entire U.S. population.

The researchers wanted to determine the number and types of arms owned and where, how, and why they were obtained. The average inmate respondent's age was 17, and 84 percent were nonwhite. The average educational level attained was 10th grade. More than half of the inmates were from cities of at least 250,000 residents. Half had committed robbery, and two-thirds had committed burglary.

Among the students, 97 percent were nonwhite and the mean (middle) age was 16. The average education level attained was 10th grade, and most were from cities of more than 250,000 people. Forty-two percent of the students reported having been arrested or picked up by the police at least once; 22 percent had been arrested or picked up "many" times. Nine percent reported having used a weapon to commit a crime.

Social Environment

The juvenile inmates had lived in an environment distinguished by gun possession and violence. Four of every 10 inmates had siblings who had also been incarcerated, and 47 percent had siblings who owned guns legally or illegally. Seventy-nine percent of the inmates came from families in which at least some of the males owned guns, and 62 percent had male family members who routinely carried guns outside the home. In this environment, 84 percent of the inmate respondents reported that they had been threatened with a gun or had been shot. Half had been stabbed with a knife.

The social world of the students was almost as dangerous. Sixty-nine percent had males in their families who owned guns. Two of five reported that males in their families routinely carried guns outside the home. More than half (57 percent) had friends who owned guns; 42 percent had friends who routinely carried guns outside the home. Like the members of the inmate sample, the student respondents were also frequently threatened and victimized by violence. Forty-five percent had been threatened with a gun or shot at on the way to or from school in the previous few years. One in 10 had been stabbed, and 1 in 3 had been beaten up in or on the way to school. Nearly a fifth (17 percent) had been wounded with some form of weapon other than a knife or a gun in or near the school.

Most inmates (70 percent) and students (68 percent) said they carried guns for self-protection. More than half of the inmates (52 percent) and almost one-third (32 percent) of the students said they carried firearms because their enemies had guns. Fewer inmates (38 percent) and students (18 percent) admitted to carrying guns in order to "get someone" or to use in a crime (37 percent of inmates). (See Table 7.9.)

The firearms of choice were high-quality, powerful revolvers, closely followed by automatic and semiautomatic handguns and then shotguns. In fact, nearly one-quarter of the students interviewed possessed a gun and 15 percent reported owning three or more guns. Eight out of 10 inmates owned at least one firearm and two-thirds owned at least three just prior to their confinement. (See Table 7.10.)

Easy to Acquire Guns

Most of those surveyed by the NIJ thought it would be easy to acquire a gun. Only 13 percent of the inmates and

TABLE 7.9

Juveniles' reasons for owning a gun

	Percent listing reason as "very important"	
	Inmates	Students
Protection	70%	68%
Enemies had guns	52	32
To get someone	38	18
Use in crimes	37	(not asked)
Friends had one	17	9
To impress people	10	9
To sell	10	5

SOURCE: *Gun Acquisition and Possession in Selected Juvenile Samples,* Office of Juvenile Justice and Delinquency Prevention, Washington, D.C., 1993

TABLE 7.10

Inmate and student gun possession (numbers in parentheses)

	Percent of inmates who owned just prior to confinement		Percent of students who owned at time of survey	
Any type of gun	83	(815)	22	(741)
Target or hunting rifle	22	(823)	8	(728)
Military-style automatic or semiautomatic rifle	35	(823)	6	(728)
Regular shotgun	39	(823)	10	(728)
Sawed-off shotgun	51	(823)	9	(728)
Revolver	58	(823)	15	(728)
Automatic or semiautomatic handgun	55	(823)	18	(728)
Derringer or single-shot handgun	19	(822)	4	(727)
Homemade (zip) handgun	6	(823)	4	(727)
Three or more guns	65	(815)	15	(741)

SOURCE: *Gun Acquisition and Possession in Selected Juvenile Samples,* Office of Juvenile Justice and Delinquency Prevention, Washington, D.C., 1993

35 percent of the students thought it would be a lot of trouble or nearly impossible. When asked how they would get a gun, 45 percent of the juvenile inmates and 53 percent of the students would "borrow" one from family or friends, while 54 percent of the inmates and 37 percent of the students said they would get one "off the streets." More than one-third of inmates (36 percent) and students (35 percent) bought guns from family members or friends. For the inmates, drug dealers (36 percent) and addicts (35 percent) were also considered good sources. (See Table 7.11.)

More than half the inmates had stolen a gun at least once, compared with 8 percent of the students. When the inmates sold or traded the guns they had stolen, they generally did so to friends or other trusted persons. Thus, these juveniles both supplied and obtained guns from an informal network of family, friends, and street sources. It seems likely that theft and burglary were the ultimate source of many of the guns acquired by the juveniles surveyed, but only occasionally was it the direct source by which the majority received their most recent weapon.

Attitudes toward Shooting Someone

The NIJ researchers asked the respondents about their attitudes toward violence. Twenty-five percent of the inmates and 10 percent of the students agreed or strongly agreed that "it is okay to shoot a person if that is what it takes to get something you want." Twenty-nine percent of the juvenile offenders and 10 percent of the students agreed or strongly agreed that it was "okay to shoot some guy who doesn't belong in your neighborhood." Sixty-one percent of the inmates and 28 percent of the students considered it "okay to shoot someone who hurts or insults you."

Gun Dealing

A large, informal street market in guns flourished in their neighborhoods. Forty-five percent of the juvenile inmates could be described as gun dealers since they had

TABLE 7.11

How juveniles obtain guns

	Percent of inmates	Percent of students
Likely source if desired*	(*N* = 738)	(*N* = 623)
Steal from a person or car	14	7
Steal from a house or apartment	17	8
Steal from a store or pawnshop	8	4
Borrow from family member or friend	45	53
Buy from family member or friend	36	35
Get off the street	54	37
Get from a drug dealer	36	22
Get from an addict	35	22
Buy from gun shop	12	28
Source of most recent handgun**	(*N* = 640)	(*N* = 211)
A friend	30	38
Family member	6	23
Gun shop/pawnshop	7	11
The street	22	14
Drug dealer	9	2
Drug addict	12	6
"Taken" from someone's house or car	12	2
Other	2	4

* Item: "How would you go about getting a gun if you decided you wanted one?" (Multiple responses permitted.)
** Item: "Where did you get your most recent handgun?"

SOURCE: *Gun Acquisition and Possession in Selected Juvenile Samples,* Office of Juvenile Justice and Delinquency Prevention, Washington, D.C., 1993

bought, sold, or traded "a lot" of guns. Of those who described themselves as dealers, the majority reported their most common source as theft from homes or cars and acquisitions from drug addicts. Sixteen percent had bought guns out of state for purposes of gun dealing, another 7 percent had done so in state, and nearly one in ten had stolen guns in quantity from stores or off trucks during shipment.

The NIJ survey found two different types of gun dealers. One group (77 percent) comprised juveniles who occasionally came into possession of surplus firearms and then sold or traded them to street sources. The other group (23 percent) was more systematic in its gun-dealing activities and was always on the lookout for a good deal.

DRUG DEALING AND GUN ACTIVITY. The majority of juvenile inmates (72 percent) and 18 percent of high school students had either sold drugs or worked for someone who did. Among those who had sold drugs or had worked for dealers, 89 percent of the inmates and 75 percent of the students had carried guns. Of the inmate dealers, 60 percent were very likely to carry guns during drug transactions, and 63 percent had fired guns during those transactions. Nearly half of the juvenile inmates who had ever stolen guns had also sold at least some of them to drug dealers. Six percent had bought guns from drug dealers.

FATAL GUNSHOT INJURIES TO CHILDREN

According the report *Protect Children Instead of Guns 2000,* by the Children's Defense Fund, gunfire killed 3,761 American infants, children, and teens in 1998, down by 35 percent from the 1994 high of 5,793 deaths. During that same time period, the number of black children and teens killed by guns declined by 45 percent, and the number of white children and teens by 28 percent. Most (58 percent) were homicides, 33 percent were suicides, and about 7 percent were unintentional. Most of the firearms that accounted for the unintentional deaths of children and teens were from the victims' homes or the homes of relatives, friends, or parents of friends.

The Centers for Disease Control and Prevention found that in 1995 firearms were the second leading cause of death among children ages 10–14 (Figure 7.7), one-quarter (24 percent) of all injury deaths for that age group. Forty-eight percent of these deaths were homicides, and 29 percent were suicides. The firearm death rate for boys ages 10–14 was 3.8 times the rate for girls.

BB GUNS

BB guns and pellet guns are often referred to as "toy guns" because they do not require gunpowder to propel ammunition. The type that has been around the longest is the spring-loaded model, which uses a spring action to propel the pellets. Technologically more sophisticated models, however, have been on the market for years. One type is an air gun (also called an air rifle or pump gun), which uses compressed air. Another type uses carbon dioxide cartridges to propel ammunition.

Many people have assumed these guns shoot at harmlessly low velocities and have bought them for children to use as toys. The Centers for Disease Control and Prevention warns that the power of some of these guns

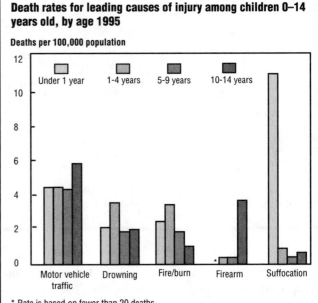

FIGURE 7.7

Death rates for leading causes of injury among children 0–14 years old, by age 1995

Deaths per 100,000 population

* Rate is based on fewer than 20 deaths.

SOURCE: Centers for Disease Control and Prevention, National Center for Health Statistics, National Vital Statistics System, Hyattsville, MD, 1997

should not be underestimated and that children with "toy" guns should never be left unsupervised. At close range, some models are capable of shooting pellets at velocities comparable to pistols and can cause death or inflict serious and permanent injury. In "BB and Pellet Gun-Related Injuries" (*Morbidity and Mortality Weekly Report,* Vol. 44, No. 49, December 15, 1995) the CDC reported that between June 1992 and May 1994 it received the following reports:

- A nine-year-old boy was struck by a BB beneath his lower left eyelid after he stepped from behind a board at which other children were shooting.

- A 16-year-old sustained a severe midbrain injury from a self-inflicted combination BB/pellet gunshot wound through the roof of his mouth.

- A nine-year-old incurred a pellet injury to the back of her right ankle after a boy fired a pellet at her from a passing car.

- A 10-year-old sustained injuries to his neck and trachea after being struck by a BB from a gun that had been fired unintentionally.

- A 13-year-old was shot in the neck with a BB gun when a friend pulled the trigger, believing the gun was not loaded.

- A 16-year-old boy sustained a penetrating injury to his right eye after being struck by a BB that ricocheted from a gun fired by a friend.

TABLE 7.12

Characteristics of children and teenagers treated in hospital emergency departments for BB and pellet gun–related injuries, June 1992–May 1994

Characteristic	No.*	(%)	Rate†	(95% CI§)
Sex				
Male	40,605	(86.1)	53.5	(45.1–61.9)
Female	6,532	(13.9)	9.0	(6.7–11.3)
Age (yrs)				
0–4¶	1,040	(2.2)	—	
5–9	8,033	(17.0)	21.6	(16.5–26.7)
10–14	24,400	(51.8)	66.6	(54.9–78.3)
15–19	13,664	(29.0)	39.6	(31.8–47.4)
Total	**47,137**	**(100.0)**	**31.8**	**(26.8–36.8)**

* Based on weighted data from 959 BB and pellet gunshot injuries reported through the National Electronic Injury Surveillance System.
† Annualized rate per 100,000 population.
§ Confidence interval.
¶ Rate was not calculated because of the small number (21) of cases in this age group; interpret estimate with caution.

SOURCE: "BB and Pellet Gun-Related Injuries—United States, June 1992-May 1994," *Morbidity and Mortality Weekly Report,* vol. 44, no. 49, December 15, 1995, Centers for Disease Control and Prevention, Atlanta, GA, 1995

During the same period, more than 47,000 children and teenagers were treated for BB or pellet gunshot wounds in hospital emergency rooms. Most were males (86.1 percent), children between the ages of 10 and 14 (51.8 percent), and teens between the ages of 15 and 19 (29 percent). (See Table 7.12.) Most victims were taken to emergency medical treatment in private cars (64.3 percent), suffering from an injury to a foot or hand (54 percent) that did not require hospitalization (95 percent). Most wounds were unintentional (65.7 percent), self-inflicted (31 percent), and in a home (45.4 percent). Some pellet or BB wounds, however, were the result of an assault (10.4 percent) or suicide attempt (0.1 percent). (See Table 7.13.)

BB Guns Can Kill

In a 1994 study the Massachusetts Department of Health ("Toy Guns: Real Injuries, Real Weapons," *Public Health Reports,* Vol. III, No. 6, November/December 1996) reported that one male (age not given) committed suicide with a non-gunpowder gun. The Massachusetts study also found that most injuries (60 percent) occurred in or around the home. According to officials with the Massachusetts Department of Health, this may reflect both the young age of the victims and consent of the parents to use the guns.

Preventing Injuries

Most, if not all, injuries from BB guns are preventable. Some injuries occur when the gun is being cleaned and the safety feature is not engaged. The CDC

TABLE 7.13

BB and pellet gun–related injuries treated in hospital emergency departments (EDs) for children and teenagers 0–19 years old, by selected characteristics, June 1992–May 1994

Characteristic	No.*	(%)
Mode of transport to ED		
Private vehicle	30,298	(64.3)
Walked in	7,788	(16.5)
Emergency medical service/Fire rescue/Ambulance	3,742	(8.0)
Police vehicle	468	(1.0)
Other/Not stated	4,841	(10.2)
Primary body part injured		
Extremity	25,453	(54.0)
Trunk	7,276	(15.4)
Face	6,788	(14.4)
Head/Neck	4,747	(10.1)
Eye	2,839	(6.0)
Other	34	(0.1)
ED discharge disposition		
Not hospitalized	44,759	(95.0)
Hospitalized	2,378	(5.0)
Victim-shooter relationship		
Self	14,636	(31.0)
Friend/Acquaintance	9,280	(19.7)
Relative	6,445	(13.7)
Stranger	1,260	(2.7)
Other/Shooter not seen	1,821	(3.9)
Not stated	13,695	(29.1)
Type of injury		
Unintentional	30,960	(65.7)
Assault	4,903	(10.4)
Suicide attempt	34	(0.1)
Not stated	11,240	(23.8)
Locale of injury incident		
Home/Apartment/Condominium	21,413	(45.4)
Street/Highway	1,821	(3.9)
Other property	1,389	(2.9)
School/Recreation area	1,104	(2.3)
Farm	90	(0.2)
Not Stated	21,320	(45.2)
Total	**47,137**	**(100.0)**

* Based on weighted data from 959 BB and pellet gunshot injuries reported through the National Electronic Injury Surveillance System.

SOURCE: "BB and Pellet Gun-Related Injuries—United States, June 1992-May 1994," *Morbidity and Mortality Weekly Report,* vol. 44, no. 49, December 15, 1995, Centers for Disease Control and Prevention, Atlanta, GA, 1995

reported that there are no nationally specified safety standards for nonpowder guns. The agency is working with the U.S. Consumer Product Safety Commission and manufacturers of nonpowder guns to develop strategies to prevent injuries from nonpowder guns.

SCHOOL SHOOTINGS

Columbine

According to *The Columbine High School Shootings: Jefferson County Sheriff Department's Investigation Report* (released May 15, 2000, by the Jefferson County Sheriff's Office), on April 20, 1999, at 11:10 A.M., senior Eric David Harris, 18, arrived alone in the student parking lot at Columbine High School in Littleton, Colorado. His classmate Dylan Bennet Klebold, 17, drove in a short time later in his 1982 black BMW. Together, they walked to the school cafeteria carrying two large duffel bags, each concealing a 20-pound propane bomb set to detonate at exactly 11:17 A.M. After placing the duffel bags inconspicuously among hundreds of other backpacks and bags, Harris and Klebold went back out to the parking lot to wait for the bombs to explode. As they waited, pipe bombs they had planted earlier three miles southwest of the high school exploded, resulting in a grass fire intended to divert the resources of the Littleton Fire Department and Jefferson County Sheriff's Office.

Minutes later, Harris and Klebold returned to Columbine High School, this time to the west exterior steps, the highest point on campus with a view of the student parking lots and the cafeteria's entrances and exits. Both were wearing black trench coats that concealed 9mm semiautomatic weapons. They pulled out shotguns from a duffel bag and opened fire toward the west doors of the school, killing 17-year-old Rachel Scott. After entering the school, they killed 13 other victims, including a teacher, before finally killing themselves.

Within days, authorities had learned that three of the guns used in the massacre were purchased the year before by Dylan Klebold's girlfriend shortly after her 18th birthday. On May 3, felony charges were filed against Mark E. Manes, 22, for admittedly selling to Eric Harris the TEC-DC9 semiautomatic handgun he used in the shooting. On August 18, Manes agreed to plead guilty to the charge.

THE VICTIMS. Cassie Bernall, 17—reportedly shot to death after answering "yes" when her killer asked if she believed in God.

Steven Curnow, 14—a soccer player whose teammates served as his pallbearers.

Corey DePooter, 17—a junior who hoped to become a U.S. Marine.

Kelly Fleming, 16—a sophomore who had moved to the Columbine area the year before and liked to spend her free hour every day at the school library, where she died.

Matthew Kechter, 16—a junior varsity lineman in his sophomore year. The following December, Columbine High School's varsity football team won its first state championship in Matthew's honor.

Daniel Mauser, 15—Daniel's death prompted his father, Tom, to take a leave of absence from his job to lobby full time for gun control.

Daniel Rohrbough, 15—Daniel's family was critical of the Jefferson County Sheriff's Department for giving Time magazine access to the killer's "farewell videotapes" before first showing the tapes to the victims' families.

Dave Sanders, 47—a teacher and coach for 25 years. Sanders died trying to save students.

Rachel Scott, 17—the first fatality in the massacre. She was killed on the Columbine lawn.

Isaiah Shoels, 18—Isaiah's family moved from Littleton after filing a wrongful-death lawsuit against the parents of Eric Harris and Dylan Klebold.

John Tomlin, 16—a sophomore who planned to join the army after graduating from Columbine High School.

Lauren Townsend, 18—a popular student who played on the school's volleyball team. Her teammates retired Lauren's uniform number, 8.

Kyle Velasquez, 16—Kyle's father, together with the father of Daniel Rohrbough, sawed down 2 of the 15 trees planted in honor of the 13 victims and their two killers.

THE SHOOTERS. On January 30, 1998, more than a year before the Columbine shootings, Harris and Klebold were arrested for breaking into a vehicle. In April 1998, both were placed in a juvenile diversion program and required to pay fines, attend anger management classes, and perform community service. Harris and Klebold successfully completed the diversion program and on February 9, 1999, were released from the program, their juvenile records cleared.

In March 1998 the Jefferson County Sheriff's Office responded to a suspicious incident report from Randy Brown. In the report, Brown alleged that his son, Brooks, had received death threats from Harris on the Internet. Brown alleged that on the same Web pages, Harris also wrote about making and detonating pipe bombs and using them against people. The information was reviewed by sheriff's investigators, but they could not gain access to Harris's Web site, and reports of the pipe-bomb writings could not be substantiated.

In the spring of 1998 Harris began a diary, later recovered by authorities. In late 1998 Harris wrote of his desire to kill. In the only entry for 1999, Harris wrote of his and Klebold's preparations for what would become the Columbine massacre, including a detailed accounting of weapons and bombs they intended to use.

After the Columbine shootings, Klebold's father, Tom Klebold, reported to investigators that his son never showed any fascination with guns. The Klebolds told authorities that their son had been accepted at the University of Arizona, where he planned on majoring in computer science. Investigators who interviewed friends and teachers of Klebold often heard him described as a nice, normal teenager.

Harris and Klebold left behind three videotapes documenting their plans and philosophies. The third tape contained eight sessions taped from early April 1999 to the morning of the Columbine shootings on April 20, and shows some of their weapons and bombs, as well as recordings of each other rehearsing for the shootings.

COLUMBINE LAWSUITS. In response to the Columbine shootings, five wrongful death lawsuits were filed in Jefferson County against the Jefferson County Sheriff's Department, alleging that the department didn't respond appropriately on the day of the shootings and that it did not fully investigate Eric Harris's Web site. Additional actions were filed in federal court in Denver, some naming other defendants such as the parents of killers Eric Harris and Dylan Klebold and those who helped supply guns to them.

On June 1, 2000, U.S. District Court Judge Lewis Babcock consolidated all Columbine-related lawsuits in federal court. In part, this was because defendants in the Jefferson County lawsuits had requested a transfer to federal jurisdiction because some of the claims against them were made under federal law. There are no limits on the amount of damages that can be awarded to plaintiffs in federal claims. Under Colorado state law, the maximum jury award for wrongful death, noneconomic losses, is $341,250.

On November 29, 2000, the families of Harris and Klebold and gun seller Mark Manes offered a $1.6 million settlement to the families of the 13 victims killed in the Columbine shooting. If accepted, the Harrises, Klebolds, and Manes would be removed as defendants from all actions brought by the families of the 13 killed, although not from other suits that are pending or yet to be filed.

Other School Shooters

Less than a year before Columbine, on May 21, 1998, 15-year-old Kip Kinkel walked into the crowded cafeteria at Thurston High School in Springfield, Oregon, and opened fire with a semiautomatic rifle. Students Mikael Nickolauson, 17, and Ben Walker, 16, were killed, and 22 of their classmates were injured. Kinkel's parents, Bill, 59, and Faith, 57, were later found shot to death at their home. The year before, Kinkel's father had bought his son a Ruger .22 semiautomatic rifle under the condition that he would use it only under adult supervision.

On September 24, 1999, as part of a plea agreement, Kip Kinkel plead guilty to four counts of murder and 26 counts of attempted murder. After a six-day sentencing hearing that included the testimony of psychiatrists and psychologists and victim's statements, on November 2, 1999, 17-year-old Kip Kinkel was sentenced to 111 years in prison without the possibility of parole.

Prompted by growing concerns over a rock-throwing incident that Kip had participated in and other behavioral problems, Faith Kinkel took her son to see a psychologist in January 1997, just over a year before the shootings. In this meeting, the psychologist concluded that Kinkel had difficulty managing anger, expressed some angry acting out, and depression.

In her report *The School Shooter: A Threat Assessment Perspective* (prepared jointly by the FBI and The Department of Justice, 1999) Mary Ellen O'Toole believes that news coverage creates a number of wrong or unverified impressions of school shooters. Among them are:

- All school shooters are alike.

- The school shooter is always a loner.

- School shootings are exclusively revenge motivated.

- Easy access to weapons is THE most significant risk factor.

O'Toole lays out a four-pronged approach in assessing "the totality of the circumstances" known about a student in four major areas: personality of the student, family dynamics, school dynamics, and social dynamics.

"If an act of violence occurs at a school," O'Toole writes, "the school becomes the scene of the crime. As in any violent crime, it is necessary to understand what it is about the school which might have influenced the student's decision to offend there rather than someplace else."

O'Toole sets forth the following factors in making that determination:

- The student's attachment to school: The student appears to be "detached" from school, including other students, teachers, and school activities.

- Tolerance for disrespectful behavior: The school does little to prevent or punish disrespectful behavior between individual students or groups of students.

- Inequitable discipline: Discipline is inequitably applied (or has the perception of being inequitably applied)—by students and/or staff.

- Inflexible culture: The school's culture is static, unyielding, and insensitive to changes in society and the changing needs of newer students and staff.

- Pecking order among students: Certain groups of students are officially or unofficially given more prestige and respect than others.

- Code of silence: Few feel they can safely tell teachers or administrators if they are concerned about another student's behavior or attitudes. Little trust exists between students and staff.

- Unsupervised computer access.

A Timeline of School Shootings

May 26, 2000: A 13-year-old honors student in Lake Worth, Florida, returned to school and fatally shot a teacher after being sent home on the last day of classes by another teacher for throwing water balloons.

February 29, 2000: A six-year-old boy used a stolen gun to kill a six-year-old female student in her classroom in front of a teacher and 22 classmates.

December 6, 1999: A 13-year-old student in Fort Gibson, Oklahoma, arrived at school and opened fire with his father's 9mm semiautomatic handgun, injuring four classmates.

November 19, 1999: A 12-year-old boy shot and killed a female classmate at the end of lunch hour outside a middle school in Deming, New Mexico. The boy was wearing a camouflage jacket when he allegedly fired the single shot from a .22-caliber handgun.

May 20, 1999: A 15-year-old student walked into Heritage High School in Conyers, Georgia, and fired into a crowd of his classmates, injuring six.

April 20, 1999: Eric Harris and Dylan Klebold opened fire in a suburban high school in Littleton, Colorado. In all, 15 were killed, including the two gunmen.

June 15, 1998: A male teacher and a female guidance counselor were shot in a hallway at a Richmond, Virginia, high school. The teacher suffered an injury to the abdomen, and the guidance counselor was reportedly grazed.

May 21, 1998: Fifteen-year-old Kip Kinkel of Springfield, Oregon, opened fire in the school cafeteria. Two students are killed. The suspect's parents are later found shot dead in their home.

May 21, 1998: A 15-year-old boy died from a self-inflicted gunshot wound to the head in Onalaska, Washington. Earlier in the day, the boy boarded a high school bus with a gun in hand, ordered his girlfriend off the bus, and took her to his home, where he shot himself.

May 21, 1998: A 15-year-old girl was shot and wounded at a suburban Houston high school when a gun in the backpack of a 17-year-old classmate went off in a biology class. The boy was charged with a third-degree felony for taking a gun to school.

May 19, 1998: Three days before his graduation, an 18-year-old honors student allegedly opened fire in a parking lot at Lincoln County High School in Fayetteville, Tennessee, killing a classmate who was dating his ex-girlfriend.

April 28, 1998: Two teenage boys were shot to death and a third was wounded as they played basketball at a Pomona, California, elementary school hours after classes had ended. A 14-year-old boy was charged in the shooting, which was blamed on rivalry between two groups of youths.

April 24, 1998: A 48-year-old science teacher was shot to death in front of students at a graduation dance in Edinboro, Pennsylvania. A 14-year-old student at James W. Parker Middle School was charged.

March 24, 1998: Four girls and a teacher were shot to death and 10 others were wounded during a false fire alarm at Westside Middle School in Jonesboro, Arkansas, when two boys, ages 11 and 13, opened fire from the woods. Both were convicted in juvenile court of murder.

December 1, 1997: Three students were killed and five others were wounded while they took part in a prayer circle in a hallway at Heath High School in West Paducah, Kentucky. A 14-year-old student pleaded guilty but mentally ill to murder and is serving life in prison. One of the wounded girls was left paralyzed.

October 1, 1997: A 16-year-old in Pearl, Mississippi, was accused of killing his mother, then going to Pearl High School and shooting nine students. Two of them died, including the suspect's ex-girlfriend. The 16-year-old was sentenced to life in prison.

February 19, 1997: Evan Ramsey, a 16-year-old student, opened fire with a shotgun in a common area at the Bethel, Alaska, high school, killing the principal and a student. Two other students were wounded. Ramsey was sentenced to two 99-year terms.

February 2, 1996: A 14-year-old boy in Moses Lake, Washington, wearing a trench coat walked into a junior high school algebra class with a hunting rifle and allegedly opened fire, killing the teacher and two students. A third student was injured.

GUN-CONTROL LEGISLATION

Since the school shootings at Columbine and Thurston High Schools, both state legislatures and the U.S. Congress have debated new gun-control laws. Much of the proposed legislation has been aimed at closing the loophole in the Brady Law that allows the sales of firearms at gun shows without background checks. On May 20, 1999, the U.S. Senate split 50-50 on a vote to amend a juvenile justice bill authored by Senator Lautenberg (D-NJ) that closed the loophole through which unlicensed dealers and private collectors sell guns at gun shows without background checks. With Vice President Al Gore casting the tie-breaking vote, the amendment passed. But on June 18, 1999, on a 218 to 211 vote, the U.S. House of Representatives endorsed a proposal by Rep. John Dingell (D-MI) to water down the Senate measure. The House then went on to defeat by 235 to 193 a competing proposal that was much closer to the Senate bill. The result is that there is still no federal legislation closing the gun show loophole.

Similar inaction by state legislatures prompted voters in Colorado and Oregon to overwhelming pass ballot initiatives aimed at closing the so-called gun show loophole. On November 7, 2000, about 70 percent of voters in Colorado passed Amendment 22, which requires background checks before any firearm transfer. Additionally, Amendment 22 requires a record of all firearm transfers once a background check is completed, and it mandates that gun show promoters post a notice stating the requirement for a background check.

Six-two percent of Oregon voters approved Measure 5, which requires a criminal background check before buying a gun at a gun show. The measure also allows for private citizens to order background checks for firearm purchases voluntarily, even if not required by law, and it requires that background records be kept for five years for use in criminal investigations.

On August 9, 2000, New York governor George Pataki signed into law a provision that closed the gun show loophole in New York State. Intentional failure to comply by a gun show operator is punishable as a Class A misdemeanor under New York law and carries a fine of up to $10,000. The law also requires firearms retailers to include a child safety locking device with every firearm purchased, post notices regarding the safe storage of guns, and include gun safety information with the purchase of any firearm. Additionally, the law established a statewide gun trafficking interdiction program and authorizes a study on "smart gun" technology.

INTEREST IN SCHOOL SHOOTINGS

According to the *Denver Post* (November 5, 2000), the Columbine High School shootings have become the most popular essay topic among college applicants in the past two years. According to the college deans surveyed, before Columbine most students wrote about such topics as favorite teachers, influential relatives, or sports achievements. College-bound students are concerned about school safety, gun control, and fear and vulnerability, according to the report, and often specifically mention Columbine in relation to these concerns.

CHANGING ATTITUDES TOWARD GUN CONTROL

Among Americans at large, attitudes about gun control appear to have shifted since the Columbine shootings. The *1999 National Gun Policy Survey of the National Opinion Research Center: Research Findings* (National Opinion Research Center, University of Chicago) measured pre- and post-Columbine attitudes toward guns. (See Table 7.14.)

The information was collected from polls taken by organizations including the Harris Poll, Associated Press, CBS/Gallup Poll, and ABC. Generally, fewer respondents were in favor of stricter gun control after Columbine than

TABLE 7.14

Pre- and post-Littleton attitudes toward guns

Harris: In general, would you say you favor stricter gun control, or less strict gun control?

	April 1998	June 1999
Stricter	69%	63%
Less strict	23	25
Neither	7	10
Not sure	1	2
	(1,011)	(1,006)

Harris: In general, do you favor stricter gun control or less strict laws relating to the control of handguns?

	April 1998	June 1999
Stricter	76%	73%
Less strict	19	25
Neither	5	5
Not sure	*	2
	(1,011)	(1,006)

AP: Which of these do you think is more likely to decrease gun violence? Better enforcement of existing gun laws or tougher gun laws.

	4/16-19/99	4/28-5/2/99	8/99
Better enforcement	47%	39%	49%
Tougher gun laws	42	51	43
Neither	—	—	5
Don't know	—	—	2
	(765)	(1,006)	(1,026)

AP: Do you favor stricter gun control laws or do you oppose them?

	4/9-12/99	4/28-5/2/99	8/99
Favor	56%	64%	56%
Oppose	34	31	39
Don't know	10	5	5
	(1,021)	(1,006)	(1,026)

CBS/Gallup: in general, do you feel the laws covering the sale of handguns should be more strict, less strict, or kept as they are now?

	Gallup 2/99	CBS 8/99
More strict	68%	67%
Less strict	6	5
Kept as they are	25	23
Don't know	1	5
	(1,054)	(736)

PSRA: Do you think stricter gun control laws would reduce the amount of violent crime in this country a lot, a little, or not at all?

	4/21-22/99	8/99
A lot	33%	33%
A little	38	35
Not at all	26	29
Don't know	3	3
	(757)	(753)

were before. For example, results from a Harris poll show that 69 percent of respondents favored stricter gun control prior to Columbine, compared with 63 percent post-Columbine. The same was true in an AP poll, when the question was asked one year prior to Columbine and again approximately two months after Columbine. The AP results showed a move from 64 percent pre-Columbine in favor of stricter gun control laws to 56 percent post-Columbine. However, the same AP poll showed a rise in

TABLE 7.14

Pre- and post-Littleton attitudes toward guns [CONTINUED]

ABC/WP: Would you support or oppose a law requiring...a nation-wide ban on the sale of handguns, except to law enforcement officers?

CBS: Would you favor or oppose a ban on the sale of all handguns, except those issued to law enforcement officers?

	CBS 4/22/99	CBS 8/99	ABC/WP 8-9/99
Favor	43%	35%	32%
Oppose	53	61	65
No opinion	4	4	3
	(450)	(736)	(1,526)

Gallup: In general, do you feel that the laws covering the sale of firearms should be more strict, less strict, or kept as they are now?

	2/99	4/26-27/99	5/23-24/99	6/99	8/99
Stricter	60%	66%	65%	62%	66%
Less strict	29	25	28	31	27
Keep as now	9	5	5	6	6
Don't know	2	2	2	1	1
	(1,054)	(1,073)	(NA)	(NA)	(NA)

ABC: Do you favor or oppose stricter gun control laws in this country? (If favor/oppose, ask:) is that strongly or somewhat favor/oppose?

	5/99	8/99	8-9/99
Strongly favor	55%	46%	52%
Somewhat favor	12	16	11
Somewhat oppose	21	22	25
Strongly oppose	10	12	11
No opinion	1	3	2
	(761)	(1,023)	(1,526)

Gallup: Which of the following statements comes closest to your view . there should be no restrictions on owning guns; There should be minor restrictions—such as a five-day waiting period to buy a gun and gun registration; There should be major restrictions that would ban ownership of some guns altogether—such as handguns and certain semi-automatic rifles; or all guns should be illegal for everyone except police and authorized persons.

	2/99	4/26-27/99
None	5%	4%
Minor	37	30
SOME (Vol.)	0	4
Major	36	38
Ban	18	22
Don't know	4	2
	(1,054)	(1,073)

* less than 0.5%
NA = not available

SOURCE: Tom W. Smith, *1999 National Gun Policy Survey of the National Opinion Research Center: Research Findings,* National Opinion Research Center, University of Chicago, Chicago, IL, 2000

TABLE 7.15

Pre- and post-Littleton issue mentions on crime and gun-related issues as most important problems

	Guns/gun control	Crime/violence
A. Harris		
1/99 - (1,008)	1%	7%
2/99 - (1,007)	1	8
4/8-13/99 - (1,006)	1	7
5/14-19/99 - (1,010)	10	19
6/99 - (1,006)	9	14
8/99 - (1,008)	9	13
B. Gallup		
1/99 - (1,009)	*	13
5/23-24/99 - (1,050)	10	17
C. CBS		
1/30-2/1/99 - (1,058)	—	6
4/13-14/99 - (878)	—	4
4/22/99 - (450)	3	16
5/1-2/99 - (1,151)	3	19

*less than 0.5%
—not listed as a category

Question wordings: Harris: What do you think are the two most important issues for the government to address?
Gallup/CBS: What do you think is the most important problem facing this country today?

SOURCE: Tom W. Smith, *1999 National Gun Policy Survey of the National Opinion Research Center: Research Findings,* National Opinion Research Center, University of Chicago, Chicago, IL, 2000

cent in the month after the Columbine shootings. A Gallup poll showed a similar rise in both categories, as did the CBS poll.

those who favored better enforcement of existing gun laws, from 39 percent prior to Columbine to almost half (49 percent) in the aftermath of Columbine.

A significant rise was also apparent in separate polls by Harris, Gallup, and CBS in how respondents rank "guns and gun control" and "crime and violence" as important issues facing the country in the aftermath of Columbine. (See Table 7.15.) In the Harris poll, the rate jumped from 1 percent pre-Columbine to 10 percent post-Columbine for guns and gun control, and from 7 percent to 13 percent for crime and violence, peaking at 19 per-

CHAPTER 8
PUBLIC ATTITUDES TOWARD GUN CONTROL

A DEEPLY PERSONAL ISSUE

The question of regulating the possession of guns, especially handguns, by federal, state, or local governments has become a major issue in the United States over the past two decades. The perception of an escalating crime rate has led some citizens to purchase guns for their own protection, while others are afraid to walk the streets for fear of gun-wielding criminals who might rob or murder them.

The significant number of political assassinations and assassination attempts over the last several decades has caused many Americans to question whether a civilized government should permit the unrestricted possession of firearms. Presidents John Kennedy, Gerald Ford, and Ronald Reagan were all victimized by assassins, as were presidential candidates George Wallace and Robert Kennedy. Civil rights leaders Martin Luther King, Jr., Medgar Evers, and Vernon Jordan were shot. In November 1994 a lone gunman fired indiscriminately on the White House, and federal authorities were considering charging the man with attempted assassination of a president. Since then, several others have shot at the White House.

In July 1998 Russell Weston, Jr., shot and killed two police officers at the U.S. Capitol after running through a metal detector and firing a handgun. Because he had once been committed to a mental institution, Weston could not, in most states, legally carry a gun. Law enforcement officials reported that Weston took his father's revolver from his parents' bedroom. According to National Rifle Association (NRA) spokesman Bill Powers, gun control laws would not have helped the situation.

MOST PEOPLE HAVE AN OPINION

Some Americans are convinced that the regulation of firearms is necessary to reduce the number of murders that are committed with guns and that every attempted or

FIGURE 8.1

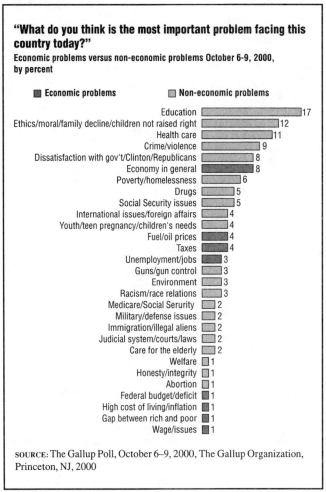

"What do you think is the most important problem facing this country today?"

Economic problems versus non-economic problems October 6-9, 2000, by percent

■ Economic problems   ▨ Non-economic problems

Education	17
Ethics/moral/family decline/children not raised right	12
Health care	11
Crime/violence	9
Dissatisfaction with gov't/Clinton/Republicans	8
Economy in general	8
Poverty/homelessness	6
Drugs	5
Social Security issues	5
International issues/foreign affairs	4
Youth/teen pregnancy/children's needs	4
Fuel/oil prices	4
Taxes	4
Unemployment/jobs	3
Guns/gun control	3
Environment	3
Racism/race relations	3
Medicare/Social Serurity	2
Military/defense issues	2
Immigration/illegal aliens	2
Judicial system/courts/laws	2
Care for the elderly	2
Welfare	1
Honesty/integrity	1
Abortion	1
Federal budget/deficit	1
High cost of living/inflation	1
Gap between rich and poor	1
Wage/issues	1

SOURCE: The Gallup Poll, October 6–9, 2000, The Gallup Organization, Princeton, NJ, 2000

successful assassination is further proof of the need for gun control. However, others who support private ownership of guns insist that the right to bear arms is guaranteed by the Second Amendment of the U.S. Constitution and that no cyclical increase in crime, no mass killing, nor any rash of political murders should lead the nation to violate the Constitution and the individual rights it guarantees. In

TABLE 8.1

Attitudes toward laws covering the sale of firearms

By demographic characteristics, 2000

Question: "In general, do you feel that the laws covering the sale of firearms should be made more strict, less strict, or kept as they are now?"

	More strict	Less strict	Kept as they are now
National	**62%**	**5%**	**31%**
Sex			
Male	52	8	39
Female	72	2	24
Race			
White	61	5	32
Black	84	0	15
Nonwhite[a]	74	2	23
Age			
18 to 29 years	69	6	24
30 to 49 years	64	5	29
50 to 64 years	49	6	44
50 years and older	57	4	37
65 years and older	64	2	31
Education			
College post graduate	68	6	25
College graduate	67	7	24
Some college	59	5	35
High school graduate or less	62	4	32
Income			
$75,000 and over	65	5	29
$50,000 and over[b]	62	6	31
$30,000 to $49,999	62	5	33
$20,000 to $29,999	62	4	33
Under $20,000	70	6	21
Community			
Urban area	67	5	27
Suburban area	65	5	28
Rural area	53	4	42
Region			
East	76	3	20
Midwest	59	5	35
South	59	5	35
West	57	7	33
Politics			
Republican	44	9	44
Democrat	81	2	16
Independent	61	4	33

Note: The "no opinion" category has been omitted; therefore percents may not sum to 100.

[a]Includes black respondents.
[b]Includes $75,000 and over category.

SOURCE: *Sourcebook of Criminal Justice Statistics, 1999,* U.S. Bureau of Justice Statistics, Washington, D.C., 1999

FIGURE 8.2

Women are more likely than men to want major restrictions on guns

Which of the following statements comes closer to your view about the ability of ordinary citizens to own guns? There should be no restrictions on owning guns, there should be minor restrictions on owning guns, there should be major restrictions on owning guns, or all guns should be illegal for everyone except police and authorized persons?

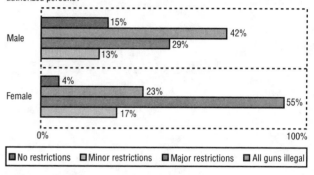

SOURCE: Reprinted by permission of Public Agenda ONLINE (www.publicagenda.org), New York, NY. Data copyrighted by source; graphics copyrighted by Public Agenda 1999.

hands of criminals. Not surprisingly, the two sides approach the issue differently. The two different strategies for gun control involve "deterrence" (discouraging by instilling fear) and "interdiction" (legally forbidding the use of). Advocates of deterrence, most notably the Second Amendment Foundation and the NRA, recommend consistent enforcement of current laws and instituting tougher penalties to discourage individuals from using firearms in crimes. They maintain that interdiction will not have any effect on crime but will strip away the constitutional rights and privileges of law-abiding Americans by taking away their right to own guns.

On the other hand, advocates of interdiction, led by such organizations as Handgun Control, Inc., the Center to Prevent Handgun Violence, and the Violence Policy Center, believe that controlling citizens' access to firearms will reduce crime. Therefore, they favor restrictions on public gun ownership.

EVALUATING PUBLIC OPINION POLLS

Public opinion polls, like all sources of information, must be used with care. It would be impossible for any pollster to interview every American on a given question. Instead, pollsters select a sample population. This selection is usually performed randomly, a process made easier today by computers. Most major pollsters interview between 1,000 and 2,000 people to establish a valid sample. Other pollsters, however, may interview far fewer than 500, and the sample could be too small to fairly represent the opinion of the American people. Generally, the larger the sample, the greater the chance for an adequate representation and a valid result.

addition, they often maintain, knives and other instruments are used to kill people, and there is no talk of banning them.

The NRA generally believes that if ordinary law-abiding citizens were allowed to carry weapons, criminals would not have a safe place to commit mass murders and other violent crimes. Many advocates of gun rights claim that most of the 23 people killed at a cafeteria in Killeen, Texas, in 1991 might not have died had a law-abiding citizen with a gun been present.

Both supporters and opponents of gun control believe that some means should be found to keep guns out of the

TABLE 8.2

To what extent do you blame gun manufacturers in the united states for gun-related crime in this country? Do you blame them completely, a lot, a little, or not at all?

	1999 Dec 9–12
Completely	4%
A lot	20%
A little	24%
Not at all	51%
No opinion	1%
	100%

As you may know, the U.S.Justice Department is considering filing alawsuit against the gun manufacture industry seeking to recover the costs associated with gun-related crime. The companies that manufacture guns in the U.S. have stated the charges have no merit. Which side do you agree with more in this dispute: the justice department or the gun manufacturers?

	1999 Dec 9–12
The Justice Department	28%
The gun manufacturers	67%
Both equally (vol.)	1%
Neither (vol.)	1%
No opinion	3%
	100%

SOURCE: The Gallup Poll, April 28–30, 2000, The Gallup Organization, Princeton, NJ, 2000

TABLE 8.3

DO YOU FAVOR OR OPPOSE THE FOLLOWING:

Holding parents legally responsible if their children commit crimes with the parents' guns

	1999 June 11–13
Favor	57%
Oppose	39%
Mixed (vol.)	3%
No opinion	1%
	100%

Requiring safety locks or trigger guards to be included with all new handgun purchases

	1999 June 11–13
Favor	85%
Oppose	14%
Mixed (vol.)	1%
No opinion	0%
	100%

Banning the import of high-capacity ammunition clips

	1999 June 11–13
Favor	68%
Oppose	29%
Mixed (vol.)	0%
No opinion	3%
	100%

Imposing a mandatory prison sentence for felons who commit crimes with guns

	1999 June 11–13
Favor	89%
Oppose	9%
Mixed (vol.)	1%
No opinion	1%
	100%

Imposing a lifetime ban on gun ownership for any juvenile convicted of a felony

	1999 June 11–13
Favor	77%
Oppose	21%
Mixed (vol.)	1%
No opinion	1%
	100%

SOURCE: The Gallup Poll, April 28–30, 2000, The Gallup Organization, Princeton, NJ, 2000

The polling errors that concern most people are those caused by "bias" in the presentation of questions. This can be a factor in how a question is answered. Is the question vague? Is it too long? Is it threatening? Were the questions asked over the telephone or by mail? If asked in an in-person interview, was the interviewer too forceful or threatening? Did respondents provide answers they thought would please interviewers? Were respondents disqualified because of membership in gun control or gun rights organizations? What was the purpose of the poll? Who hired the polling organization, and what is its stand on the issue? While pollsters are not purposely or even consciously slanted, they are subject to the same influences as everyone else. Finally, polling does not always determine how important a person considers an issue. The issue may be of absolutely no concern to the respondent, but when asked, the respondent then thinks about the topic and provides an answer. Five minutes after having been asked the question, the issue will completely disappear from his or her mind.

The polling organization might not include the number of times there was no response. If these "no replies" come predominantly from one group, it might influence the answers so that they do not truly represent national opinion on a given issue. Pollsters are aware of these weaknesses and, for that reason, usually indicate how reliable they consider their polls. Many polls indicate a plus or minus (+/-) 2 to 4 percent accuracy rate.

IS GUN CONTROL AN IMPORTANT ISSUE?

In October 2000 when the Gallup Poll asked an open-ended question about the most important problem facing this country today, only 3 percent thought gun control was one of the most important. Respondents' answers were scattered across a wide variety of social and economic issues. (See Figure 8.1.) This compares with only 1 percent in a similar Gallup poll conducted in 1998. In 2000 the most frequent response to the "most important problem" question was education at 17 percent (13 percent in 1998), followed by "Ethics/morals/family decline/children not raised right" at 12 percent (16 percent in 1998), and health care at 11 percent (6 percent in 1998). Only 9 percent of the 2000 respondents ranked crime and violence as the top problem facing the country, less than half of the 20 percent who thought so in 1998. By contrast, in 1994 about half of Americans said crime and violence was the most important problem facing the country.

TABLE 8.4

Attitudes toward a law requiring a police permit prior to gun purchase
By demographic characteristics, selected years 1974–98

Question: "Would you favor or oppose a law which would require a person to obtain a police permit before he or she could buy a gun?"

	1974 Favor	1974 Oppose	1975 Favor	1975 Oppose	1976 Favor	1976 Oppose	1977 Favor	1977 Oppose	1980 Favor	1980 Oppose	1982 Favor	1982 Oppose	1984 Favor	1984 Oppose	1985 Favor	1985 Oppose
National	75%	24%	74%	24%	72%	27%	72%	26%	69%	29%	72%	26%	70%	27%	72%	26%
Sex																
Male	66	33	66	32	64	35	64	35	63	36	68	31	62	37	65	34
Female	83	15	80	17	78	20	78	19	74	23	75	23	76	20	78	20
Race																
White	75	24	73	25	71	27	70	28	68	30	71	27	69	29	72	27
Black/other	77	22	81	15	74	24	81	17	81	15	78	19	79	18	76	22
Age																
18 to 20 years	75	23	74	26	78	22	69	31	71	29	77	23	71	24	71	29
21 to 29 years	77	23	79	19	71	27	72	26	73	27	76	24	73	25	74	25
30 to 49 years	76	24	70	27	73	25	70	29	70	29	72	26	70	29	71	28
50 years and older	74	24	73	24	70	29	74	24	67	29	69	29	70	26	72	26
Education[a]																
College	77	22	76	22	71	27	74	25	70	29	76	23	74	25	75	24
High school graduate	75	23	74	24	72	27	70	28	69	29	71	27	68	30	71	28
Less than high school graduate	71	27	68	26	71	28	72	25	70	27	64	30	72	23	69	26
Income																
$50,000 and over	NA	NA	NA	NA	NA	NA	NA	NA	NA	NA	NA	NA	NA	NA	NA	NA
$30,000 to $49,999	NA	NA	NA	NA	NA	NA	NA	NA	NA	NA	NA	NA	NA	NA	NA	NA
$20,000 to $29,999	NA	NA	NA	NA	NA	NA	NA	NA	NA	NA	NA	NA	NA	NA	NA	NA
Under $20,000	NA	NA	NA	NA	NA	NA	NA	NA	NA	NA	NA	NA	NA	NA	NA	NA
Occupation																
Professional/business	74	25	73	24	74	25	76	23	70	28	75	23	71	27	75	24
Clerical	84	16	81	18	78	20	75	22	77	21	77	23	76	23	79	21
Manual	74	24	70	27	68	30	68	30	67	32	69	29	68	29	68	31
Farmer	52	48	60	33	56	44	66	31	53	47	36	60	48	48	43	57
Region																
Northeast	88	12	85	12	86	13	85	14	86	13	85	13	80	18	82	17
Midwest	77	22	76	22	72	27	67	31	71	27	73	24	70	25	73	25
South	70	28	66	30	63	35	69	28	64	34	62	36	66	31	67	32
West	66	32	70	29	68	30	68	31	60	38	69	30	67	32	71	29
Religion																
Protestant	71	28	70	27	67	31	67	30	64	34	68	30	66	31	68	30
Catholic	85	14	83	15	82	18	80	20	83	16	81	17	79	20	79	20
Jewish	98	2	96	4	89	11	89	9	88	12	89	5	93	7	94	6
None	70	29	71	28	68	28	73	26	71	28	72	28	78	22	74	26
Politics																
Republican	74	25	74	23	71	27	71	26	64	35	66	33	66	32	70	28
Democrat	78	22	77	20	74	25	73	26	74	25	75	24	75	23	74	25
Independent	73	25	70	28	69	29	71	28	68	29	72	26	70	28	72	27

Note: The "don't know" category has been omitted; therefore percents may not sum to 100.

[a]Beginning in 1996, education categories were revised slightly and therefore are not directly comparable to data presented for prior years.

SOURCE: *Sourcebook of Criminal Justice Statistics, 1999,* U.S. Bureau of Justice Statistics, Washington, D.C., 1999

SUPPORT FOR GUN CONTROL AND REGISTRATION

Stricter Laws

The Gallup organization has periodically surveyed the public for its opinion on many gun control measures and has consistently found that Americans generally support stricter gun laws. In 2000, 62 percent said they would like to see stricter laws, and 31 percent thought they should be kept the same. Only 5 percent believed that the laws should be less strict. (See Table 8.1.)

CHARACTERISTICS OF RESPONDENTS. Women (72 percent) were significantly more likely than men (52 per-

cent) to want stricter gun laws. A greater percentage of blacks (84 percent) preferred stricter legislation than whites (61 percent). Nearly three-quarters of nonwhites (including blacks) wanted stricter gun laws. Respondents aged 18 to 29 years (69 percent) and those living in urban areas (67 percent) were more likely to support stricter legislation than those ages 50 to 64 years (57 percent) and those living in rural areas (53 percent). Four out of 10 Republicans (44 percent) supported stronger laws, compared with 61 percent of independents and 81 percent of Democrats.

GUN OWNERS. Not surprisingly, gun owners were more likely to oppose stricter gun control laws than

TABLE 8.4

1987		1988		1989		1990		1991		1993		1994		1996		1998	
Favor	Oppose	Favor	Oppose	Favor	Oppose	Favor	Oppose	Favor	Oppose	Favor	Oppose	Favor	Oppose	Favor	Oppose	Favor	Oppose
70%	**28%**	**74%**	**24%**	**78%**	**21%**	**79%**	**20%**	**81%**	**18%**	**81%**	**17%**	**78%**	**20%**	**80%**	**18%**	**82%**	**16%**
62	36	66	33	69	30	72	27	74	25	73	26	70	29	73	25	76	22
76	22	79	17	85	13	84	14	86	12	87	11	84	14	86	12	86	12
69	29	74	24	77	21	77	21	81	18	80	18	77	22	80	19	80	18
74	23	75	23	81	18	86	12	84	15	84	15	84	14	84	13	88	10
69	29	73	24	66	34	91	9	70	30	83	17	85	15	69	29	82	16
76	23	73	26	81	17	83	15	82	18	83	17	78	20	78	21	82	16
68	30	72	26	74	25	76	23	82	17	82	17	77	22	83	15	82	16
69	29	75	20	81	17	78	19	80	17	80	18	79	19	80	19	81	16
74	25	76	22	80	19	81	18	85	14	84	15	79	19	83	16	84	14
67	31	74	24	75	23	77	20	79	20	79	19	76	22	79	19	79	19
70	27	66	27	82	17	73	22	70	24	76	20	78	18	76	20	80	17
NA	NA	NA	NA	NA	NA	NA	NA	NA	NA	84	15	79	20	82	16	83	15
NA	NA	NA	NA	NA	NA	NA	NA	NA	NA	83	16	74	25	82	17	81	18
NA	NA	NA	NA	NA	NA	NA	NA	NA	NA	84	15	80	19	81	18	83	15
NA	NA	NA	NA	NA	NA	NA	NA	NA	NA	79	20	80	18	78	19	84	14
74	24	77	21	82	17	78	20	89	11	84	15	79	20	82	17	83	14
77	22	78	19	80	16	84	15	84	15	89	10	85	14	83	16	84	14
64	33	71	26	72	26	77	22	75	23	75	23	74	24	80	18	79	19
48	50	24	65	73	27	56	39	72	28	72	24	56	38	53	43	80	20
83	15	84	13	90	10	85	15	84	15	90	9	85	15	84	13	88	10
68	31	76	22	80	19	78	20	81	17	82	16	78	21	84	14	79	18
66	31	69	28	72	26	77	20	78	21	75	22	77	21	78	20	79	18
67	31	68	28	74	24	75	24	85	15	82	17	74	25	77	21	82	17
67	31	72	26	75	23	76	22	78	20	79	19	75	23	81	17	80	18
74	24	77	20	84	16	84	14	84	15	84	14	84	15	83	15	85	12
85	10	100	0	100	0	100	0	100	0	96	4	94	6	89	11	88	9
77	20	73	25	70	26	76	23	87	13	80	20	76	22	72	26	80	17
71	27	68	29	76	22	78	21	81	18	76	22	71	28	77	22	75	23
70	29	79	19	84	15	83	15	82	16	86	13	85	14	86	12	86	13
70	28	73	24	71	26	76	23	80	19	81	17	77	21	79	19	83	14

nonowners, although a large number still supported some gun control measures. In 1997 a nationwide Harris poll found that 57 percent of gun owners surveyed wanted stricter laws, compared with 76 percent of those who did not own guns. An even larger majority of gun owners (66 percent) favored stricter control of handguns.

WILL TOUGHER GUN LAWS DECREASE GUN VIOLENCE? A Gallup poll conducted in April 2000 asked, "In order to significantly reduce the amount of gun-related violence in America do you think it is sufficient to enforce current gun laws more strictly, or do you think it is also necessary to pass new gun laws?" Respondents were split down the middle. Forty-six percent believed it sufficient to enforce current laws more strictly, while 46 percent favored the passing of new laws.

Restrictions on Guns

When the Gallup organization asked if there should or should not be restrictions on owning guns, 9 percent wanted no restrictions while 15 percent wanted guns to be illegal for everyone except police and authorized personnel. Forty-three percent of respondents supported major restrictions on gun ownership, while almost one-third (32 percent) wanted minor restrictions. Women (55 percent) were far more likely than men (29 percent) to want major restrictions on guns. (See Figure 8.2.)

Holding Gun Manufacturers Accountable

In December 1999 a Gallup poll asked to what extent blame could be placed on gun manufacturers in the United States for crimes committed with guns in this country. A mere 4 percent of respondents held gun manufacturers completely responsible, while, at the other end of the spectrum, 51 percent said that gun manufacturers were not at all responsible. Of those in between, 20 percent thought gun manufacturers bore "a lot" of the responsibility, and 24 percent said they bore "a little" responsibility. When the same respondents were asked who they would side with if the Justice Department filed a lawsuit against gun manufacturers seeking to recover the costs associated with gun-related crimes, over two-thirds (67 percent) sided with the manufacturers, while little more than one-fourth (28 percent) said they would side with the Justice Department. (See Table 8.2.)

In other results 57 percent favored, and 39 percent opposed, holding parents legally responsible if their children commit crimes with their guns. More than four out of five (85 percent) wanted to see safety locks or trigger guards included with all new handgun purchases. Sixty-eight percent favored and 29 percent opposed banning the importing of high-capacity ammunition clips. Almost 9 out of 10 respondents (89 percent) wanted mandatory prison sentences for felons who commit crimes with guns, and 77 percent would impose a lifetime ban on gun ownership for any juvenile convicted of a felony. (See Table 8.3.)

Attitudes Concerning Gun Permits

Since 1972 the Roper Center for Public Opinion Research, while not specifying a particular type of gun, has been asking respondents whether they would favor or oppose a law which would require a person to obtain a permit from the police before he or she could buy a gun. During the years between 1974 and 1998, on average, 75 percent of the respondents favored the permit, while 25 percent opposed it. (See Table 8.4.)

Many observers believed the 1981 attempted assassination of President Ronald Reagan would increase the already significant proportion of Americans favoring permits. John Hinckley, the convicted gunman, had a history of mental problems that might have been uncovered through a background search for a permit. It was not until 1989, however, that the percentage of Americans favoring a permit increased significantly. In that year 78 percent of those polled favored requiring a police permit before the purchase of a gun. The proportion of those in favor of a permit has continued to increase slightly since, with 82 percent favoring a police permit in 1998. (See Table 8.4.)

CHARACTERISTICS OF RESPONDENTS. In 1998, although 82 percent of the population favored a police permit to purchase a gun, there was a difference between the sexes—76 percent of the men and 86 percent of the women were in favor. Since 1975 minorities have consistently supported gun permits. The differences in opinion between whites and minorities were often pronounced in the early 1980s. By 1998, eight percentage points separated their opinions (88 percent versus 80 percent). The differences between college-educated respondents (84 percent) and those with a grade-school education (80 percent) were slight. (See Table 8.4.)

Professional/business people (83 percent), clerical workers (84 percent), and manual workers (79 percent) and farmers (80 percent) were largely in favor of gun permits. The proportion of farmers favoring permits significantly increased from 1996, when 53 percent advocated permits. There was no significant difference in opinion between income levels. Surveys taken prior to 1993 used different categories, with the highest income being $15,000 and over, so this survey did not include past results because of the difficulty in comparing the statistics. (See Table 8.4.)

In 1998 the polls showed a significant increase from 1996 among the 18- to 20-year-old group concerning police permits. Eighty-two percent of those 18 to 20 years of age supported gun permits, compared with 69 percent in 1996. In 1998 support was slightly stronger in the Northeast (88 percent) and West (82 percent) than in the Midwest and South (79 percent). (See Table 8.4.)

Among religious groups, Jews (88 percent) remain the strongest supporters of gun permits. Along with Catholics (85 percent), they were somewhat more likely to favor permits than Protestants or those reporting no religious affiliation (80 percent). Republicans (75 percent) and independents (83 percent) were less likely than Democrats (86 percent) to back gun permits. (See Table 8.4.)

HANDGUN CONTROLS

A 2000 poll conducted by Harris Interactive found that almost three in four (72 percent) of the respondents favored stricter laws relating to the control of handguns, with 20 percent favoring laws that are less strict. (See Table 8.5.)

Characteristics of Respondents

Women (79 percent) were more likely than men (63 percent) to favor stricter restrictions on handguns. The survey also showed differences between racial groups: 89 percent of blacks and 80 percent of Hispanics favored stricter laws for handguns, compared with only 68 percent of whites. The youngest of the respondents (18 to 24) were 87 percent in favor of stricter laws on handguns, but the next age group (25 to 29) dropped to 65 percent in favor. Col-

TABLE 8.5

Attitudes toward handgun control

By demographic characteristics, United States, 2000

Question: "In general, do you favor stricter or less strict laws relating to the control of hand guns?"

	Stricter	Less strict	Neither[a]
National	72%	20%	6%
Sex			
Male	63	28	8
Female	79	13	4
Race, ethnicity			
White	68	23	7
Black	89	10	1
Hispanic	80	19	1
Age			
18 to 24 years	87	12	1
25 to 29 years	65	33	2
30 to 39 years	76	17	4
40 to 49 years	72	19	7
50 to 64 years	63	25	11
65 years and older	69	17	7
Education			
College post graduate	75	19	4
College graduate	68	22	6
Some college	71	22	6
High school graduate or less	73	18	6
Income			
Over $75,000	72	19	7
$50,001 to $75,000	69	24	6
$35,001 to $50,000	67	23	8
$25,001 to $35,000	75	20	4
$15,001 to $25,000	82	12	5
$15,000 or less	76	17	2
Region			
East	82	13	4
Midwest	68	22	7
South	67	23	6
West	73	19	7
Politics			
Republican	64	27	8
Democrat	84	11	3
Independent	64	26	8

Note: The "don't know" and "refused" categories have been omitted; therefore, percents may not sum to 100.

[a] Response volunteered.

SOURCE: *Sourcebook of Criminal Justice Statistics, 1999*, U.S. Bureau of Justice Statistics, Washington, D.C., 1999

lege graduates (75 percent), those with the lowest incomes (82 and 76 percent), and Democrats (84 percent) were more likely to favor stricter laws on the control of handguns. Respondents living in the South and Midwest were less likely to favor stricter handgun controls than those living in other regions of the United States. (See Table 8.5.)

Registering Handguns

When respondents to an April 2000 Gallup Poll Online were asked, "Would you favor or oppose the registration of all handguns?" almost three-fourths (76 percent) were in favor of registration, while 22 percent opposed the registration of all handguns. These results were then compared with responses as far back as 1938,

TABLE 8.6

Would you favor or oppose the registration of all handguns?

	Favor	Oppose	No opinion
2000 Apr 28–30	76%	22%	2%
2000 Jan 13–16	73%	26%	1%
1999 Feb 8–9	79%	19%	2%
1993 Dec	81%	18%	1%
1991	80%	17	3
1990	81%	17	2
1985	70%	25	5
1982	66%	30	4
1938*	84%	16	—

*Question wording: Do you think all owners of pistols and revolvers should be required to register with the government?

SOURCE: The Gallup Poll, April 28–30, 2000, The Gallup Organization, Princeton, NJ, 2000

TABLE 8.7

Would you favor or oppose the registration of all firearms?

	Favor	Oppose	Mixed (vol.)	No opinion
1999 Jun 11–13	79%	20%	1%	—
1998 Sep 25–Oct 1	67%	30%	—	3%
1998 Sep 9–11	67%	30%	—	3%
1980 Sep 12–15	60%	37%	—	3%
1975 Mar 28–31	67%	27%	—	6%

SOURCE: The Gallup Poll, April 28–30, 2000, The Gallup Organization, Princeton, NJ, 2000

when 84 percent of respondents favored the registration of "pistols and revolvers with the government." Since 1982 the proportion of respondents favoring registration of handguns has ranged from a low of 66 percent in 1982 to a high of 81 percent in 1990 and 1993. (See Table 8.6.)

Of respondents in a Gallup poll conducted in June 1999, 79 percent said they favored the registration of all firearms, while 20 percent were opposed. This represented a significant change over previous years. In two separate polls conducted in 1998, 67 percent favored the registration of all firearms and 30 percent were opposed. Similar results were obtained in 1985 (60 percent in favor, 37 percent opposed) and in 1975 (67 percent in favor, 27 percent opposed.) (See Table 8.7.)

College Freshmen Responses

The Higher Education Research Institute at the University of California at Los Angeles annually surveys college freshmen across the country on various issues. In the 1999 survey, when asked if the federal government should do more to control the sale of handguns, an overwhelming majority (82.3 percent) said yes. This proportion has been fairly consistent since 1989. Female students (90.5 per-

TABLE 8.8

College freshmen reporting that the federal government should do more to control the sale of handguns
By sex, United States, 1989-99

(Percent indicating "agree strongly" or "agree somewhat")

	The federal government should do more to control the sale of handguns		
	Total	Male	Female
1989	78.2%	67.2%	87.6%
1990	77.1	65.5	87.0
1991	78.1	66.8	87.8
1992	80.4	69.4	89.6
1993	81.8	71.8	90.2
1994	79.9	69.2	89.2
1995	80.8	70.2	89.7
1996	81.6	71.6	89.5
1997	81.3	70.8	90.1
1998	82.5	72.7	90.8
1999	82.3	72.6	90.5

SOURCE: *Sourcebook of Criminal Justice Statistics, 1999*, U.S. Bureau of Justice Statistics, Washington, D.C., 1999

TABLE 8.9

Attitudes toward referendum on selected criminal justice issues
United States, 1996

Question: "Suppose that on election day this year you could vote on key issues as well as candidates. Please tell me whether you would vote for or against each one of the following propositions. Would you vote for or against . . . ?"

	For	Against
The legalization of marijuana	24%	73%
The death penalty for persons convicted of murder	79	18
Life imprisonment without parole for major drug dealers	80	17
A law which would make it illegal to manufacture, sell, or possess semi-automatic guns known as assault rifles	57	42

Note: The "no opinion" category has been omitted; therefore percents may not add to 100.

SOURCE: Kathleen Maguire and Ann L. Pastore, eds. *Sourcebook of Criminal Justice Statistics—1995*, U.S. Department of Justice, Bureau of Justice Statistics, Washington, D.C., 1996

TABLE 8.10

Attitudes toward a ban on assault rifles
By demographic characteristics, United States, 1995

Question: "Please tell me whether you would favor or oppose the following proposal which some people have made to reduce crime: a ban on the manufacture, sale and possession of certain semiautomatic guns known as assault rifles."

	Favor a ban	Oppose a ban
National	68%	29%
Sex		
Male	61	36
Female	74	23
Race		
White	68	29
Black	68	27
Nonwhite[a]	73	24
Age		
18 to 29 years	61	34
40 to 49 years	67	30
50 to 64 years	76	21
50 years and older	73	24
65 years and older	70	27
Education		
College post graduate	77	23
College graduate	77	21
Some college	66	32
No college	64	32
Income		
$50,000 and over	76	22
$30,000 to 49,999	63	37
$20,000 to 29,999	70	26
Under $20,000	64	32
Community		
Urban area	69	27
Suburban area	71	28
Rural area	61	37
Region		
East	68	26
Midwest	73	26
South	67	30
West	64	34
Politics		
Republican	65	33
Democrat	76	23
Independent	64	30

Note: The "don't know/refused" category has been omitted: therefore percents may not sum to 100.

[a] Includes black respondents.

SOURCE: Kathleen Maguire and Ann L. Pastore, eds. *Sourcebook of Criminal Justice Statistics—1995*, U.S. Department of Justice, Bureau of Justice Statistics, Washington, D.C., 1996

cent) were more likely to agree that the government should take more control over handgun purchases than male students (72.6 percent). (See Table 8.8.)

BANNING ASSAULT RIFLES

In a 1996 survey the Gallup Poll found that 57 percent of respondents would vote for a law criminalizing the manufacture, sale, or possession of "semi-automatic guns known as assault rifles." More than 4 of 10 (42 percent) respondents reported they would vote against such a measure. (See Table 8.9.) When asked how they felt about a ban on the sale, manufacture, or possession of "certain types of semi-automatic guns known as assault rifles," 68 percent favored such a ban. (See Table 8.10.) Gallup also found that respondents were highly opposed to a repeal of the ban on selling semiautomatic assault rifles. (See Table 8.11.) Females, people over the age of 40 and those with yearly incomes of more than $35,000 were most likely to have opposed the sale of "assault rifles." Those from urban areas and Democrats were also likely to favor a ban.

KIDS WITH GUNS

Juvenile arrests for violent crime have decreased since 1994. Though many Americans are particularly con-

TABLE 8.11

Attitudes toward making it legal to sell semiautomatic assault rifles

By demographic characteristics, United States, 1996

Question: "The house of representatives recently voted to repeal the ban on the sale of semi-automatic assault rifles and to allow their sale in the future. do you favor or oppose making it legal to sell semi-automatic assault rifles?"

	Favor	Oppose
National	17%	81%
Sex		
Male	28	70
Female	8	91
Race, ethnicity		
White	19	79
Black	4	93
Hispanic	16	84
Age		
18 to 24 years	25	75
25 to 29 years	30	70
30 to 39 years	18	82
40 to 49 years	15	84
50 to 64 years	14	82
65 years and older	12	85
Education		
Less than high school graduate	12	83
High school graduate	20	79
Some college	15	83
College graduate	20	80
College post graduate	14	86
Income		
$15,000 or less	18	81
$15,001 to $25,000	19	79
$25,001 to $35,000	20	80
$35,001 to $50,000	14	85
Over $50,000	18	81
Community		
Central city	15	84
Metropolitan area[a]	18	81
Small town	14	82
Rural area	26	71
Region		
East	16	83
Midwest	17	80
South	15	84
West	24	75
Politics		
Repulbican	26	73
Democrat	10	89
Independent	17	81

Note: The "not sure/refused" category has been omitted; therefore percents may not sum to 100.

[a] Excluding central city.

SOURCE: Kathleen Maguire and Ann L. Pastore, eds. *Sourcebook of Criminal Justice Statistics—1995*, U.S. Department of Justice, Bureau of Justice Statistics, Washington, D.C., 1996

FIGURE 8.3

People say they support mandatory sentences for youngsters with guns

Would you favor or oppose mandatory time in a juvenile detention facility for any youth who has a gun without parental supervision?

Favor (73%)
Oppose (17%)
Not sure (10%)

SOURCE: Reprinted by permission of Public Agenda ONLINE (www.publicagenda.org), New York, NY. Data copyrighted by source; graphics copyrighted by Public Agenda 1999.

cides and 67 nongun murders. All 50 states have responded with laws making it easier to prosecute juveniles in adult criminal courts.

In 1995 Massachusetts approved legislation that imposes mandatory confinement for all children found carrying a firearm. Though critics call the law overly harsh, the public seems to agree with the crackdown on kids. In a Fox News/Opinion Dynamics poll, Americans were asked whether they would favor or oppose mandatory time in a juvenile detention facility for any juvenile who has a gun without parental supervision. Nearly three-quarters (73 percent) of the respondents favored mandatory sentences. (See Figure 8.3.)

NATIONAL OPINION RESEARCH CENTER *SECOND ANNUAL GUN POLICY SURVEY*

The *Second Annual Gun Policy Survey* (National Opinion Research Center, University of Chicago, September 1998) questioned adults about gun ownership and issues (see Chapter 2), including their opinions about guns. The survey found that in response to the high level of gun violence in America, the public generally supports a wide range of gun control measures to regulate firearms in order to make them safer and less easily available. They do not, however, favor banning guns.

Safety in Gun Design

When asked about the safety of guns, about half the people polled thought that all or some guns were regulated by federal safety standards. However, guns manufactured in the United States are, for the most part, not regulated for safety. After respondents were told that imported handguns did have to meet federal safety standards, they were asked whether they thought handguns made in the United States should have to meet the same standards. Ninety-four percent of all Americans agreed; 93 percent of gun owners surveyed (28 percent of respondents) also agreed. (See Figure 8.4.)

cerned about juvenile crime, Robert Shepherd, Jr., a law professor at the University of Richmond in Virginia, says he has not seen much change in the numbers of violent crimes committed by children over the 30 years he has been involved in juvenile justice issues. The thing that has changed is the role of guns in juvenile violence. A 1997 report from the Department of Justice studied homicides by juveniles aged 13 and 14. In 1980 there were 74 murders committed with guns and 68 with other weapons by that age group. In 1995 there were 178 gun-related homi-

FIGURE 8.4

FIGURE 8.5

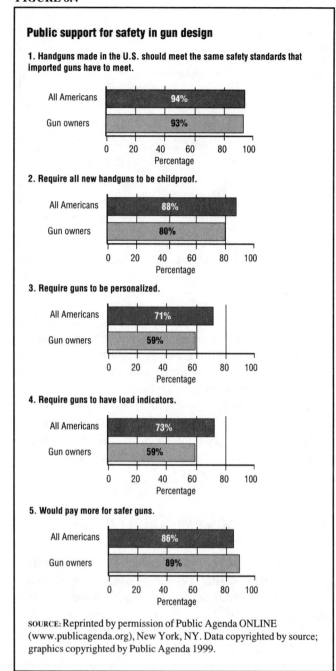

Public support for safety in gun design

1. Handguns made in the U.S. should meet the same safety standards that imported guns have to meet.

2. Require all new handguns to be childproof.

3. Require guns to be personalized.

4. Require guns to have load indicators.

5. Would pay more for safer guns.

SOURCE: Reprinted by permission of Public Agenda ONLINE (www.publicagenda.org), New York, NY. Data copyrighted by source; graphics copyrighted by Public Agenda 1999.

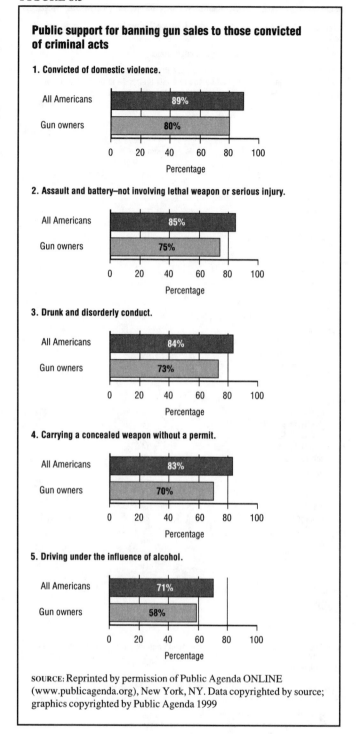

Public support for banning gun sales to those convicted of criminal acts

1. Convicted of domestic violence.

2. Assault and battery–not involving lethal weapon or serious injury.

3. Drunk and disorderly conduct.

4. Carrying a concealed weapon without a permit.

5. Driving under the influence of alcohol.

SOURCE: Reprinted by permission of Public Agenda ONLINE (www.publicagenda.org), New York, NY. Data copyrighted by source; graphics copyrighted by Public Agenda 1999

One option for regulating the safe design of guns is to require all new handguns to be childproof. When asked if they would favor or oppose legislation requiring guns to be made so they could not be fired by a young child with small hands, 88 percent favored this legislation, with 67 percent strongly in favor. Eighty percent of gun owners approved. Personalization of handguns, which allows operation of the gun by an authorized user only, is another safety option. Overall, 71 percent of those surveyed favored a law requiring personalization, and among gun owners, 59 percent favored such a law. (See Figure 8.4.)

Guns can be designed with magazine safeties to prevent unintentional firing. Eighty-two percent

favored mandating these safety designs in new guns. When asked about load indicators, described as "a device in some handguns that shows if the handgun contains ammunition," 73 percent favored a law requiring load indicators in all new handguns. A majority of gun owners (59 percent) also favored this measure. (See Figure 8.4.)

Requiring these safety measures would likely make guns more expensive to buy. Asked if they would be willing to pay more for safer guns, 86 percent of all of those

FIGURE 8.6

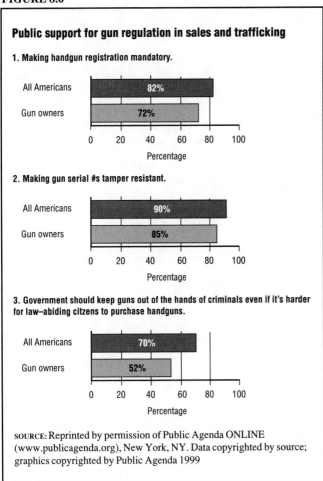

Public support for gun regulation in sales and trafficking

1. Making handgun registration mandatory.

2. Making gun serial #s tamper resistant.

3. Government should keep guns out of the hands of criminals even if it's harder for law–abiding citzens to purchase handguns.

SOURCE: Reprinted by permission of Public Agenda ONLINE (www.publicagenda.org), New York, NY. Data copyrighted by source; graphics copyrighted by Public Agenda 1999

crimes should or should not be able to purchase handguns. Respondents saw many reasons for denying permits. The greatest percentage of respondents (89 percent) thought that persons who had been convicted of domestic violence should not be allowed to purchase handguns. More than 8 out of 10 wanted to deny handguns to persons convicted of assault and battery, drunk or disorderly conduct, and carrying a concealed weapon without a permit. Seventy-one percent felt anyone convicted of drunk driving should not be able to buy a handgun. (See Figure 8.5.)

Gun Regulation in Sales and Trafficking

Most respondents wanted to prevent criminals from obtaining guns. Seventy percent of all those polled and 52 percent of gun owners wanted the government to "do everything it can to keep handguns out of the hands of criminals even if it means that it will be harder for law-abiding citizens to purchase handguns." Eighty-two percent of all respondents and 72 percent of gun owner respondents supported mandatory handgun registration. Nine out of 10 Americans wanted mandatory tamper-resistant serial numbers on handguns, as did 85 percent of gun owners. (See Figure 8.6.)

surveyed said yes. An even larger percent of gun owners (89 percent) were willing to pay more (Figure 8.4).

Banning Gun Sales to Persons Convicted of Crime

Survey respondents were read a list of crimes and asked if persons who had been convicted of each of those

CHAPTER 9

THERE SHOULD BE STRICTER GUN CONTROL LAWS

This chapter presents a sample of the arguments used by the proponents of strong federal gun control to support their position over the last several decades. Please see Chapter 10 for the arguments put forward by opponents of strong federal gun control.

STATEMENT OF PRESIDENT WILLIAM JEFFERSON CLINTON IN AN INTERVIEW WITH ABC'S *GOOD MORNING AMERICA* (MAY 14, 1999)

I think the Brady Bill has made a real difference; having background checks matters. We know that 250,000 people, from the time I signed the Brady Bill in 1994 until last year, were unable to get handguns. We know just since the Insta-Check went in last year, another 36,000 people have been denied the right to get handguns. So closing the gun show loophole matters. You know... even the NRA says, well, we ought to prosecute crimes. Well, we ought to make the right things crimes, and we ought to make it unlawful for children to possess weapons; we ought to make it unlawful for people to sell them to them or to transfer to them; and we ought to close the loopholes in the law. And as we do that, we will make a difference. This is not just about school shootings, although they're very important, but 13 children are killed every day by guns on the streets, in the neighborhoods and various circumstances. So I think there are basically three problems. You have more kids that are kind of at risk of violence. You have a culture that desensitizes and glorifies violence, and desensitizes people to it. And it's way too easy to get guns.

STATEMENT OF FRANK R. LAUTENBERG (D-NJ) BEFORE THE SENATE ON OCTOBER 2, 1998

As a result of the Brady Act, we have helped prevent thousands of guns from getting into the hands of the wrong people. Since the Brady Act went into effect in 1994, more than 242,000 handgun purchases have been denied to convicted felons, fugitives, drug addicts, and other dangerous persons. The Domestic Violence Gun Ban in the Brady Act... has prevented more than 6,800 firearms sales to people convicted of abusing a spouse or child.

However, the Brady Law has not completely stopped the flow of handguns to those who should not have them. Gun traffickers continue to supply an illegal gun market by buying large quantities of guns in states with lax gun laws and then reselling them on the streets—often in cities and states with strict gun laws.

If these traffickers cannot legally buy a gun themselves, or if they do not want to have their name turn up if the gun is later found at a crime scene, they find others to make the purchases for them. The trafficker pays a straw purchaser, in money or drugs, to buy 25, 50 or more handguns at a time and then resells the guns to those who otherwise could not buy them—such as convicted felons, drug addicts or children.

In fact, the Maryland State Police official testified that multiple gun purchases by straw purchasers were the source of the majority of firearms used in the commission of violent crime.

My bill would make it far more difficult and less profitable for traffickers to conduct their deadly business, by prohibiting an individual from buying more than one handgun a month. We know this approach works because three states—Virginia, Maryland, South Carolina—have passed one-gun-a-month laws and the results have been dramatic. Gun trafficking from these states has plunged.

For instance, officers from the Virginia State Police testified that after Virginia passed its one-handgun-a-month limit in 1993, the number of crime guns traced back to Virginia from the Northeast dropped by nearly 40 percent. Prior to one-gun-a-month, Virginia had been among the leading supplier of weapons to the so-called "Iron Pipeline" that feeds the arms race on the streets of Northeastern cities.

In 1995, the Virginia Crime Commission conducted a comprehensive study of the one-handgun-a-month limit to determine if the law had achieved its purpose. That study found, and I quote, "Virginia's one-gun-a-month statute... has had its intended effect of reducing Virginia's status as a source state for gun trafficking."

Maryland and South Carolina showed similar results.... "Prior to the passage of the one-gun-a-month law, South Carolina was a leading source state for guns traced to New York City, accounting for 39 percent of guns recovered in criminal investigations. Following the implementation of the law, South Carolina virtually dropped off the statistical list of source states for firearms trafficked to the Northeast."

Maryland... passed its law in 1996 and has already seen the results. According to the testimony from the Maryland State Police:

> In 1991, Maryland was nationally ranked second in terms of suppliers of crime guns to the City of New York. By 1997, one year after the passage of Maryland's one-gun-a-month law, Maryland moved out of the top ten suppliers of crime guns to New York City.

And most significant is the drop in crime that has followed enactment of limits on handgun sales. For example, in Virginia, the number of murders, robberies and aggravated assaults committed with a firearm significantly dropped after 1993 when the limit went into effect....

Limits on handgun purchases, while disrupting gun traffickers, have little or no effect on the sportsman or law-abiding citizen because a very small percent of all handgun purchases involve multiple sales. Virginia State Police reported only 6 percent of handgun purchases were multiple sales. But of these, nearly 75 percent were semi-automatic weapons, the weapon of choice among gun traffickers. Mayor Rendell testified that less than 1 percent of handgun purchasers in Philadelphia bought more than 12 handguns in a 12-month period....

STATEMENT OF HIGH SCHOOL STUDENT, ABIGAIL NESSON, FROM VERMONT, SUBMITTED TO THE HOUSE OF REPRESENTATIVES FROM BERNARD SANDERS (I-VT), AUGUST 7, 1998

I believe that our forefathers had the right idea. Their wish was to create a safe and free nation for all of us to live in, and they wrote this to prove it: "We the people of the United States, in order to form a more perfect union, establish justice, ensure domestic tranquillity, provide fore the common defense, promote the general welfare, and secure the blessings of liberty to ourselves and our posterity, do ordain and establish this Constitution of the United States of America."

I am here today to talk to you about guns. The widespread availability of these weapons is frightening and wrong. Thousands are killed every year in our country by guns bought legally, guns made not to hunt animals but to hunt humans. Many have killed or have been killed by the time they reach my age, if they ever do.

I am a strict constructionist when it comes to the preamble and the Second Amendment, meaning I believe that our forefathers wrote just what they meant. They meant for the Constitution to increase domestic tranquillity and general welfare and, especially, common defense. I believe—I know—that the guns that are available today do none of these things. I believe and I know that our forefathers would agree, because I refuse to think that the intention of the ones who wrote the Constitution was to put lethal weapons in the hands of every person who wanted one. That is not "a well-regulated militia." No, their intention was to ensure that safety and freedom for us, their posterity.

I propose that we follow the words of the preamble and of our constitution. I propose that we take a step to make our nation safe again, for me and for the children I want to have some day. I propose we remove the guns from our streets, our homes and our hands.

STATEMENT OF SYLVESTER DAUGHTRY, JR., CHIEF OF POLICE, GREENSBORO, NC, AND PRESIDENT OF THE INTERNATIONAL ASSOCIATION OF CHIEFS OF POLICE, BEFORE THE HOUSE SUBCOMMITTEE ON CRIME AND CRIMINAL JUSTICE, APRIL 25, 1994

On January 25 of last year... in Langley, Virginia, an individual with no criminal record went on a shooting spree outside CIA headquarters, killing two and wounding three. On the other side of the country, on July 1 of last year, another individual with no criminal record entered a San Francisco law firm with over 450 rounds of ammunition, eventually killing eight and seriously wounding six. With these examples, the argument by gun control opponents that we will be restricting the rights of law-abiding citizens rings very hollow. As we have said, we in law enforcement cannot make such a simplistic and dreamy distinction.

The reason there is no decrease in gun-related mayhem as a result of stringent state and local gun control laws is that guns are easily purchased in less stringent locations and brought into the stricter areas. As you can imagine, chiefs do not have a patrol to prevent firearms purchased elsewhere from entering and being used in our jurisdictions. This is one of the logical reasons why the IACP supports federal legislation in the area of gun control. Gun control will work only if all the states are required to observe it.

STATEMENT OF HOWARD METZENBAUM (D-OH), *CONGRESSIONAL RECORD*, SENATE, MARCH 1, 1994

...[T]here is a gun crisis in this country. There are over 200 million guns in America. An American is killed by a gun every 14 minutes. Every 50 seconds, someone is raped, robbed, or assaulted with a handgun.

And we are all paying the price. Our children are paying the price. Foreign tourists are paying the price. Shopkeepers are paying the price. Innocent bystanders are paying the price. We are all victims.

Since 1968, more than 300,000 Americans have been murdered by guns. In 1992, more than 35,000 people were killed by gunfire. Today, only cars cause more fatal injuries than guns, and guns are expected to take the lead very soon....

Aside from the toll on human lives, the economic costs from gun violence are staggering. A 1989 study by the Centers for Disease Control and Prevention estimated the lifetime economic cost of gun violence in 1985 at $14.4 billion. And that was 1985.

And what kind of country are we creating for our children? What can we say when our children are afraid to go to school? When we are afraid to let them go outside to play?

Gun violence takes the life of a child every 2 hours.... The number of 10- to 17-year-olds who used guns to commit murder skyrocketed 79 percent during the 1980s....

STATEMENT OF BILL BRADLEY (D-NJ), *CONGRESSIONAL RECORD*, SENATE, APRIL 26, 1994

Every year, more than 24,000 Americans... are killed with handguns.... Some will argue that these grim statistics are the result of weak law enforcement, light sentencing, legitimate fear, and the waning of family values. Others will argue that they are the result of joblessness, poverty, and long term neglect of our most violent neighborhoods. I have no doubt that the growing rate of violent activity has been aggravated in part by all these factors. But accepting many of these causes of handgun violence does not erase the reality that crime and deviant behavior have become much more of a burden on our society because of the explosive growth in handguns. Disputes that were settled with fists and knives 10 years ago are now being settled with guns.

STATEMENT OF N. T. "PETE" SHIELDS, CHAIRMAN OF HANDGUN CONTROL, INC., ACCOMPANIED BY MATTHEW FENTON IV, BEFORE THE SUBCOMMITTEE ON CRIMINAL LAW, U.S. SENATE, MAY 5, 1982

As Americans become increasingly concerned about the threat of nuclear war, they are also understanding the threat from within, the threat of America's handgun war.

Yes, war is a proper analogy for America's domestic violence which is far worse than our most recent foreign war. During the Vietnam war, more American civilians were murdered with handguns here at home in America

than American soldiers killed in action in Vietnam. And I repeat, that is murder. That is not accidents or suicides. And that is handguns. That is not rifles and shotguns.

Your colleagues are well aware that six Presidential Commissions, as well as the Reagan administration's Task Force on Violent Crime, have urged Congress to pass tougher handgun laws. Our Nation's leading law enforcement organizations—the Police Executive Research Forum, the International Association of Chiefs of Police, and the National Association of Attorneys General—also support tougher handgun control laws.

The handgun waiting period... has two important features: First, it would provide an opportunity for law enforcement officials to insure that the prospective purchaser was who he said he was and did not have a criminal record, a history of mental illness or drug addiction, was at least 21, and was a state resident. Second, it would provide a "cooling off" period for individuals intent on buying handguns to commit crimes of passion....

Your colleagues are no doubt aware of the growing handgun violence which has prompted a ground swell of public outrage across the country. Simply put, Americans are fed up with the handgun violence that is changing our lives and changing our country. And, to understate their outrage, they are growing impatient with congressional inaction. This explosion of State and local action shows that our citizens recognize the difference between handguns and long guns. They know that handguns are used by criminals, that long guns are used by hunters.

STATEMENT OF JUDGE MARVIN E. ASPEN, CRIMINAL DIVISION, CIRCUIT COURT OF COOK COUNTY, IL, BEFORE THE SUBCOMMITTEE ON CRIME, HOUSE COMMITTEE ON THE JUDICIARY, APRIL 14, 1975

This myth goes something like this: "Gun control legislation will disarm the law-abiding citizen, leaving him the helpless prey of the crook who will not be affected by the legislation."

My response to this contention, although statistically supportable, is based on my courtroom observations over the past 4 years, where more than 1,000 accused felons have appeared before me for trial. I believe that a strong Federal gun control bill will, in the long run—not overnight—disarm the criminal. I believe that the law enforcement needs of the law-abiding citizen are not best served by possession of a firearm.

I am not convinced that restricting or banning the sale and possession of handguns to the general public will have no effect on the criminal... restricting the import and interstate sale of handguns will dry up the potential arsenal readily available at the local gun shops to the criminal and the potential criminal.

Reducing or eliminating the private ownership of handguns by private citizens will also serve to reduce this potential arsenal. It is my impression that a significant number of handguns used in crimes are taken in burglaries from the homes and businesses of law-abiding citizens.... 500,000 guns are stolen every year from homes and businesses of law-abiding citizens....

Therefore, it is clear to me that the criminal, whether or not he initially turns in his handgun, will, in the long run, be adversely affected by proposed Federal legislation.

No responsible law enforcement officer would argue that weapons in the private sector have been significantly effective in combating crime. On the contrary, weapons in the private sector pose a constant threat to the law-abiding citizen.

STATEMENT OF DAVID SCOTT, GEORGIA HOUSE OF REPRESENTATIVES, BEFORE THE SUBCOMMITTEE ON CRIME, HOUSE COMMITTEE ON THE JUDICIARY, JULY 21, 1975

America is simple: We live in a society in which the highest priority is the preservation of life; the freedom to live! We have, through our ingenious efforts, developed an instrument that reflects man's greatest inhumanity to man: the handgun, the expressed purpose of which is to kill people. There is no other purpose. The least we can do is to see to it that persons who buy and/or possess the handgun meet minimum qualifications, such as age, mental competency, residency, no previous felony crime with a gun, not having killed anyone before. Is that asking too much for each of our fifty states to insure? Is it not our first responsibility as government to do all we can to enhance the public's safety? In the name of God, we must love our fellow man enough to insist, if this deadly instrument must be tolerated in our society, that we take as much precaution as possible to protect the safety of our public. This can be done most effectively by licensing, registration, [instituting] a waiting period before purchase, and by requiring each of the fifty states to administer such provisions through their departments of public safety.

This gun lobby's special interest must be exposed to the American people for what it is; a very tragic but effective, very deadly but powerful, group of combined industrial giants in the ammunition and arms industries along with sportsmen clubs, hunting clubs, wholesale and retail gun and ammunition dealers and NRA members throughout the country who realize that if meaningful laws are enacted to stop making the handgun so easily accessible and available, sales will go down.... Most major anti-gun control groups are sponsored and encouraged, directly or indirectly, by these special interests.

STATEMENT OF ABNER J. MIKVA (D-IL), BEFORE THE SUBCOMMITTEE ON CRIME, HOUSE COMMITTEE ON THE JUDICIARY, FEBRUARY 18, 1975

We must realize the pervasive consequences that violent crime—both the threat and reality—has had on our society. It has changed our lives to a degree most often associated with the revolutionary technological changes of the post World War II period—television, the growth of the automobile and commercial air travel, and computers. Yes, this society has had a long history of violence, but the magnitude of the present situation is unprecedented and intolerable....

The vast majority of Americans... understand that the problem of violent crime and the use and availability of handguns are directly related. Every public opinion poll on handguns shows that an overwhelming majority of Americans favor strong controls. And in recent years, police officials throughout the country have been calling repeatedly for strong national handgun control legislation.

Critics of gun control argue that guns do not kill people.... But two facts sharply limit the truth to this argument. First, most killers do not plan in advance to kill their victims. According to the FBI... almost two-thirds of all killings resulted from a family dispute or other arguments between friends or acquaintances and not because of premeditated murder. Most of these killings would have ended as nothing more serious than a shouting match or a fistfight, except for the presence of a gun. Second, one of every five gun attacks ends in death while only one of every 20 knife attacks ends in death. Thus, if the attacker is intent on murder, he is four times less likely to be successful if he cannot get a gun. It is much more difficult to kill somebody with a garrote by accident, or by mistaken identity.

Many people claim that they need a handgun around the house to protect themselves against intruders. Yet statistics show that a gun kept around the house is six times as likely to kill a family member as it is to kill an intruder. And the National Committee on Violence found that in one year, more homeowners were killed in gun accidents alone than were killed by robbers and burglars in the four preceding years combined. Thus, keeping a handgun in the house is itself a dangerous practice and should be discouraged.

...Another favorite argument of gun control opponents is that the Second Amendment guarantees the right to bear arms. But the Supreme Court has held on at least four occasions that this right is limited to state militias and does not extend to private citizens. Those who use this argument ignore an even more basic right that has been denied many citizens because of the lack of adequate handgun control laws—the right of citizens not to be gunned down in the streets or in their homes.

As for sportsmen, under my proposal any legitimate gun club will be allowed to obtain and use handguns on the club premises. This may be a slight inconvenience to the relatively few people who like to shoot at targets in their backyards, but when measured against the lives that will be saved, this seems a small concession for sportsmen to make.

Secondly, as to the contention that the states and not the federal government should enact handgun legislation, it seems almost pointless to ban the sale of handguns in Illinois if a person can buy one with no trouble just over the state line in Indiana, Wisconsin, or Missouri. Further, since most handgun killings are crimes of passion, long prison sentences and stiff fines—another proposal of some—would not serve as an effective deterrent, whether such sentences or fines are imposed at the state or federal level.

CHAPTER 10
THERE SHOULD NOT BE STRICTER GUN CONTROL LAWS

This chapter presents a sample of the arguments used by the opponents of strong federal gun control to support their position over the last several decades. Please see Chapter 9 for the arguments put forward by supporters of strong federal gun control.

STATEMENT OF STROM THURMOND (R-SC), UNITED STATES SENATE, JANUARY 5, 1995

Let me first say that I strongly support our Constitutional right to own firearms under the Second Amendment. However, I do not believe this is an absolute right which would allow convicted criminals and other miscreants to lawfully own firearms. In fact, federal law currently prohibits gun ownership by those persons who are, among other things, a fugitive from justice, convicted of a felony, addicted to controlled substances, an illegal alien, or those who have been committed to a mental institution.

Restrictions on gun ownership have been debated by the U.S. Congress and state legislatures for some time. It is my belief that efforts to fight crime are best served by focusing on the criminal element and not with gun control legislation. Criminals should know that when they break the law there will be swift apprehension, prosecution, and punishment. This must be a virtual certainty and not just a mere possibility.

STATEMENT OF RICHARD G. LUGAR (R-IN), UNITED STATES SENATE, DECEMBER 20, 1994

As crime and firearms legislation comes before the U.S. Senate, I carefully evaluate each bill's merits on reducing and discouraging criminal violence and the effect on the rights of law-abiding citizens to own firearms. A large majority of members, including myself, support the Second Amendment.

I will vote against sweeping proposals such as Sen. Chafee's [R-RI] bill to "prohibit the manufacture, importa-

tion, exportation, sale, purchase, transfer, receipt, possession, or transportation of handguns and hand ammunition," or Sen. Moynihan's (D-NY) bill for "regulating or restricting the availability of ammunition," or Sen. Metzenbaum's (D-OH) proposal to make it "unlawful to transfer or possess a semi-automatic assault weapon."

I believe in the rights of law-abiding citizens to possess firearms for sporting and defensive purposes, and I support Indiana law related to the purchase and ownership of firearms. I also remain committed to diminishing the threat of criminal violence for the benefit of our families in Indiana and the nation.

REPRESENTATIVE JACK R. KINGSTON (R-GA) ON THE FLOOR OF THE HOUSE OF REPRESENTATIVES, APRIL 18, 1994

...I think because there is emotion, it is important for members of Congress to look at gun control not based on philosophical bias but based on empirical data and objectivity....

I am going to talk about an article that was in the March Journal of Medicine, which is the publication of the Georgia Association of Medicine [David B. Kopel, "The Lure of Foreign Gun Laws"]....

In it he talks about countries that have strict gun control laws and what it has meant in terms of the crime rate....

Today you cannot own a gun or rifle in Japan. You can own a shotgun only through very rigorous licensing laws.

Is it a safe country? It certainly is a safe country. They have a very low crime rate. What does that mean? Maybe if we look at it at first glance, get rid of the guns and you get rid of the crime problem, if you only look at the law and the crime rate.

...Switzerland ...actually has a lower murder rate than Japan. They have strict gun control laws, but in a completely different way. Every male in Switzerland has to join the militia. If you are between the age of 20 and 50 and you are male, you are a member of the militia. You spend three or four weeks per year training, and as part of your duty in the militia you are given a fully automatic assault rifle which you take home. You do not leave that at the National Guard armory for weekend duties. You do not pick it up for your three weeks of summer training. You take that home to suburban Zurich or wherever you live and keep it at home. Every male must be proficient in marksmanship. Every male between the ages of 20 and 50 will get tested on marksmanship.

In a country which is about two-thirds the size of West Virginia, there are over 3,000 shooting ranges. Ammunition, while we have one proposal right now to tax it, is subsidized in Switzerland. To get a handgun or rifle, there is a very easy permitting process. Just about any adult can get one. You can get an antitank gun, antiaircraft gun, and you can buy some types of cannons. This is just the folks on the street.

I would submit that they are not more responsible, they are not safer, and they are not smarter, but what they do have in Switzerland, and they also have in Japan, is a strong family structure, tightly knit communities, and good relationships from generation to generation.

In short, in these two countries culturally young people are socialized into noncriminal behavior....

If we just superficially kid ourselves and say we are going to get rid of the guns, we are going to get rid of the problems, the statistics do not show that at all. They show it to be a cultural socializing process which we are not doing a good job at in America, particularly in the inner cities, where we have the highest murder rates.

In Britain, they have very tough gun control laws. They have had those ...for about 30 or 40 years ...despite that, in a country where only 4 percent of the households legally have guns, their murder rates are higher now than they were before the strict gun control laws went into effect.

Let us talk about Jamaica because one of the things we hear so often from Second Amendment proponents is that you are not necessarily owning a gun to defend yourself against a burglar, but you are doing it to defend yourselves against the government.

In 1974, Jamaica enacted very strict gun control laws, which include house-to-house searches randomly, secret trials, detention, incommunicado, mandatory life sentences for possession of a single bullet, very strict gun control laws.

What happened? Violent crime dropped significantly for about six months, but then, within a year, it went back up to the level it was before the gun control laws, and in fact has been increasing since.

What is the most significant is that one-third of the murders in Jamaica were perpetrated by the police. Think about that in terms of the Second Amendment people who are saying, "You have to worry about the government, not just the burglar."

...Why is it that police can have guns, but you and I and the average American citizen cannot?

STATEMENT OF ORRIN HATCH (R-UT), BEFORE THE COMMITTEE ON THE JUDICIARY, UNITED STATES SENATE, OCTOBER 4, 1983

I have constantly been amazed by the indifference or even hostility shown the Second Amendment by courts, legislatures, and commentators. James Madison would be startled to hear that his recognition of a right to keep and bear arms, which passed the House by a voice vote without objection and hardly a debate, has since been construed in but a few, and most ambiguous, Supreme Court decisions, whereas his proposals for freedom of religion, which he made reluctantly out of fear that they would be rejected or narrowed beyond use, and those for freedom of assembly, which passed only after a lengthy and bitter debate, are the subject of scores of detailed and favorable decisions. Thomas Jefferson, who kept a veritable armory of pistols, rifles, and shotguns at Monticello, and advised his nephew to forsake other sports in favor of hunting, would be astounded to hear supposed civil libertarians claim firearm ownership should be restricted. Samuel Adams, a handgun owner who pressed for an amendment stating that the "Constitution shall never be construed ...to prevent the people of the United States who are peaceable citizens from keeping their own arms," would be shocked to hear that his native state today imposes a year's sentence, without probation or parole, for carrying a firearm without a police permit.

This is not to imply that courts have totally ignored the impact of the Second Amendment in the Bill of Rights.... They argue that the Second Amendment's words "right of the people" mean "a right of the state"— apparently overlooking the impact of those same words when used in the First and Fourth Amendments. The "right of the people" to assemble or to be free from unreasonable searches and seizures is not contested as an individual guarantee. Still they ignore consistency and claim that the right to "bear arms" relates only to military uses. This not only violates a consistent constitutional reading of "right of the people" but also ignores that the Second Amendment protects a right to "keep" arms. These commentators contend instead the amendment's preamble regarding the necessity of a "well-regulated militia ...to a free state" means that the right to keep and bear arms applies only to a National Guard. Such a reading fails to note that the Framers used the term "militia" to relate to every citizen capable of bearing arms, and that Congress has established the present National Guard under its power to raise armies, expressly stating that it was not doing so under the power to organize and arm the militia.

STATEMENT OF NEAL KNOX, EXECUTIVE DIRECTOR, INSTITUTE FOR LEGISLATIVE ACTION, NATIONAL RIFLE ASSOCIATION, BEFORE THE SUBCOMMITTEE ON CRIMINAL LAW, UNITED STATES SENATE, MARCH 4, 1982

Gun laws fail because they do not address the issue. The issue is not possession of firearms, but misuse of firearms. We cannot expect criminals to abide by gun laws when they have already shown a disregard for law and order by their criminal activity. The only people ever affected by gun laws are peaceful, law-abiding citizens, who never abuse their firearms right.

Recent research is finding gun laws do not reduce the amount of violent crime in our society....

Gun laws have succeeded only in disarming the law-abiding and making the criminals' work environment safer. I submit that our concern should be to make the environment safer for honest citizens, and this, gun laws have failed to do.

In response to violent crime, people buy guns. Those purchases do not adversely affect the problem of violent crime. Indeed, the persons most likely to own handguns solely for protection are among the persons most likely to be victimized by violent crime and least likely themselves to commit violent crime: poor, black, female heads of households.

People will acquire handguns for protection in response to violent crime. Laws will, if anything, simply encourage faster gun purchases out of fear of more restrictive future legislation....

Law-abiding citizens are purchasing handguns for self-defense; to provide the protection the government and the police cannot provide....

As with any gun law currently on the books, or being proposed, it has the clear effect of making millions of peaceful citizens criminals overnight. Any restrictive gun law inherently provides for increased police and Government power over people.

Every restrictive gun law ever passed inherently infringes on the civil liberties that Americans hold dear—the constitutional protections of privacy, freedom from unreasonable search and seizure, due process, and the right to keep and bear arms. Yet, some would have you believe that more gun laws are justified.

STATEMENT OF DR. DAVID I. CAPLAN, PH.D., LL.B., NEW YORK, BEFORE THE SUBCOMMITTEE ON CRIMINAL LAW, UNITED STATES SENATE, MAY 5, 1982

The constitutional right of the people to keep arms has deep roots in common law and constitutional history, and it remains of fundamental importance to this day. This right is explicitly guaranteed in the Second Amendment in the Bill of Rights and includes the keeping by private citizens of any hand-carried arms commonly used by private individuals and police for personal defense.

Because "a man's house is his castle and his defense," and because the Third Amendment in the Bill of Rights prohibits Government from quartering soldiers in a person's house during times of peace without his consent, the constitutional right of the people to keep arms must guarantee at its core the legally unfettered ability of the householder to acquire speedily and to keep permanently and anonymously in his house such arms as are commonly used for home defense, not only as a means for resistance against violent burglars but also as a strong moral check and deterrent against illegal quartering of troops in his house.

In short, the arms protected under the common law, and hence under the Constitution, in the hands of the citizenry are all those arms which are "hand-carried weapons commonly used by individuals and police for personal defense." Thus, firearms such as pistols, revolvers, rifles, and shotguns are all clearly within the ambit of constitutional protection, and none can logically be excluded.

STATEMENT OF JAMES M. COLLINS, (R-TX), HOUSE OF REPRESENTATIVES, BEFORE THE SUBCOMMITTEE ON CRIME, HOUSE COMMITTEE ON THE JUDICIARY, FEBRUARY 20, 1975

[There should be] legislation designed to reduce crimes committed with weapons by instituting mandatory, strict sentences for any person convicted of using a gun during the commission of a crime ...[and] prohibit[ing] the granting of a suspended sentence or a probationary sentence for any Federal felony committed with a firearm.

Gun control laws will only result in a large criminal network of illegal firearms sales, thereby denying guns to all but criminals. Americans must maintain the right to own guns for the defense of their families and for sporting purposes. Without this right, our Country would be a virtual police state with arbitrary control rights vested in the government. Let us put the criminal behind bars, keep him there, and work to rehabilitate him ...instead of trying to pass legislation against the large majority of the solid citizens who own guns because of their interest in sports.

STATEMENT OF HAROLD W. GLASSEN, REPRESENTING THE MICHIGAN RIFLE AND PISTOL ASSOCIATION, BEFORE THE SUBCOMMITTEE ON CRIME, HOUSE COMMITTEE ON THE JUDICIARY, JUNE 9, 1975

The problem of crime is criminals, not guns. Less than two-tenths of 1 percent of all firearms in the United States are used for illegal purposes.... The other 99 8/10 percent are used legally for hunting, target shooting, for protection. The crime problem is created by the small percentage of people who have discovered that our lenient legal system makes it easier for them to prey on innocent victims than to work a respectable job at a good salary.

To a criminal, a firearm is a tool of the trade. He would no more register or turn in his gun than a doctor would turn in his stethoscope. Obviously, a law or laws requiring registration and/or confiscation would only affect the law-abiding. Like the era of prohibition, organized crime would find ways to turn this into a wholesale nationwide money-making and crime-making venture.

...We feel that the citizen has a right to be protected from the criminal by invoking mandatory penalties for the commission of a crime with a firearm, speedy and decisive adjudication of criminal cases, and appropriate incarceration for recidivists.

...The handgun is to kill only. I want to give a rebuttal to this assertion.... There are five handgun events in the shooting portion of each of the famous Pan American and Olympic Games, plus a pistol-shooting competition as one part of the Modern Pentathlon event of those games.

STATEMENT OF LARRY MCDONALD (D-GA), BEFORE THE SUBCOMMITTEE ON CRIME, HOUSE COMMITTEE ON THE JUDICIARY, JULY 21, 1975

They are not rights which are granted to us by the federal government, but rights with which the Constitution forbids the federal government to interfere.

Thus the Second Amendment does not "grant" the right to keep and bear arms, but protects it from usurpation. Note that the Amendment doesn't say this right may not be abolished. It goes farther. It says it may not even be infringed. That is, this right is so important it may not be tampered with, or trespassed upon, or transgressed, or chiseled away by any method or means Washington might devise. The Constitution is unequivocal on this point.

Allegedly, in order to control the acts of our criminal minority, the gun-controllers demand that tens of millions of law-abiding Americans be restricted, harassed, and eventually deprived of their constitutional right as well as their legal property. In defiance of all logic, such gun-controllers express a far greater fear of those tens of millions of Americans who are not criminals than they do of the hoodlums actively terrorizing our cities. The reason is that their attitudes and opinions are not the product of logic but of ideology.

STATEMENT OF STEVEN SYMMS (R-ID), BEFORE THE SUBCOMMITTEE ON CRIME, HOUSE COMMITTEE ON THE JUDICIARY, FEBRUARY 21, 1975

Men such as Samuel Adams and Patrick Henry were very emphatic about the need for such an Amendment prior to ratification of the Constitution, protesting that as first submitted, the document did not guarantee "the right of having arms in your own defense." So important was the right to bear arms to our forefathers that it was placed second in the Bill of Rights, with freedom of expression the only Amendment ahead of it. Recognition of the individual's right to bear arms was by no means a new idea, however. In fact, it dates all the way back to the seventeenth century English Common Law.

My second objection to federal gun laws is purely practical—they do not work.... Common sense tells us that the reason they are classified criminals in the first place is because they are in the habit of breaking laws. There is no reason to assume that they will obey federal gun laws any more than other laws they have broken.

...What would be the effect of outlawing the so-called "Saturday Night Special?" The only lasting effect would be to once again disarm the law-abiding citizen. But in this case, primarily the poor would be penalized— the people who generally live in high-crime neighborhoods but who can scarcely afford an expensive Smith and Wesson for protection. By outlawing inexpensive handguns, we would in effect be denying lower income people their basic right to self-defense.

STATEMENT OF JAMES VALENTINO, PRESIDENT, ILLINOIS STATE RIFLE ASSOCIATION, BEFORE THE SUBCOMMITTEE ON CRIME, HOUSE COMMITTEE ON THE JUDICIARY, APRIL 15, 1975

Protecting the citizens is not disarming them. To properly protect the citizens, we cannot deny them the right to protect themselves. The handgun in the dresser drawer should remain a legitimate means of self-protection to the honest citizen. Why talk about gun laws when our federal government has so miserably failed at all other attempts to ban products or commodities? Our prohibition of alcohol was notoriously unsuccessful and produced an organized underworld unsurpassed in history. Our narcotic bans have failed to reduce the flow and operate to protect underworld profits. If we attempt to ban any desired type of guns, the underworld will be manufacturing before the Congressional ink is dry.

APPENDIX I
STATE CONSTITUTION ARTICLES CONCERNING WEAPONS

The Second Amendment of the Bill of Rights of the U.S. Constitution reads: "A well regulated militia being necessary to the security of a free State, the right of the people to keep and bear arms shall not be infringed."

Alabama: That every citizen has a right to bear arms in defense of himself and the state. Art. I, sect. 26.

Alaska: A well-regulated militia being necessary to the security of a free state, the right of the people to keep and bear arms shall not be infringed. Art. I, sect. 19.

Arizona: The right of the individual citizen to bear arms in defense of himself or the State shall not be impaired, but nothing in this section shall be construed as authorizing individuals or corporations to organize, maintain, or employ an armed body of men. Art. II, sect. 26.

Arkansas: The citizens of this State shall have the right to keep and bear arms for their common defense. Art. II, sect. 5.

Colorado: The right of no person to keep and bear arms in defense of his home, person and property, or in aid of the civil power when thereto legally summoned, shall be called in question; but nothing herein contained shall be construed to justify the practice of carrying concealed weapons. Art. II, sect. 13.

Connecticut: Every citizen has a right to bear arms in defense of himself and the state. Art. I, sect. 15.

Delaware: A person has the right to keep and bear arms for the defense of self, family, home and state and for hunting and recreational use. Art. I, sect. 20.

Florida: The right of the people to keep and bear arms in defense of themselves and of the lawful authority of the state shall not be infringed, except that the manner of bearing arms may be regulated by law. Art. I, sect. 8.

Georgia: The right of the people to keep and bear arms, shall not be infringed, but the General Assembly shall have power to prescribe the manner in which arms may be borne. Art. I, sect. 1.

Hawaii: A well regulated militia being necessary to the security of a free state, the right of the people to keep and bear arms shall not be infringed. Art. I, sect. 15.

Idaho: The people have the right to keep and bear arms, which right shall not be abridged; but this provision shall not prevent the passage of laws to govern the carrying of weapons concealed on the person nor prevent passage of legislation providing minimum sentences for crimes committed while in possession of a firearm, nor prevent the passage of legislation providing penalties for the possession of firearms by a convicted felon, nor prevent the passage of any legislation punishing the use of a firearm. No law shall impose licensure, registration or special taxation on the ownership or possession of firearms or ammunition. Nor shall any law permit the confiscation of firearms, except those actually used in the commission of a felony. Art. I, sect. 11.

Illinois: Subject only to the police power, the right of the individual citizen to keep and bear arms shall not be infringed. Art. I, sect. 22.

Indiana: The people shall have a right to bear arms, for the defense of themselves and the State. Art. I, sect. 32.

Kansas: The people have the right to bear arms for their defense and security; but standing armies, in time of peace, are dangerous to liberty, and shall not be tolerated, and the military shall be in strict subordination to the civil power. Bill of Rights, sect. 4.

Kentucky: All men are, by nature, free and equal, and have certain inherent and inalienable rights, among which may be reckoned: ...The right to bear arms in defense of themselves and of the State, subject to the power of the General Assembly to enact laws to prevent persons from carrying concealed weapons. Bill of Rights, sect. 1.

Louisiana: The right of each citizen to keep and bear arms shall not be abridged, but this provision shall not prevent the passage of laws to prohibit the carrying of weapons concealed on the person. Art. I, sect. 11.

Maine: Every citizen has the right to keep and bear arms for the common defense; and this right shall never be questioned. Art. I, sect. 16.

Massachusetts: The people have a right to keep and bear arms for the common defence [sic]. And as, in times of peace, armies are dangerous to liberty, they ought not to be maintained without the consent of the legislature; and the military power shall always be held in an exact subordination to the civil authority, and be governed by it. Pt. I, Art. 17.

Michigan: Every person has a right to keep and bear arms for the defense of himself and the state. Art. I, sect. 6.

Mississippi: The right of every citizen to keep and bear arms in defense of his home, person, or property, or in aid of the civil power where thereto legally summoned, shall not be called in question, but the legislature may regulate or forbid carrying concealed weapons. Art. III, sect. 12.

Missouri: That the right of every citizen to keep and bear arms in defense of his home, person and property, or when lawfully summoned in aid of the civil power, shall not be questioned; but this shall not justify the wearing of concealed weapons. Art. 1, sect 23.

Montana: The right of any person to keep or bear arms in defense of his own home, person, and property, or in aid of the civil power when thereto legally summoned, shall not be called in question, but nothing herein contained shall be held to permit the carrying of concealed weapons. Art. II, para. 12. "Militia forces shall consist of all able-bodied citizens of the state except those excepted by law." Art. VI, para. 14.

Nebraska: All persons are by nature free and independent and have certain inherent and inalienable rights; among those are life, liberty, the pursuit of happiness, and the right to keep and bear arms for security or defense of self, family, home, and others, and for lawful common defense, hunting, recreational use, and all other lawful purposes, and such rights shall not be denied or infringed by the state or any subdivision thereof. To secure these rights, and the protection of property, governments are instituted among people, deriving their just powers from the consent of the governed. Bill of Rights, Art. I, sect. 1.

Nevada: Every citizen has the right to keep and bear arms for security and defense, for lawful hunting and recreational use and for other lawful purposes. Art. I, para. 11, subsection 1.

New Hampshire: All persons have the right to keep and bear arms in defense of themselves, their families, their property, and the state. Part I, Art. 2a.

New Mexico: No law shall abridge the right of the citizen to keep and bear arms for security and defense, for lawful hunting and recreational use and for other lawful purposes, but nothing herein shall be held to permit the carrying of concealed weapons. Art. II, para. 6.

North Carolina: A well regulated militia being necessary to the security of a free State, the right of the people to keep and bear arms shall not be infringed; and, as standing armies in time of peace are dangerous to liberty, they shall not be maintained, and the military shall be kept under strict subordination to, and governed by, the civil power. Nothing herein shall justify the practice of carrying concealed weapons, or prevent the General Assembly from enacting penal statutes against that practice. Art. I, sect. 30.

North Dakota: All individuals are by nature equally free and independent and have certain inalienable rights, among which are those of enjoying and defending life and liberty; acquiring, possessing and protecting property and reputation; pursuing and obtaining safety and happiness; and to keep and bear arms for the defense of their person, family, property, and the state, and for lawful hunting, recreational, and other lawful purposes, which shall not be infringed. Art. I, sect. 1.

Ohio: The people have the right to bear arms for their defense and security; but standing armies, in time of peace, are dangerous to liberty, and shall not be kept up; and the military shall be in strict subordination to the civil power. Art. I, sect. 4.

Oklahoma: The right of a citizen to keep and bear arms in defense of his home, person, or property, or in aid of the civil power, when thereunto legally summoned, shall never be prohibited; but nothing herein contained shall prevent the Legislature from regulating the carrying of weapons. Art. II, sect. 26.

Oregon: The people shall have the right to bear arms for the defense of themselves, and the State, but the Military shall be kept in strict subordination to the civil power. Art. I, sect. 27.

Pennsylvania: The right of the citizens to bear arms in defence [sic] of themselves and the State shall not be questioned. Art. I, sect. 21.

Rhode Island: The right of the people to keep and bear arms shall not be infringed. Art. I, sect. 22.

South Carolina: A well regulated militia being necessary to the security of a free State, the right of the people to keep and bear arms shall not be infringed. As, in times of peace, armies are dangerous to liberty, they shall not be maintained without the consent of the General

Assembly. The military power of the State shall always be held in subordination to the civil authority and be governed by it. Art. I, sect. 20.

South Dakota: The right of the citizens to bear arms in defense of themselves and the state shall not be denied. Art. VI, sect. 24.

Tennessee: That the citizens of this State have a right to keep and to bear arms for their common defense; but the Legislature shall have power, by law, to regulate the wearing of arms with a view to prevent crime. Art. I, sect. 26.

Texas: Every citizen shall have the right to keep and bear arms in the lawful defense of himself or the State; but the Legislature shall have power, by law, to regulate the wearing of arms, with a view to prevent crime. Art. I, sect. 23.

Utah: The people have the right to bear arms for their security and defense, but the Legislature may regulate the exercise of this right by law. Art. I, sect. 6.

Vermont: That the people have a right to bear arms for the defence [sic] of themselves and the State—and as standing armies in time of peace are dangerous to liberty, they ought not to be kept up; and that the military should be kept under strict subordination to and governed by the civil power. Ch. I, Art. XVI.

Virginia: That a well regulated militia, composed of the body of the people, trained to arms, is the proper, nat-ural, and safe defense of a free state, therefore, the right of the people to keep and bear arms shall not be infringed; that standing armies, in time of peace, should be avoided as dangerous to liberty; and that in all cases the military should be under strict subordination to, and governed by, the civil power. Art. I, sect. 13.

Washington: The right of the individual citizen to bear arms in defense of himself, or the state, shall not be impaired, but nothing in this section shall be construed as authorizing individuals or corporations to organize, maintain, or employ an armed body of men. Art. I, sect. 24.

West Virginia: A person has the right to keep and bear arms for the defense of self, family, home, and state, and for lawful hunting and recreational use. Art. III, sect. 22.

Wisconsin: The people have the right to keep and bear arms for security, defense, hunting, recreation, or any other lawful purpose. Art. 1, sect. 25.

Wyoming: The right of citizens to bear arms in defense of themselves and of the state shall not be denied. Art. I, sect. 24.

STATES WITHOUT CONSTITUTIONAL PROVISIONS

Six states do not have constitutional provisions on the right to keep and bear arms: California, Iowa, Maryland, Minnesota, New Jersey, and New York.

IMPORTANT NAMES AND ADDRESSES

Bureau of Alcohol, Tobacco and Firearms
650 Massachusetts Ave. NW
Washington, D.C. 20226
(202) 927-8480
FAX (202) 927-8866
URL: http://www.atf.treas.gov

Center to Prevent Handgun Violence
1225 Eye St. NW, Suite 1100
Washington, D.C. 20005
(202) 289-7319
FAX (202) 408-1851
URL: http://www.cphv.org

**Centers for Disease Control and
Prevention (CDC)**
1600 Clifton Rd. NE
Atlanta, GA 30333
(404) 639-3534
URL: http://www.cdc.gov

**Citizens' Committee for the Right to Keep
and Bear Arms**
Public Affairs Director
1090 Vermont Ave. NW, Suite 800
Washington, D.C. 20005
(202) 326-5259
FAX (202) 898-1939
URL: http://www.ccrkba.org

Coalition to Stop Gun Violence
1023 15th St. NW, Suite 600
Washington, D.C. 20005
(202) 408-0061
FAX (202) 408-0062
URL: http://www.csgv.org

**Educational Fund to End
Handgun Violence**
Box 72
110 Maryland Ave. N.E.
Washington, D.C. 20002
(202) 544-7227
URL: http://www.bitsnet.com/agca/efehv.htm

Federal Bureau of Investigation
935 Pennsylvania Ave. NW
Washington, D.C. 20535
(202) 324-3691
FAX (202) 324-684
URL: http://www.fbi.gov

Gun Owners of America
8001 Forbes Pl., Suite 102
Springfield, VA 22151
(703) 321-8585
FAX (703) 321-8408
URL: http://www.gunowners.org

Handgun Control, Inc.
1225 Eye St. NW, Suite 1100
Washington, D.C. 20005
(202) 898-0792
FAX (202) 371-9615
URL: http://www.handguncontrol.org

House Judiciary Committee
Subcommittee on Crime and Criminal Justice
207 Cannon House Office Bldg.
Washington, D.C. 20515
(202) 225-3926
FAX (202) 225-3737
URL: http://www.house.gov/judiciary/
sub106.htm

National Institute of Justice
810 7th St. NW
Washington, D.C. 20531
(202) 307-2942
FAX (202) 307-6394
URL: http://www.ojp.usdoj.gov/nij

National Rifle Association
11250 Waples Mill Rd.
Fairfax, VA 22030
(703) 267-1000
FAX (703) 267-3973
URL: http://www.nra.org

National Safety Council
1121 Spring Lake Dr.
Itasca, IL 60143-3201
(630) 285-1121
URL: http://www.nsc.org

**Office of Juvenile Justice and
Delinquency Prevention**
810 7th St. NW
Washington, D.C. 20531
(202) 307-5911
FAX (202) 307-2093
URL: http://ojjdp.ncjrs.org

The Second Amendment Foundation
The James Madison Bldg.
12500 NE 10th Pl.
Bellevue, WA 98005
(425) 454-7012
FAX (425) 451-3959
URL: http://www.saf.org

Senate Judiciary Committee
Subcommittee on Crime and
Justice Oversight
Room SD-157, Dirksen Senate Office Bldg.
Washington, D.C. 20510
(202) 224-4135
FAX (202) 228-0463
URL: http://judiciary.senate.gov/criminal.htm

Supreme Court of the United States
1-1st St. NE
Washington, D.C. 20543
(202) 479-3211
URL: http://www.supremecourtus.gov

Violence Policy Center
1140 19th St. NW, Suite 600
Washington, D.C. 20036
(202) 822-8200
FAX (202) 822-8205
URL: http://www.vpc.org

RESOURCES

The Bureau of Alcohol, Tobacco and Firearms (ATF) monitors alcohol, tobacco, and firearms production and regulation and is the major source of statistical and technical information on these categories. The annual *Firearms State Laws and Published Ordinances* provides a complete overview of firearm regulations of local towns, cities, states, and the federal government. The ATF also publishes periodic press releases with vital information about licensing, domestic gun manufacturing, and importing and exporting statistics. "War Between the States: How Gunrunners Smuggle Weapons Across America," a congressional study based on data from the ATF, provided information on gun trafficking.

The Bureau of Justice Statistics (BJS) and the Federal Bureau of Investigation (FBI), both in Washington, D.C., maintain crime statistics in the United States. The FBI's annual *Crime in the United States* is based on crime statistics reported through its Uniform Crime Reports program. The FBI also produces *Law Enforcement Officers Killed and Assaulted.*

The annual Bureau of Justice Statistics' *Sourcebook of Criminal Justice Statistics* 1999 is the most complete source of statistical information published on crime. The annual *Criminal Victimization in the United States* is based upon periodic sampling surveys of about 50,000 Americans. *Presale Handgun Checks,* a report of data collected on background checks of applicants for handguns, is also published annually. The BJS's *Homicide Trends in the U.S., Guns Used in Crime,* and *Firearm Injury from Crime* provides valuable information on handgun crime, handgun victimization, and handgun theft.

The Office of Juvenile Justice and Delinquency Prevention (OJJDP; Washington, D.C.), a branch of the National Institute of Justice, reported on young offenders in *Juvenile Offenders and Victims: 1999 National Report* and on students and young inmates in *Gun Acquisition and Possession in Selected Juvenile Samples*(1993). The OJJDP also published *Combating Fear and Restoring Safety in Schools* (1998) and *Kids and Guns: From Playgrounds to Battlegrounds* (1997). The National Institute of Justice published *High School Youths, Weapons and Violence: A National Survey* (1998) and *Guns in America: National Survey on Private Ownership and Use of Firearms* (Philip J. Cook and Jens Ludwig, 1997).

Information on background checks for firearms purchases was provided in *Gun Control—Implementation of the Brady Handgun Violence Prevention Act* (prepared by the General Accounting Office [GAO], Washington, D.C., 2000). The ATF's *Commerce in Firearms 1999* reported on the number of federal firearms applications and renewals.

The Centers for Disease Control and Prevention (CDC) published several informative studies in its *Morbidity and Mortality Weekly Review,* including "Rates of Homicide, Suicide, and Firearm-Related Death Among Children—26 Industrialized Countries" (February 7, 1997), "Youth Risk Behavior Surveillance—United States, 1997" (August 1998), and "BB and Pellet Gun-Related Injuries—United States, June 1992–May 1994" (December 15, 1995). The National Center for Health Statistics (NCHS) provided both national and international data on injury mortality.

The Gale Group would like to express its continuing appreciation to The Gallup Organization of Princeton, New Jersey, for its kind permission to publish its surveys and the National Opinion Research Center of the University of Chicago for use of its material, especially the 1999 *National Gun Policy Survey* by Tom Smith (2000). Louis Harris Associates (The Harris Poll, New York) generously allowed use of material from its surveys. Public Agenda Online granted permission to use several graphics.

The *New England Journal of Medicine* granted permission to use information from "Injuries Due to

Firearms in Three Cities" by Arthur Kellermann et al. (November 7, 1996) and "Protection or Peril? An Analysis of Firearm-Related Deaths in the Home" (June 12, 1986). The *New England Journal of Medicine* also gave permission to use data from "Gun Ownership as a Risk Factor for Homicide in the Home," by Arthur Kellermann et al. (October 7, 1993). *The Public Health Reports* published "When Bullets Don't Kill" (November/December 1996) by Catherine W. Barber et al.

The Violence Policy Center provided helpful information in its press releases and publications and granted permission to use a table from *Paper Tiger? Will the Brady Law Work After Instant Check?* (November 1998). The Handgun Epidemic Lowering Plan (HELP) allowed us to use tables from *Missing in Action: Health Agencies Lack Critical Data Needed for Firearm Injury Prevention* (The HELP Network, Chicago, IL, 1999).

Other sources used in the preparation of this book include *Making a Killing* by Tom Diaz (New York: The New Press, 1999), *More Guns, Less Crime* by John R. Lott, Jr. (Chicago, IL: The University of Chicago Press, 1998), *Crime, Deterrence, and Right-to-Carry Concealed Handguns,* a study by John R. Lott, Jr., and David B. Mustard (University of Chicago, 1996), and *The Politics of Gun Control* by Robert Spitzer (Chatham House, New Jersey, 1995).

INDEX

*Page references in italics refer to pho-
tographs. References with the letter* t *following them indicate the presence of a table.
The letter* f *indicates a figure. If more than
one table or figure appears on a particular
page, the exact item number for the table or
figure being referenced is provided.*

A

Accessibility of firearms, 94–95, 95(*t*7.11)
Accidental deaths, 54, 55(*t*5.6)
Accidental shootings, 73–74, 74*t*
Accu-Tek, Hamilton v., 48–49
After-school programs, 92
Age
    arrests, 61*t*
    auto accidents, 78(*f*6.4)
    death by firearms, 70*t*, 74, 75*t*–77*t*, 77,
      78(*f*6.5)
    gun control, 109(*t*8.5)
    injuries from firearms, 69*t*, 91(*t*7.4)
    murder offenders, 87(*t*7.2), 88*f*
    murder victims, 87(*t*7.3), 88*f*, 89*f*
    ownership of firearms, 11, 90–91
    victimization, 58*t*
Aggravated assault. *See* Assault
Alcohol, 10
Amendments to the United States
    Constitution, 2
    Second amendment, 3–4, 18, 20, 35–36,
      122–123
    Tenth amendment, 39
American colonists, 2–3
American Indians and Alaska Natives
    arrests, 62*t*–64*t*
    auto accidents, 79*t*–82*t*
    death by firearms, 75*t*–77*t*
American Revolution. *See* Revolutionary
    War
*American Shooting Sports Council, Inc. v.
    Harshbarger,* 42
Ammunition, 17
Andrade v. Baptiste, 47–48
Antigun lawsuits, 48–49
Armed robbery, 54–55, 56(*t*5.8), 58*t*

Armijo v. Ex Cam, Inc., 46–47
Armor-piercing ammunition, 17
Arrests, 61*t*, 62*t*–64*t*
Asian and Pacific Islander Americans
    arrests, 62*t*–64*t*
    auto accidents, 79*t*–82*t*
    death by firearms, 75*t*–77*t*
Aspen, Marvin E., 117–118
Assassinations, 103
Assault, 56–57, 68, 73(*t*6.4)
    law enforcement officers as victims,
      56(*t*5.7)
    victimization, 58*t*
    weapons, 56(*t*5.9)
Assault weapons. *See* Semiautomatic assault
    weapons
Attempted suicides. *See* Suicides
Auto accidents
    deaths, 74, 77, 78(*f*6.3), 78(*f*6.4)
    injuries, 79*t*–82*t*
Availability of firearms, 83

B

Background checks, 101
    Brady Law, 21, 22, 39
    gun shows, 23
    inquiries/rejections, 22(*t*3.2), 22(*t*3.3), 23
Bailey, Benjamin v., 41
Bailey, U.S. v., 37–38
Bans
    Benjamin v. Bailey, 41
    handguns, 33, 43–44
    Kalodimos v. Village of Morton Grove, 44
    Oregon v. Boyce, 42–43
    Quilici v. Village of Morton Grove,
      43–44, 45
    *Second Amendment Foundation v. City of
      Renton,* 43
    semiautomatic assault weapons, 33, 41,
      42, 110, 110(*t*8.10)
    states, 28
Baptiste, Andrade v., 47–48
"BB and Pellet Gun-Related Injuries"
    (*Morbidity and Mortality Weekly Report,*
    Vol. 44, No. 49, December 15, 1995),
    96–97

BB guns, 96–97, 97(*t*7.12), 97(*t*7.13)
Benjamin v. Bailey, 41
Black/African Americans
    arrests, 62*t*–64*t*
    auto accidents, 79*t*–82*t*
    death by firearms, 75*t*–77*t*
    injuries, 88
    murder, 86, 90*f*
    murder offenders, 88*f*
    murder victims, 89*f*
    victimization, 58*t*
    victimization, juvenile, 72
Blaksley, City of Salina v., 42
Boston (MA), 89–90
Boyce, Oregon v., 42–43
Bradley, Bill, 117
Brady Handgun Purchase Form, 19*f*
Brady Handgun Violence Prevention Act of
    1993. *See* Brady Law
Brady Law, 18, 20–23, 57–58
    background checks, 21, 22
    changes, 22(*t*3.4)
    Clinton, Bill, 115
    compliance, 21*f*
    Mack v. U.S., 39
    National Rifle Association (NRA), 23
    permits, 31*t*
    Printz v. U.S., 39
    waiting period, 39
Bryan, U.S. v., 39–40
Byrne, Sklar v., 44–45

C

California
    Saturday night specials, 45
    semiautomatic assault weapons bans, 42
    Stockton school yard murders, 33
Caplan, Dr. David L., Ph.D., 123
Car accidents. *See* Auto accidents
Centers for Disease Control and Prevention
    (CDC), 71
Chief law enforcement officials (CLEOs), 39
"Child Access Prevention" (CAP) law. *See*
    Safe storage of firearms
China, 6–7, 7(*t*2.4)
City health departments, 71*f*